GETTING STARTED IN

STOCK

ANALYSIS

ILLUSTRATED EDITION

BOOKS IN THE *GETTING STARTED IN* SERIES

GETTING STARTED IN
STOCK
ANALYSIS

ILLUSTRATED EDITION

MICHAEL C. THOMSETT

WILEY

Other Wiley Editorial Offices
John Wiley & Sons, 111 River Street, Hoboken, NJ 07030, USA
John Wiley & Sons, The Atrium, Southern Gate, Chichester, West Sussex, P019 8SQ, United Kingdom
John Wiley & Sons (Canada) Ltd., 5353 Dundas Street West, Suite 400, Toronto, Ontario, M9B 6HB,
    Canada
John Wiley & Sons Australia Ltd., 42 McDougall Street, Milton, Queensland 4064, Australia
Wiley-VCH, Boschstrasse 12, D-69469 Weinheim, Germany

ISBN 978-1-118-93786-0 (Paperback)
ISBN 978-1-119-01951-0
ISBN 978-1-119-01952-7

Typeset in 11/15 pt, Adobe Garamond Pro by Aptara India
Printed in the United States by Courier Digital Solutions

10 9 8 7 6 5 4 3 2

CONTENTS

ACKNOWLEDGMENTS

Many thanks to the editorial and publishing staff at John Wiley & Sons, including Nick Wallwork, Jeremy Chia, and Syd Glanaden; to the production staff in Singapore and Hoboken, notably Chris Gage; and to the illustrator, who has brought this book to life with creative additions.

ELEMENT KEY

Definitions
This symbol is found in boxed notations providing specific definitions of options terms. These are placed within the book to accompany and augment discussions relevant to each definition.

Key Points
These highlighted sections emphasize key points or add observations, rules of thumb, resources, and added points that options traders can use.

Valuable Resources
These sections provide links to websites where you will find added value for particular options discussions, to further expand your options knowledge base.

Examples
Numerous examples illustrate points raised in context and provide a view of how the issues might apply using actual options trades. This is intended to demonstrate practical application of the principles being presented.

INTRODUCTION

Throughout history, people with new ideas—who think differently and try to change things—have always been called troublemakers.
—Richelle Mead, *Shadow Kiss,* 2008

Do you favor fundamental or technical analysis?

Many market observers favor either fundamental analysis or technical analysis, exclusively. But both offer value, in different ways. This book makes a case for using *both* systems together to identify quality companies and their stocks, and to then time trades to increase profits and improve timing of trades.

Fundamental analysis is often associated with conservative and long-term investing. It is the reliance on financial statements and other financial information about a company, intended to identify the levels of capital safety and strength, as well as earnings potential. The drawback of fundamentals is that the information is outdated by the time it is used; for example, financial statements normally are issued several months after the end of the fiscal year.

Technical analysis is focused exclusively on current price and trading volume information: the study of price movement in the stock versus the fundamental emphasis on financial attributes of the company. Price is judged on charts, with the shape and speed of price movement used to anticipate trends and reversals. Reliance is not only on the price level itself but also on volume of trading, moving averages of the price over time, and momentum of trading. The drawback of technical analysis is that none of the indicators can be relied on consistently; short-term price movement is random, so technical analysis is not an exact science.

Even with the drawbacks of fundamental and technical analysis, many analysts recognize that the two disciplines affect one another, and are clearly related. Used together, investors and traders may improve the selection of stocks and the timing of trades to improve profitable outcomes in their portfolios.

The idea that combined use of two different approaches to analysis could produce improved results is intriguing. For many years, great energy has been put into perfecting analysis, notably with widespread use of automated systems and advanced algorithms, methods of calculating likely movement of price based on variables. The algorithm is too complex to calculate by hand, so high-frequency traders (HFTs) rely on sophisticated programs to time large-dollar value trades based on very small changes in price. This technical system today accounts for as much as 50 percent of all trades on U.S. markets. Other issues surrounding the problems associated with HFTs and regulating them highlight the growing importance of this trading trend. Interest in automated systems that give an edge to some traders over others has led to controversy and even regulatory steps to curtail high-frequency trading activity.[1]

The advantage that HFT trading provides is clear; but it is less clear how much negative impact the practice has on individual trading. The high concentration of dollars traded has led to many losses among institutions, but for individuals the impact is not as clear. This book is concerned with methods that investors and traders can use to improve overall profitability in investing and trading stocks, not as part of larger-volume trading practices but in the management of an individual portfolio. The premise is that a typical individual does not have access to algorithms and other tools, and must rely on exceptional analytical methods to beat the averages of market investing and trading. To accomplish this goal, the book is designed to present the basics of both fundamental and technique analysis in two parts.

Part I (Fundamental Analysis) contains seven chapters designed to introduce and examine the essential fundamental sources—financial statements, annual reports, and fundamentals not found in reports. This section also explores the many ratios and trends that are valuable to anyone employing the fundamentals to select companies as viable investment candidates. The section also devotes an entire chapter to a detailed analysis of five key trends every investor needs to track, including an explanation of how to track and interpret them.

Part II (Technical Analysis) provides an equally in-depth examination of the major technical attributes and indicators and has eight chapters.

---

[1] Carol Clark, "How to Keep Markets Safe in the Era of High-Speed Trading," *Chicago Fed Letter*, October, 2012, www.chicagofed.org/digital_assets/publications/chicago_fed_letter/2012/cfloctober2012_303.pdf.

It includes analysis of market theories and what they mean; charting analysis and interpretation, trends; and moving averages. This section also provides chapters on price indicators, volume indicators, momentum oscillators, and confirmation.

The purpose of this book is beyond explaining the indicators and their meaning. It is designed to show how the combined use of fundamental and technical indicators can be put into action to create an effective program to build a portfolio, manage its risks, and time entry and exit based on ever-changing indicators. This helps generate additional income while preserving the conservative standards that most investors need and want.

GETTING STARTED IN

STOCK ANALYSIS

ILLUSTRATED EDITION

PART 1

FUNDAMENTAL
ANALYSIS

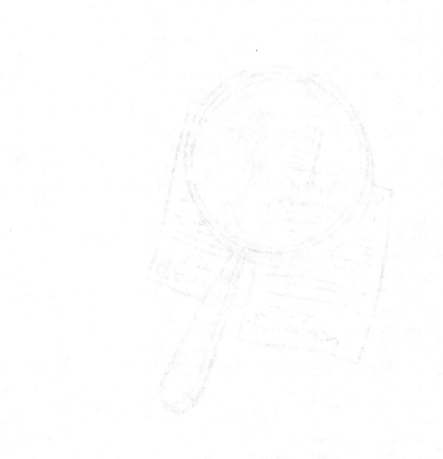

1

FINANCIAL STATEMENTS IN OVERVIEW

Money is always there but the pockets change.
　　　　　　—Gertrude Stein, quoted in *Time*, October 13, 1975

Financial statements are poorly understood by some investors. Many believe statements to be overly complex for anyone without an accounting education to understand. Others know all about statements in adequate detail, but discount their importance.

In both cases, realizing the powerful value of statements is essential. By knowing how to translate the raw data of the financial statement into a comparative tool, investors make better choices. Statements test capital strength, cash management, and profitability. They can be used to spot emerging changes in long-term *trends*, both positive and negative. The information on statements can also be reduced to a shorthand version of the dollar value, the all-important *ratios* that financial analysts use to quantify and compare value. This makes it easier to identify *value investments* and also to spot companies whose strength is beginning to diminish.

trends

the directional movement of a specific financial statement account balance or ratio that reveals growing or falling strength or profitability.

ratios

reduced
expressions
of financial
data, for the
purpose of trend
analysis and
used to clarify
the meaning
behind dollar
values; ratios
are expressed
as percentages
or comparative
numerical sets
(a / b).

The ratio is used to express trends or ending values of outcomes on statements. Knowing how trends are developed and what they mean helps to analyze financial information, not only for accounting experts but also for the typical investor.

The ratios used to develop trends in the study of fundamental attributes (capital strength, cash management, and profitability) not only refer to the historical outcomes but also provide clues about likely futures levels of those same attributes. Many critics of fundamental analysis point out that financial statements are historical and may not be much help in studying today's price structure. In this regard, the critics contend, fundamental analysis does not help to find high-quality investments.

Example

Yesterday's news – You are reviewing financial statements for two companies, both recently published. One is for a fiscal year ending two months ago and the other is from four months ago. While both of these are outdated, the four-month one is quite old, now at one-third of the new fiscal year. This is a major disadvantage in fundamental analysis.

Key Point

Fundamentally based ratios are much more than historical results. Properly applied, they can help to better estimate likely future movement in a trend.

This criticism misses the point about what financial statements provide. No one should expect to review a single year's financial statements and be able to draw accurate conclusions about a company. By studying long-term trends (preferably over 5 to 10 years), you can estimate the future changes in financial status and profitability.

So financial statements cannot be relied upon for a single year, but should be viewed as the latest entry in a longer-term trend. The important fundamental tests investors apply to pick one company over another may be viewed as a starting point for making informed decisions, and never as the last word in whether to buy stock of a particular company.

THE GAAP SYSTEM

Financial statements are prepared under a set of uniform and widely agreed-upon rules. These are called *GAAP* or Generally Accepted Accounting Principles.

Although GAAP has been a standard in the U.S. for decades, the system may soon be replaced with another, called *IFRS* (International Financial Reporting Standards). A move away from GAAP toward IFRS is planned to occur in the near future.

value investments

those investments that may be undervalued by the market, but whose fundamental strength is exceptional; the deflated price posture of such companies indicates good timing to purchase shares, and also indicates lower than average risk of loss due to the fundamental strength of the company.

The differences between GAAP and IFRS are not substantial enough to concern most nonaccountant investors. However, some important differences are worth noting. The so-called "international convergence" from GAAP to IFRS includes the direct involvement of the Securities and Exchange Commission (SEC) as the primary U.S.–based regulatory board; and of the industry policy-setting and monitoring organizations. These include the Financial Accounting Standards Board (FASB), the American Institute of Certified Public Accountants (AICPA), and the International Accounting Standards Board (IASB), the home page of IFRS.

GAAP

Generally
Accepted
Accounting
Principles, a
complex set
of policies,
standards
and reporting
formats used by
all publicly listed
companies; the
system is not
centrally located,
but is the sum
of regulations,
published
opinions, and
policies, as well
as long-standing
methods for
recording
and reporting
transactions
and setting
valuation.

Valuable Resources
Securities and Exchange Commission (SEC): **www.sec.gov**
Financial Accounting Standards Board (FASB): **www.fasb.org**
American Institute of Certified Public Accountants (AICPA):
www.aicpa.org
International Accounting Standards Board (IASB), operated
by the International Financial Reporting Standards (IFRS):
www.ifrs.com

The merging of GAAP with IFRS was announced by the Securities and Exchange Commission (SEC) in 2010:

The Securities and Exchange Commission today voted to issue a statement that lays out its position regarding global accounting standards and makes clear that the Commission continues to believe that a single set of high-quality globally accepted accounting standards would benefit U.S investors.

As a step toward achieving the goal of a single set of high-quality global accounting standards, the statement notes that the Commission continues to encourage the convergence of U.S. Generally Accepted Accounting Principles (U.S. GAAP) and International Financial Reporting Standards (IFRS) in order to narrow the differences between the two sets of standards.[1]

Two primary areas in which the conversion from GAAP to IFRS is likely to have the greatest impact are in calculations of tax liabilities and year-to-year trend tracking. The two systems have substantial differences in treatment of some transactions for the purpose of taxes, and once the changes are put in place, the continuation of existing trends may be distorted.

Example

The deadly trend: You have been tracking several trends on the income statement. You notice a shift in some of the trends, but you are not sure why. And then you discover that the company changed its accounting system and assumptions two years ago. That's when the trends seemed to move in an unexpected manner. Obviously, the company did not restate its previous years.

---

[1] SEC, "SEC Approves Statement on Global Accounting Standards," *SEC News Digest*, February 24, 2010.

Key Point

If conversion from GAAP to IFRS does occur, it is not likely to have a large impact on most investment decisions. Changes will be the greatest in a small number of valuation methods, but a big impact on investors is unlikely.

IFRS

International Financial Reporting Standards, a system for the uniform reporting of financial transactions and valuation, which is scheduled to replace the GAAP system in coming years.

With these potential distortions in mind, investors who rely on long-term ratios and trend analysis will need to ensure that the historical valuation methods have been updated so that an entire period is reported on the same overall standards. However, no matter how much care is taken, a period of adjustment should be expected before a revised, international system will work well.

AUDITING OF THE BOOKS: PURPOSE AND PROCESS

The independent audit is intended as an objective examination of the decisions made on the corporate level, the identification of specific valuation and reserve levels, and determination of net profits.

To an outsider, it might seem that a uniform set of standards ensures that a properly calculated net profit is going to be correct, and that an audit will confirm this assumption. However, even when the audit certifies the latest set of financial statements, there could be room for interpretation that might make a significant difference in what is reported. How is this possible?

The GAAP system gives corporations great leeway in how they interpret and report their annual profit and loss. For example, corporations are able to make *elections* about how to value inventory, set up reserve for bad debts, and place value on intangible assets, like goodwill or a brand name.

Acknowledging that corporations have the ability to interpret their transactions conservatively or liberally, the question remains: What is the value of the independent audit?

elections

decisions made by corporations to treat certain transactions, set up reserves, or determine value, under one of several allowed processes; these elections affect the calculation of net profits as well as capitalization of the company.

The purpose of the audit is not to arrive at a single correct interpretation, but to ensure that the range of decisions made by the corporation is reasonable and accurate—within the latitude allowed by the GAAP system. Auditing firms provide a range of service in addition to audits, including tax consultation, internal control development, computer systems, bookkeeping, and other forms of consulting services. An argument could be made that offering nonaudit services poses a conflict of interest for an auditing firm. A counterargument can also be made that being familiar with a range of corporate matters improves the auditor's ability to understand the corporate culture and how accounting determinations are made inside the company.

Key Point

There is not a single, correct interpretation of financial statements. The rules are broad enough so that a number of different outcomes are acceptable; investors have to rely on the fairness of both the corporation and its auditors to end up with a reasonable set of financial statements.

Another auditing service is that of identifying outright fraud or misrepresentation by a corporation. There have been cases in which the audit has revealed deep problems and even falsification of the financial reports; and others in which the audit has concluded that a company is not a "going concern," meaning profits are inadequate for a company to expect to continue in business.

Example

Cooking the books: An audit revealed that the company has been booking revenue early, by using initial orders not yet filled as earned income. If the company will not accept the auditor's adjustments to correct this, then it is a form of falsification. If the auditor has integrity, this will not be allowed, or the audit opinion letter will explain the difference and label the results as unqualified.

These are important aspects of the audit, because without the outside involvement, the regulators (primarily the SEC and state securities agencies) would have to reply on the financial statements that the corporation issues. These agencies do not have the resources to perform in-depth audits of their own, so they are more likely to respond once violations have been discovered.

In the past, the system has not always worked as intended. The deep problems of Enron and dozens of other companies often included culpability among auditing firms, and not just within the corporation. The case of Enron was one of deep abuse and included hiding of evidence by the auditing firm as well as corporate officers. The senior auditor at Arthur Andersen admitted to shredding incriminating documents. As a consequence, Arthur Andersen was forced to close down all of its operations. How does this happen?

The conflict of interest among auditing firms was a result of the pressure on senior audit partners to produce revenues beyond audits. Thus, a partner performing an audit had a lot at stake, and this compromised objectivity. In the case of Arthur Andersen, audit partners were expected to create nonaudit revenue at twice the rate of audit revenue. This system was called 2X. So if a particular client paid $4 million for auditing services, senior partners were also expected to generate $8 million in nonaudit work. This system was much more than just a goal. It formed the basis of performance evaluation inside of Arthur Andersen. Partners not meeting this goal often were fired.

Key Point

Once auditing firms began mixing independent and objective auditing practices with marketing, the conflict of interest became glaring. In the case of Arthur Andersen, this decision robbed the company of its objectivity; it was no longer independent.

This set up a system in which a client could threaten to go to a different auditing company unless the Arthur Andersen partner went along with the client's decisions, even those that were clearly misrepresentations in violation of GAAP standards. A partner who did not want a career-ending decision had incentive to look the other way and to sign off even on fraudulent transactions. That is what happened in the case of Enron.

Reforms since those times include a law intended to curtail abuses and eliminate conflicts of interest. The Sarbanes-Oxley Act of 2002 was intended as a measure to prevent fraud, both by corporations and auditors. The effectiveness of this law is not certain. It has probably had a chilling effect on corporate officers and auditors who might have once believed they could get away with a loose interpretation of the accounting rules, or even with fraud. But the degree of this cannot be known. Other, specific problems persist, however:

In some ways, Sarbanes-Oxley has not done enough to change the accounting and audit industry, critics say. It did not resolve an inherent tension within the industry's "client pays" business model—that is, an auditor's basic conflict between serving the paying client and serving the greater good.

Nor has it brought increased competition to an industry that still is an oligopoly, now dominated by the so-called Big Four firms: Ernst & Young, PricewaterhouseCoopers, KPMG and Deloitte. Former Enron auditor Arthur Andersen is history.

Auditors have become more independent of clients, but not entirely so. The law limited the types of consulting that accounting firms can do for their audit clients, but left them free to do lucrative tax work. It made lead audit partners rotate off accounts after five years, but let audit firms serve the same clients indefinitely.[2]

---

[2] Kevin Drawbaugh and Dena Aubin, "Analysis: A Decade on, Is Sarbanes-Oxley Working?," *Reuters*, July 30, 2012.

As with all laws meant to prevent abuses of the system, it is reactive rather than proactive. The flaws in Sarbanes-Oxley point out the problem all investors face when relying on certification by an independent auditing firm: Ultimately, everyone has to study trends over time to decide whether the financial reports make sense. This does not demand a high-level accounting education—just the basic skill to compare and analyze the numbers.

Example

Staying with the basics: Any investor can track a trend as long as the results are available. This can include calculating a percentage of change, placing the results on a graph in Excel, or comparing two trends to each other (e.g., revenue and earnings). The point? You do not need a finance or accounting education to document your own trends.

Even the clever accounting distortion eventually shows up in the long-term trend, and this is where fundamental analysis is the most valuable. You can spot trends and any distortions they include by studying the long-term trends reported in a set of financial statements.

STOCKHOLDER RELIANCE ON THE AUDIT

Anyone who invests in the *equity markets* (equity referring to ownership, usually of shares of stock) becomes a stockholder. Every stockholder relies on the accuracy and integrity of the financial statements, which are the primary means for deciding whether a company is solvent, profitable, and well managed.

equity markets

the markets for publicly traded stock, or exchanges set up to facilitate trading in equities; an equity holder is part owner of the corporation, compared to the debt markets, in which a bondholder is a lender to the corporation.

Even those who acknowledge that a wide range of interpretations make financial statements less than specific agree that within the range of accounting interpretations, a fair and complete financial statement is possible, even though different observers may draw different conclusions about a company's capital strength, management, and profitability.

So under the range of possible outcomes, there may be a number of accurate reports for the same company and in the same year. Because there is no single right interpretation, investors rely on trends and ratio analysis to decide whether a company's statements are to be accepted. No matter how skillfully the numbers might be manipulated, the trend eventually tells the complete story. So reviewing a 10-year history reveals at least one important outcome: If the latest year is fair and within the range of acceptable interpretations, the numbers will fall in line with the trend. If the numbers do not look right, it could be due to several reasons, including a change in the market, an overall change in economic circumstances, or some form of manipulation of the numbers.

Key Point

A surprising and puzzling change in the trend could be due to many causes. It does not always mean the numbers have been manipulated, but a wise starting point is a study of the audited financial statements.

Relying on the independent audit is a starting point for every investor. However, given the history of the audit and of financial distortions among publicly listed companies, investors have to remain diligent and should never accept the audited statements with 100 percent confidence. It is always wise to ask questions and to be able to examine the trends to make sure it all looks right.

METHODS OF HIDING OR DISTORTING DATA

Many tactics can be used to alter the way the financial statements come out. Any method that does not accurately reflect the true summary of operations, valuation, or capital value of a business is a disservice to stockholders.

These methods include:

Cookie jar accounting (also called *sugar bowl accounting*): In this practice, a company has had an exceptionally good year, with net profits far above average. But in order to keep the trends level without any spikes in the numbers, the company defers some of those profits for future years. When a poor year occurs with profits below average, some or all of the deferred profits in the cookie jar are taken and put back on the books.

While it's true that stockholders like to see predictable, steady growth in revenue and earnings, cookie jar accounting presents a false picture of the year. Stockholders deserve to see the truth, that chaos often is the real picture of a company's revenue and earnings. When stockholders believe that a company is growing at the same rate every year, but the truth is something else, it creates a false sense of security. Many investors will hold onto shares believing the company's profits are predictable, when they actually are not.

cookie jar accounting (also known as sugar bowl accounting)

a form of manipulation of financial statements, in which exceptionally favorable profits are put aside in the current year to level out the long-term trend, and to be used in a later year when results are below average.

Example

Hands in the jar: A company had an exceptionally profitable year, but you notice that the income statement results are amazingly accurate from one year to the next. You also notice an item in the liability section of the balance sheet called "deferred credits." When you investigate, you become suspicious that the company might be manipulating revenue to keep results steady from year to year. They are storing revenue some years and then putting their hands in the cookie jar in other years.

Key Point

Altering the true outcome of profits, even by understating them, is deceptive and leads to trouble. Once this is justified, it is just as easy to move numbers in the opposite direction as well.

A problem related to cookie jar accounting is an ethical one. Some analysts will argue that deferring income does no real harm. But it is not accurate; if management is willing to defer income in an exceptionally good year, what is to prevent them from exaggerating income when a year is below average?

Booking revenue in the wrong year: One of the most frequent forms of manipulation involves adjustments to revenue, or the top line on the income statement. In a year with lower than expected revenues, a company might book revenues at the end of the year that actually will not be earned until the following year. This is seen in many forms, including *recognition* of current-year income based on orders that have been placed but not filled, on estimated future revenue, or on outright made-up numbers.

Revenue in excess of the trend average might also be deferred to a future accounting year (see cookie jar accounting earlier).

Both examples are distortions of the real numbers, and are intended to mislead stockholders into believing results that are not accurate. In the case of early booking of revenue, the inflated profits that result are especially dangerous because they indicate the corporation's willingness to mislead stockholders and auditors.

Key Point

One of the basic ideas of good accounting is that all transactions should be placed in the applicable year. Once this rule is broken, the financial statements lose all integrity.

Booking costs or expenses in the wrong year: Another method of distorting the true revenue and earnings picture is to manage expenses by recognizing them in the wrong year. The accounting rules state that expenses are to be recognized in the year of *accrual*, meaning the year the money was spent or the commitment made.

For example, at the end of a calendar year, a company has ordered thousands of dollars of supplies, signed contracts for advertising, and has accumulated telephone bills. None of these will actually be paid for

recognition

booking transactions for revenue, costs, and expenses; the year in which these transactions are booked should be the proper accounting period. The process of booking transactions is called recognition because it indicates that all of these are booked into the proper accounting period.

until next month. However, by making an accrual for these expenses in the current period, the expenses are recognized.

Key Point

The usual method for booking transactions in the proper fiscal year is by way of accrual journal entries. Unfortunately, the same process can also be used to control and misstate the outcomes.

accrual

recognition of an expense in the current year when the purchase was made, but when actual payment will not occur until the following period. This places expenses in the applicable year even though actual cash transactions often are not made until later.

This is where manipulation can come into the picture. A company wanting to boost earnings may fail to accrue expenses that properly belong in the current year. This artificially creates the appearance of lower expenses, and thus higher profits.

The opposite can also occur. A company that has had an unusually profitable year may overaccrue current expenses, creating a cushion for next year, when net profits might be below average. This evening out of reported profits is another form of misrepresentation.

Capitalizing expenses: Some companies have practiced the art of *capitalizing* expenses that should be *written off* in the current year. This defers expenses, boosting current-year profits.

When the company capitalizes current expenses and treats them like capital assets, it distorts the profit picture by increasing the amount reported as profits.

Examples

Expenses turned into assets—a miracle?: A company has had unusually large general expenses this year, mainly due to poor internal controls on spending. Rather than reporting these properly as current-year expenses, the company set up some of the total as a capital asset called "other assets" and plans to write off one-third over the next three years. This might also be found in a different asset account called prepaid assets or deferred assets.

Not reporting liabilities: Some liabilities are called "off book" because they are not reported as current debts of the company. This affects the capital value of the organization and, when some liabilities are treated as off book, they disappear entirely.

For example, a company may form a subsidiary overseas and transfer liabilities to it, excluding those liabilities from the balance sheet. This distorts the true debt and equity picture of the organization, because the debts are very real but they do not show up on the balance sheet. Even so, the proceeds of a loan may be included, so the borrowed funds are reported as assets, but the debt is nowhere to be found.

capitalizing

setting up a transaction as a long-term asset subject to depreciation or amortization over a period of years, rather than being written off in the current year; the tax rules state that capital assets (with a useful life of more than one year) must be capitalized and depreciated, and that current-year expenses are to be written off in the year those expenses are accrued.

Key Point

Any time a company knowingly leaves liabilities off the balance sheet, it is manipulation. Investors have the right to expect full disclosure, and they rely on that to make investing decisions.

This manipulation is used when a company wants to appear to have more equity than it does. This deceives stockholders as well as bondholders, both of whom rely on the integrity of the financial statements.

These forms of misrepresentation do not occur with regularity, because when a company is caught, the penalties may include both civil and criminal charges. However, these kinds of abuses are found in some companies every year. A stockholder able to study long-term trends may spot questionable volatility, and that can be a danger signal. However, for the most part, the combination of honest corporate officers, diligent auditors, and a vigilant regulatory environment makes misrepresentation rare.

Even so, it is always wise to know how distortions may occur, and to look for examples that distort trends or lead to irregular spikes and changes in the numbers.

THE REGULATORY ENVIRONMENT

The regulatory environment for investing is complex and exists on many levels. This includes governmental regulators as well as self-regulatory organizations within the industry.

The auditing industry, consisting of accounting firms, is meant to ensure that published financial statements of publicly traded companies meet the standards under Generally Accepted Accounting Principles (GAAP). This system exists in an informal collection of agencies, published opinions and papers, standards, and practices within the industries. Central to this standard-setting is the American Institute of Certified Public Accountants (AICPA).

This is the world's biggest accounting membership organization, with nearly 400,000 members in over 125 countries. The AICPA sets standards for accounting practice as well as ethical auditing standards for its members. The organization also administers the CPA exams and issues credentials for specialties within the CPA universe.

written off

the act of recognizing expenses in the current year, and applying them to reduce net profits; the accumulated annual costs and expenses are deducted from revenue to arrive at operating profit.

Valuable Resource
To learn more about the AICPA, visit its website at **www .aicpa.org.**

A second and equally important organization providing oversight in the accounting industry is the Financial Accounting Standards Board (FASB). This organization works with the AICPA and federal and state regulators in the development of uniform standards of accounting and financial reporting.

Valuable Resource
The website for FASB is **www.fasb.org/home**.

The AICPA and FASB provide standards in cooperation with state and federal regulators. Every state has its own securities oversight organizations. These audit broker dealers and investment companies within their borders and cooperate with the Securities and Exchange Commission (SEC) when questions arise about possible violations of the law by those companies.

Example

Monitoring the monitors: Auditing firms are set up to audit publicly listed companies and to provide a range of accounting and legal services. But if a company or an auditing firm breaks the rules, the incident is reported to the regulatory agencies. This protects investors and the general public.

A central organization focused on protecting investors is the North American Securities Administrators Association (NASAA). This organization works with regulators to ensure compliance among investment companies and broker-dealers with state and federal laws and also functions as a consumer protection agency within the securities industry.

Valuable Resource

The website for NASAA also lists the contact information for securities regulators in every state: **www.nasaa.org/about-us/contact-us/contact-your-regulator**.

Overseeing the entire industry, including listed companies, exchanges broker-dealers, accounting firms, and financial advisors, is the Securities and Exchange Commission (SEC). The SEC was formed as a response to the lack of regulation existing before the Great Crash of 1929. At that time, financial disclosure and the means to prevent fraud in stock trading were practically nonexistent.

Franklin D. Roosevelt was president when Congress passed the landmark Securities Act of 1933 and Securities Exchange Act of 1934. Under the 1934 Act, the SEC came into existence under its first chairman, Joseph Kennedy, father of future president John F. Kennedy.

In this newly formed regulatory environment, two major and new standards were set: First, any company offering securities to be traded publicly is required to disclose all important facts about its business and investment risks involved in buying its securities. Second, organizations selling securities, including brokers, dealers, and exchanges, are required to treat investors fairly.

From its founding until today, the SEC is the primary federal regulator of the securities industry and all of its participants.

Valuable Resource
The Securities and Exchange Commission (SEC) provides many useful resources and explanations of regulations on its website, **www.sec.gov**.

Several laws govern the range of participants and practices in the securities industry. These include:

Securities Act of 1933

The act, also called the "truth in securities" law, requires disclosure of significant information by anyone selling securities, prohibits misrepresentation or fraud when selling securities.

The full text is available at www.sec.gov/about/laws/sa33.pdf.

Securities Exchange Act of 1934

This law created and funded the SEC, and granted it authority over the entire securities industry. This includes brokerage firms, exchanges, agents, and self-regulatory organizations. The act also provided the SEC the authority to require reporting from companies trading securities publicly.

The full text can be viewed at www.sec.gov/about/laws/sea34.pdf.

Trust Indenture Act of 1939

This law identifies requirements for debt securities, such as bonds and notes, offered to the public; these may not be sold unless an agreement (a trust indenture) is created and put into effect.

The act's full text is found at www.sec.gov/about/laws/tia39.pdf.

Investment Company Act of 1940

This law provides oversight of investment companies (e.g., mutual funds) engaged in securities trading on behalf of the public. It requires full disclosure of risks and financial information as well as financial objectives. The text of the law can be seen at www.sec.gov/about/laws/ica40.pdf.

Investment Advisers Act of 1940

This law regulates activities of professionals offering investment advice. Advisers must register with the SEC (with at least $100 million under management). The full text is found at www.sec.gov/about/laws/iaa40.pdf.

Sarbanes-Oxley Act of 2002

The act (SOX) reformed the industry following the period of widespread abuses, on the part of both corporations and auditing firms, and created a new Public Company Accounting Oversight Board (PCAOB).

The text can be found at www.sec.gov/about/laws/soa2002.pdf.

Dodd-Frank Wall Street Reform and Consumer Protection Act of 2010

This act is intended to revise the securities industry in terms of consumer protection, trading restrictions, credit ratings, corporate governance, and more. The full text can be viewed at www.sec.gov/about/laws/wallstreetreform-cpa.pdf.

For every investor, the laws determine how companies report their transactions, and what they must report. Although a lot of background has gone into this, it all comes down to the communication of information every investor receives in the form of notices, such as a prospectus, earnings reports, and, of course, financial statements.

TYPES OF FINANCIAL STATEMENTS

Three types of financial statements are published quarterly, and these are set up in a standard manner. However, many other financial news stories, announcements, and specialized reports are also issued.

The emphasis here is on two of the three financial statements: the *balance sheet* and the *income statement*. More detailed explanations are provided in Chapter 3 (Balance Sheet Ratios) and Chapter 4 (Income Statement Ratios). And Chapter 6 explains the contents of the annual report.

The third financial statement is called the *Statement of Cash Flows*. This is a restatement of transactions during the year on a cash basis, showing the amount of cash received (from income, sale of assets, and loans) and paid (to buy assets, repay loans, or for losses). For the purposes of fundamental analysis, this book focuses on the first two financial statements and on ratios and trends about *working capital* and will not devote more space to this third and more technical financial statement.

Example

Go with the flow—The Statement of Cash Flows is merely a summary of cash that trades hands. So income is restated to exclude any accrued revenue and earnings, remove depreciation and other noncash expenses, and reflect the activity on a purely cash basis. For those wondering where all the money went last year, this is a useful summary.

Statement of Cash Flows

a financial statement that summarizes all of the company's cash-based transactions for the year, including breakdowns of cash received and cash paid; sources of funds include cash-based income, proceeds from loans or the sale of assets, and nonoperating items, such as currency exchange gains or interest received. Applications of funds include repayments of loans, money spent to buy assets, or any losses.

ANNUAL REPORTS

The annual statement includes all of these standardized financial statements as well as an extensive list of footnotes. These footnotes often take up more space in the annual report than any other section. For example, a comparison between three companies and their 2012 annual reports shows how much space is devoted to footnotes:[3]

IBM:

146 pages total

63 pages footnotes (43%)

Johnson & Johnson:

83 pages total

45 pages footnotes (54%)

General Motors:

182 pages total

103 pages footnotes (57%)

---

[3] Annual reports at www.ibm.com, www.jnj.com, and www.gm.com.

These footnotes often are complex and technical, written by accountants for other accountants. However, if you are reviewing an annual report and questions arise, you might find the answer in the footnotes.

The problem every individual investor faces is understanding these complex but necessary footnotes. For this reason, relying on ratios and trend analysis often provides a greater benefit; these are summarized versions of outcomes without detailed explanation, but often with benefit and insight about both positive and negative changes in a company's financial strength.

working capital

the amount of funds a company has available to fund ongoing operations, used as a measurement of how effectively it manages its money; the dollar value of working capital is equal to the total of current assets (cash and those assets convertible to cash within 12 months), minus current liabilities (money due and payable within 12 months).

Valuable Resource

Contact the *shareholder services* department for a listed company if you need help understanding a footnote or for any other questions about financial statements. Many online brokerage firms also provide a free analytical service through *S&P Stock Reports*, a highly detailed summary of 210 years' financial data as well as explanations.

The financial statements and the annual report are essential for developing insight about a company and how it succeeds (or fails) in a competitive market. The annual report has an additional difficulty to overcome, however: It is part financial disclosure and part self-promotional. So you need to distinguish between the basic financial information and the spin a company is likely to put on the negatives.

ANALYSIS: THE IMPORTANCE OF TRENDS

You do not need an accounting education to analyze the fundamentals on a financial statement. You need to be able to identify the trends that matter, and in coming chapters these trends will be examined and demonstrated. Chapter 5 presents an approach in which a short list of five key trends should be adequate to select high-quality companies as potential investments.

This does not mean you must use these five, or that other trends should be ignored. This is only one approach, but it makes the point that you do not need a comprehensive list of 20 or 30 tests. You can narrow your search with as few as five indicators, for those trends that are the most revealing.

shareholder services

a department in a company designed to respond to customer questions, and to ensure that financial information is fully disclosed.

Key Point

Trend analysis does not have to be highly technical. In fact, the easier and clearer a trend can be expressed, the greater its value. Investors should be able to develop and interpret most trends without the help of an accountant or financial adviser.

Trend analysis should be based on a few sound principles of statistics. These rules help you to ensure that the conclusions you reach in

net return

net profit divided by revenue; one of the most widely used income statement ratios, expressed in the form of a percentage.

tracking financial trends make the most sense and are accurate. These include the following:

1. **Remember, ratios represent relationships.** The ratio is a shorthand representation of a bigger number, and every financial ratio will be presented in one of several forms. A trend in dividend yield or *net return* is expressed as a percentage; some trends, like the debt ratio or P/E ratio, are also percentages but the percentage sign is left off.

   Other ratios are expressed as single numbers. The current ratio, for example, may be expressed as "2," which means current assets are twice the dollar value of current liabilities; when the ratio is "1" it means the two sides are approximately the same.

   As you study ratios, remember they represent relationships between much larger dollar values. They make it easier to understand a trend. For example, 3:1 is much clearer than $16,773,303 to $5,591,101, but both of these are the same relationship to one another.

2. **Be aware of spikes.** In statistics, a trend is recognized as containing typical entries in a data field, as well as untypical ones. These are spikes, or outcomes that are not normal. In developing a trend, spikes should be ignored because they distort an otherwise predictable trend.

   To qualify as a spike, a number has to be exceptionally different than those preceding it; once a spike occurs, it should be excluded only if the next entries are more within the normal range.

3. **Watch for leveling out of trends over time.** Every trend will plateau and level out over time. This is not

a significant change in the trend, but it is expected to occur. A change from one period to the next can never be expected to continue indefinitely. So over a large number of periods (such as fiscal years) you are likely to see a trend's growth line begin to level out. When revenue, for example, has been climbing at a rate of 20 percent per year, if it starts to rise only 10 or 15 percent that does not mean that the positive trend is reversing; it does mean that the growth curve is behaving in a normal manner.

4. **Make distinctions between dollar amounts and percentages.** Some trends are easily misinterpreted because analysts confuse the dollar amount with the percentage. This is why relying on ratios makes more sense than trying to interpret dollar values. So when comparing net earnings to revenues, it is easy to make a common mistake: If earnings are continuing to rise along within revenues, an initial conclusion may be that the trend is positive; but in some cases, the trend is turning negative. Here's an example:

Year	Revenues	Earnings	%
1	$425,860	$40,501	9.5%
2	517,006	47,681	9.2
3	553,569	48,714	8.8
4	603,356	51,285	8.5
5	656,991	53,873	8.2

At first glance, both revenues and earnings are rising every year. This appears as a positive trend based on the dollar values. But in fact, the net return is declining every year, from 9.5 percent in year 1 to 8.2 percent in year 5.

Key Point

Trend analysis helps spot what's really going on. The raw numbers are not easily comprehensible, so analysts and investors have to rely on the shorthand of a ratio.

While some leveling out might be expected, as explained in point 3, this looks more like a negative trend often seen during periods of growth. The top line (revenue) and the bottom line (earnings) dollar values are both on the rise, so it all looks positive. However, when analysis goes deeper, it often is discovered that internal controls are relaxed due to the positive growth, resulting in higher expenses and a lower net return. So from a statistical basis, be very aware of how the ratio trend is moving, because it often is not apparent in the trend of dollar values alone.

SIMPLIFYING THE FINANCIAL STATEMENT

The intention of ratios used for trend analysis is to simplify the process. The raw numbers are difficult to decipher, and abbreviated forms of expression are not only easier to comprehend but also easy to create.

Example

Math phobia: An investor has avoided using ratios in the belief that they are simply too complex. One day, a friend told him that the ratio is just a shorthand version of the larger numbers. A lightbulb went on in his head and he began using ratios effectively.

Another method for greatly simplifying trends is the use of graphs. For example, the previous example of a five-year trend in revenues and earnings can be greatly simplified with a visual aid, as shown in Figure 1.1.

In Figure 1.1, all three of the relationships are shown together—the revenue dollar amount, earnings dollar amount, and net return. At a glance, you can see that the curve of the earnings trend has not kept up with the curve of the revenue trend.

The next chapter discusses the levels of reliability in financial statements, and provides guidelines for deciding how much trust you can place in this source of fundamental information.

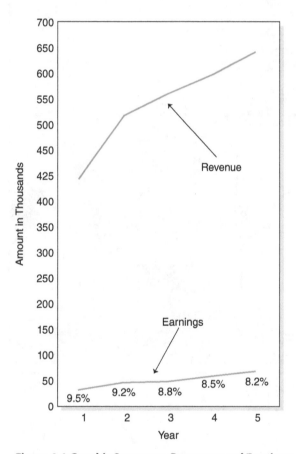

Figure 1.1 Graphic Summary, Revenues and Earnings

ORDER!
CALLING THE MEETING
TO ORDER!

MAIN ST.

FUN·DA·MEN·TAL
CLUB EMPHASIS
ON THE
MENTAL.

LET'S GET
STARTED.

NO
SMOKING

FIRST OF ALL,
DO WE HAVE ANYONE
WHO IS HERE FOR THE
FIRST TIME?

YES, ME.
MY NAME IS
MICHAEL.

I CAME TO
SEE WHAT THIS
GROUP WAS
ALL ABOUT.

MATH
IS SEXY

WELCOME,
MICHAEL. THIS IS
THE FUN-DA-MENTAL
CLUB AND EVERYONE
IS WELCOME.

ARE YOU
AN INVESTOR?

YES I AM,
BUT...

...I WANT TO
MAKE SURE WE
HAVE THE SAME
DEFINITION
OF WHAT
FUNDAMENTALS
ARE...

STALE COOKIES

NON-SPECIFIC AND ODD-TASTING SNACK

TERRIBLE COFFEE

SO MICHAEL, WHAT BRINGS YOU TO OUR LITTLE CLUB?

I'M A *WRITER* AND I HAVE WRITTEN BOOKS ABOUT FUNDAMENTALS.

FUN-DA-MEN EMPHA

NO, *REALLY*: WHY DID YOU COME TODAY?

WELL, ANOTHER REASON IS THAT I ENJOY PLAYING *CHESS*...

...AND I HEARD YOU SOMETIMES *PLAY* CHESS AFTER MEETINGS.

YES, WE DO. IN FACT, *CHESS* IS VERY MUCH LIKE *FUNDAMENTAL ANALYSIS*.

REALLY? WHY IS THAT?

CHAPTER 2

HOW RELIABLE ARE THE FINANCIAL REPORTS?

There are no whole truths; all truths are half-truths. It is trying to treat them as whole truths that plays the devil.
—Alfred North Whitehead, *Dialogues*, 1954

PUBLICLY TRADED COMPANY REPORTING

A *publicly traded company* is one whose stock can be bought or sold by individual investors as well as by large *institutional investors* and *insiders*. All publicly traded companies are required by law and regulation to publish audited financial statements; this is where the question of reliability has to be raised.

By definition, a publicly traded company offers shares to the general public and, as a result, has a special responsibility to ensure the public is given the information it needs to make an informed decision about whether to buy and hold shares of stock.

publicly traded company

a company whose stock is available to the public as investment or for short-term trading, usually through one of the public stock exchanges or electronically.

institutional investors

those investors that are not individuals, but larger institutions, such as mutual funds, insurance companies, or pension and profit-sharing organizations.

Institutions account for the largest amount of shares traded for publicly traded companies. Because institutions have much more cash to trade than most individuals, they also tend to have a greater influence on prices of stock. However, the larger size also makes it difficult to buy or sell shares as quickly as individuals can, simply because they own so many shares. A large block of shares, traded at the same time, would drive prices up or down immediately; the market might not be able to accommodate an exceptionally large trade. Consequently, institutions often have to spread buy or sell trades over a period of time.

Example

Should you be institutionalized?: Two investors each own shares in the same company. One is an individual with under $100,000 invested in various stocks; this is not an institutional investor. The other is a mid-sized mutual fund that manages a portfolio consisting of many stocks; this is an institutional investor, because it pools the capital of many shareholders into a single portfolio.

An insider—a corporate officer or major shareholder, for example—has information available about a company's future plans, new products, mergers and acquisitions, and other issues. However, trading on that knowledge is not wrong as long as the general public has access to the same information. The well-publicized insider trading problems that arise from time to time are references to insiders making trades based on information not available to the general public.

THE NEED FOR FINANCIAL REPORTING

Financial disclosures are needed by investors, as a means for selecting from a group of potential companies in which to invest. Fundamental analysis is based on the idea that strongly capitalized, well-managed companies are better investments than those not even reporting net income each year.

insiders

individuals who hold or trade shares of stock as primary shareholders or officers of the company.

Key Point

The entire system of reporting financial results relies on complete disclosures of material facts; withholding these facts would mislead investors, so great emphasis is placed on disclosure.

However, beyond the individual investor's interests, many other stakeholders are equally interested in financial reporting, and rely on it in many ways. These include:

1. Regulators: Federal and state regulatory agencies are responsible for ensuring the safety of investors' funds, and that financial reporting is consistent and fair. The Securities and Exchange Commission (SEC) is a primary oversight agency for this. The industry itself also has a self-regulatory agency called the Financial Industry Regulatory Authority (FINRA), which is a watchdog for the entire industry. It publishes rules for securities firms and brokers, conducts compliance exams, and educates investors through its online programs.

2. Credit rating agencies: The three largest agencies are Standard & Poor's, Moody's, and Fitch. Together, these three publish approximately 95 percent of all credit ratings of publicly listed corporations, their equity and debt securities, and government solvency and debt. These are among the agencies designated as nationally recognized statistical rating organizations (NRSROs). They examine the financial reports of companies as well as management, markets, and more, to set ratings as a measurement of

retail investors

all individuals investing and trading for their own account, excluding institutional investors.

bond underwriter

an organization that assesses a corporate bond issuer's creditworthiness and helps set the terms of a debt issue, acting as go-between for the issuer and debt investor.

market risk. This creates a layer of outside critical analysis beyond the independent audit and federal and state securities agencies.

3. Institutional investors: Financial reports are essential to the investors beyond so-called *retail investors*, or individuals. Included among institutional investors are mutual funds, pension and profit-sharing programs, insurance companies, and other large-scale money management companies.

4. Auditors: Among the hundreds of public auditing firms in the world, most provide not only audit work but also consultation on taxes, actuarial, internal controls, and legal and other services. The "Big Four" auditing firms work with a majority of the biggest publicly traded companies. These firms are Deloitte, PricewaterhouseCoopers (PwC), Ernst & Young, and KPMG.

5. Stock exchanges: The stock exchanges also have oversight for those companies they list, and impose financial reporting and other requirements. As part of the need to execute this function, the exchanges also rely on publicly issued financial statements and on quarterly and annual reports filed with the SEC.

6. Bond underwriters: A *bond underwriter* is an institution that funds debt issues by corporations, based on their credit rating. The underwriter is a go-between for the issuing company and eventual debt investor, and assists in setting interest rates and other terms based on the issuer's credit.

THE VALUE AND PURPOSE OF FUNDAMENTAL ANALYSIS

Even the most cautious investor may fall for a current popular fad, resulting from perceptions of value rather than real value itself. In the past, the tech bubble was one example. Fads in the markets come and go with predictable outcomes: They last a while, and then fade, and the more speculative traders may lose big.

Example

Following the crowd: A fad is likely to hit the market at any time. Are you interested in tulips? In the seventeenth century, speculators drove up the prices of tulip bulbs to ridiculous levels, and then the entire market for tulips crashed. So-called tulipmania is an example of a fad.

Fundamental analysis helps you to spot and understand the difference between a fad and a real value opportunity. Fads include not only specific market sectors but also "sure thing" systems. These ideas, often ways to get rich quick, never work; they appeal to some people who want easy answers, do not want to do any work, and think they can profit in the market without having to do any research of their own. This is not a wise method for investing in the market.

Key Point

One of the biggest mistakes investors make is in forgetting to ask a few basic questions, such as, "Has this company reported a profit?"

Fundamental analysis is far from perfect, but it is a system for applying known facts about a company, to make comparisons and to pick companies whose stock may be well priced and whose future competitive and market position is promising. Anyone using fundamental analysis is likely to make decisions based on the strength or weakness and long-term trends found in the numbers. In comparison, buying stock based on what you hear among coworkers, relatives, or friends is a poor method for finding the next good deal.

In fact, getting those "tips" can be as misleading and inaccurate as any other gossip. As a starting point, when you are given a free tip about a stock to buy, ask a few questions:

1. What kind of business is the company in?
2. Have its earnings per share increased this year, and by how much?
3. What is the current price and target price?
4. How much dividend does the company pay per share? And what is the current dividend yield?
5. What is the latest price/earnings ratio range?

You will be likely to discover that the bearer of the stock tip won't have these answers and might not have *any* of them. That should tell you all you need to know.

Relying on hard facts rather than rumors or opinions is one of the major benefits and uses of fundamental analysis. In addition, once you learn how to track a company's fundamental trends, you will be able to spot changes, both positive and negative. When a trend slows down or reverses, it is a signal to buy (if a negative turns positive) or to sell (if a positive turns negative). While this form of analysis more often is used in technical analysis, it also applies to fundamental trends.

Key Point

One primary reason to perform analysis is to spot when trends slow down or begin moving in the opposite direction.

multiple

the number of years' earnings in the current price per share, based on a calculation of the price/earnings ratio.

Ultimately, the value of the fundamentals is that they help you to decide whether a company is well priced. This is determined by a number of tests. For example, the price/earnings (P/E) ratio compares the current price per share to earnings per share. The result, called the *multiple*, represents the number of years' earnings that are reflected in the current price (see Chapter 5 for more information about the P/E ratio).

For example, a company's current earnings per share are $1.85 (total dollars earned, divided by common shares outstanding). The closing price of the company's stock was $35.75 per share. The P/E is 19.3 ($35.75 ÷ $1.85). This result, 19.3, is also called the multiple, and it means that the current price is equal to 19.3 years of earnings.

A general standard for P/E states that a moderate range is between 10 and 25. So if a company's P/E falls anywhere within that range, it is thought that the stock is well priced.

Key Point

The P/E ratio is the calculation of a multiple, representing the numbers of years of profits in the current stock price. The higher the multiple, the more expensive the stock.

FINANCIAL STRENGTH   WORKING CAPITAL   PROFITABILITY

Fundamentals generally have three broad classifications, and the value of each of these adds to the overall conclusions you reach about a company:

1. Financial strength: This may describe a company's asset value, brand name, or in a larger sense, its capitalization size.
2. Working capital: This is the liquidity of a company—the amount of cash it has available to fund growth and pay its bills.
3. Profitability: Is the company making a profit? Or is it losing money every year? Profits are essential in order for a company to survive.

Example

Three buckets of goodies: Among fundamentals, you decide to review a company's net worth and assets (testing financial strength), debt ratio (quantifying working capital), and revenue and earnings (profitability). These three cover each type of indicator.

LONG-TERM TRENDS AND RATIOS

Any form of analysis is improved with the addition of more data. In statistics, an attempt is made to draw conclusions about a large data set, with the selection of a small sample. This sample should represent the characteristics of the larger body of data; if so, then the conclusions will be accurate.

The same rule applies to the analysis of fundamental values. You cannot rely on any one dollar value fixed in time to understand its longer-term significance. You need to study trends to better grasp where the conclusions are and how they are moving. These are most often expressed in the form of ratios.

Key Point

Analysis is easier to follow when dollars and cents are reduced to simplified ratios. This makes trends easier to track.

Trends usually refer to movement of value over a period of time. Using a three-year trend is not as reliable as a five-year trend or a ten-year trend. The longer the trend is allowed to run, the better you understand how that trend is evolving and where it is likely to move next.

Trends used in fundamental analysis may consist of several different types:

1. *Changes in a single value:* For example, when tracking revenue or earnings from one year to another, the dollar value can be tracked and graphed so that the trend itself becomes highly visible.

2. *Percentages of change in a single value:* Another form of trend analysis is to track the degree of change from one year to another. For example, revenues and earnings may be tracked in terms of dollar value changes, or in percentage or change

from one period to another. While this adds a different perspective to the trend analysis, it may also distort the true significance of changes. For example, because it is not realistic to expect a trend to continue on the same level of change every year, a natural evening out over time could appear as a negative change in what actually is a positive trend.

3. *Calculation of two related items and the changes in their values:* When revenue and earnings are tracked together in a single graph, you can further spot whether the relationship between these two single values is widening or narrowing. Of course, fundamental analysts want to see both revenue and earnings grow every year, but if the net return (percentage of earnings to revenues) is declining even as the dollar values grow, that is a negative trend. The net return cannot grow indefinitely, but it is desirable to see a similar net return each year while revenue and earnings both increase. A long-term trend displaying this tendency is a positive one.

4. *Analysis of changes in a range of values:* Another type of trend tracks a range of outcomes. For example, the P/E ratio usually is reported by annual high and low levels. This enables you to track the trend in the range each year as well as the general level of the multiple itself. So a trend can be graphed with a comparison between high and low P/E for each year, allowing you to judge how much or how little volatility there is in both price and earnings.

Types of ratios also vary, depending on what is being reported. These types include:

1. *A to B:* A summary of the trend in terms of how the numbers relate to one another helps to clarify the meaning at once. When two dollar values are compared, $17.625 million versus $5.875 is less clear than the ratio of 3 to 1. So some ratios are always expressed in the lowest form of A to B to make the true relationships clearer.

2. *Percentage:* A favorite method for reporting outcomes is to calculate the percentage. Net return is a good example. Dividing earnings by revenue produces the percentage of net return. Within a long-term trend, changes in the percentage of net return are more easily comprehended in this way.

3. *Percentage reduced to single digits:* Some ratios are expressed as single digits. For example, the current ratio (a comparison between current assets and current liabilities) is usually expressed as a single digit. So if current assets are $10.664 million and current liabilities are $5.332, the current ratio is 2. This means the assets are twice as much as the liabilities. This relationship is usually either rounded to a single digit or reported with one decimal place. Another example is the debt ratio (comparison of long-term debt to total capitalization). This is a percentage, but it is reported as a number without percentage signs, usually to one digit. For example, if long-term debt is $36.4 million and total capitalization is $106.4 million, the debt ratio is 34.2 ($36.4 ÷ $106.4).

FUNDAMENTAL RISKS

Many discussions of fundamental analysis focus solely on the techniques of calculating trends and ratios and then interpreting them. The purpose is to create relative understandings of value, profitability, working capital, and financial strength.

Example

Crunching the trend numbers: You spend a lot of time analyzing the trends a company exhibits on the balance sheet and income statement. But one day you start to wonder: Am I just trying to pick stocks, or am I also developing an analysis of the risks?

> **Key Point**
>
> It is not enough to create an accurate fundamental trend; you also need to develop the ability to interpret the trend's significance.

This is a worthwhile pursuit; however, what is easily overlooked is the evaluation of the risks involved in relying on fundamental analysis. Among these risks are:

1. *Relying on reported financial results with one-time or non-core items:* The reported financial results can be in compliance with GAAP rules but still contain inaccuracies; this is a problem with the GAAP system. For example, items of income or expense that don't recur will include accounting valuation changes, capital gains or losses from selling equipment or real estate, writing off one-time losses, or gains and losses from changed value in currency exchange. Any of these can easily distort the profit picture. For this reason, Standard & Poor's developed an adjustment called core earnings in order to remove these extraordinary and nonrecurring items. This adjustment is included in the S&P Stock Report that most online brokerage services provide their customers free of charge. The core earnings after making adjustments (which might be substantial) is a more accurate profit based on isolating the revenues, costs, and expenses of the company's core business.

2. *Using flawed, incorrect or misleading data:* If the information on a financial statement contains errors or misleading information, relying on it can lead to higher risks as well. In the past, many investors, including professional institutional ones, were misled by falsified statements published by Enron and other companies. It was especially disturbing in some of those cases that the auditing firms were part of the problem. The once largest independent firm, Arthur Andersen, was forced to go completely out of business because of its cooperation with Enron's management in presenting a false picture of profit and loss.

Investors can only hope that such high levels of deception are rare. New laws (specifically Sarbanes-Oxley) were designed to police both companies and accounting firms to remove conflicts of interest. However, everyone relying on financial statements needs to remain diligent. Ultimately, the trend reveals everything and no deception can remain hidden for many years without the trends becoming distorted.

3. *Drawing inaccurate conclusions:* Even when financial statements are completely accurate and fair, you might draw conclusions not supported by the numbers. There are instances in which increasing net profits look positive,

but with declining net return, the trend is actually quite negative. (This is explained in more detail in Chapter 4, with examples.)

As complex as financial statements are, you may need to rely on interpretations provided by professional analysts, and to limit the indicators you rely on to draw conclusions. It is not reasonable to try to analyze all aspects of an income statement; even if you did, the results might not yield better information than you can achieve with a short list of focused ratios and trends. (Chapter 5 offers a few key indicators worth following.)

4. *Relying on past trends when, in fact, the current trend has changed:* Trends might last a long time, but no trends go on forever. Just as it matters that you can spot trends, it also matters that you can spot when they begin to change. The momentum of a trend eventually slows down, then stops, and then turns in the opposite direction or resumes after a pause.

   As trends evolve, they slow down for several reasons. As a matter of statistical averaging, no trend can continue to change at the same rate forever; the tendency is to regress toward the mean. This refers to the tendency of evolving trends to become ever closer to the overall average, rather than to continue changing in the same direction. Another reason for a trend slowing down is changed business or market conditions. A company cannot expect to increase revenues and earnings by the same dollar amount or percentage every year. The market for any product or service is limited in size and is shared with competitors. This means that unless a company is able to expand its markets or products, its revenue and earnings trends eventually slow down and stop growing.

5. *Ignoring market-wide influences on a stock's price:* The specific influences within a company's fundamentals are a primary reason for trends to develop or to reverse. However, beyond this a number of market-wide influences also may directly affect a company's fundamental trends. Market sentiment tends to move back and forth from bullish to bearish; economic strength and weakness have market-wide influence on overall prices as well as on the market health of individual companies. A specific industry may move in favor or out of favor with investors, not for any company-specific reason but just as a matter of what is popular in today's market.

6. *Failing to diversify due to strong fundamentals in one company:* You may develop a list of fundamental indicators that you consider the strongest of all, apply these to locating candidates, and find a company that perfectly suits your requirements. However, this does not ensure that your investment will be profitable, for a number of reasons.

First, indicators are just that. They indicate but do not guarantee how a stock's price will perform. So if your timing is off and the stock price declines after you buy shares, it could be a matter of timing that contradicts what your fundamental indicators reveal. For this reason, it makes sense to pick companies based on fundamentals, but time trades based on technical signals related to price, volume, and momentum.

Second, even if you find a company that meets all of your tests, it makes no sense to overinvest in one place. You need to spread risks by diversifying among several dissimilar companies. Relying on a set of indicators and then investing all of your capital in one company is not advisable, given the fact that prices may move up or down, and for many reasons beyond the fundamentals.

Third, some influences on a company's value and its stock price will not appear on the financial statements. Changes in management, problems related to product safety, or competitive forces can all adversely affect even the strongest fundamentals of a company, so many variables have to be considered when using fundamental analysis.

CONTRARIAN INVESTING FROM A FUNDAMENTAL PERSPECTIVE

contrarian

an investor who decides when to buy or sell based on an analytical study of fundamental (and technical) signals, as opposed to following the majority or making decisions emotionally.

Fundamental investors tend to focus narrowly on the dollars and cents found on the financial statements. However, this does not limit how you apply strategies within the market.

One system that has proven successful for all types of investors, including those relying on the fundamentals, is to take a *contrarian* approach to investing. This is a widely misunderstood approach. Many believe that contrarians make decisions opposite those of the market at large, meaning they sell when everyone else is buying, and they buy when everyone else is selling. This is not the actual process for a contrarian.

The most popular systems of trading are based on emotional responses to market activity. So when the market rises, the emotion of greed inspires many investors to jump into the market, often without even analyzing the fundamentals of a company. When the market falls, another emotion takes over—panic. Investors tend to sell to cut their losses, fearing that prices will fall even further.

> **Key Point**
>
> A contrarian does not do the opposite of the broader market just to be different; the contrary part is *why* that individual decides to buy or sell—based on logic and reason rather than on emotion.

A contrarian does not act out of greed or panic, but times trades based on an unemotional analysis of the fundamental and technical signals. A company with strong fundamentals is placed on a list of possible investments, and the time of buy and sell decisions is made based on price movement. This is where the contrarian outperforms the crowd of the market.

A majority of traders act in concert, buying when prices rise and selling when prices fall. The opposite makes more sense, buying when prices decline to bargain levels and selling to take profits if prices rise too quickly. But is this truly fundamental investing?

Some investors equate fundamental with conservative because fundamental investors do tend to be conservative in how they trade. But this does not mean you have to just buy good stocks and then take no further action, holding for the long term. In fact, it makes more sense to time trades based on not only the fundamental value of a company but also how other investors behave. This is the essence of contrarian investing.

Example

A "quite contrary" view: You don't consider yourself ultraconservative but you believe in the fundamentals. You make your decisions based on cold, hard facts and avoid emotional trading. You are a contrarian. (No, you're not.) (Yes, you are.)

Some market observers confuse contrarian investing with the efficient market theory (EMT). This is a theory stating that all current prices of stocks have already taken all known information into account and, as a result, markets act efficiently. Anyone who has traded in the market already knows that the market and price movement in the market are anything but efficient. In fact, pricing in the short term is highly chaotic. But EMT has nothing to do with contrarian investing; in fact, whereas a fundamental investor is likely to act as a contrarian in how and when a company is selected as an investment candidate, EMT refers more to the technical side and refers to the price of stocks, when and why they move, and whether it is possible to outperform the market.

Key Point

Contrarian investing as a fundamental approach has nothing to do with the efficient market theory, a technically based belief.

So make a distinction between the fundamental concept of contrarian investing and the technical theory of an efficient market. These are different and not even remotely related to one another. For more about the technical theories about the market, check Chapter 8.

IS BUY AND HOLD DEAD?

The traditional conservative approach to the market was *buy and hold*, which means just that—buying shares of stock and holding on to them for the long term. Today, the trend is moving away from buy and hold, and favoring much shorter holding periods than in the past.

buy and hold

a method for investing, in which high-quality companies are located and shares bought to be held for the long term.

The average holding period for stocks has been declining dramatically over the past several decades. For example, in 1945, the average holding period for stock was about nine years. By 1980, it had been cut to three years, about one-third the holding period 35 years before. Today, the average is under one year and can be measured in a matter of months and even weeks.

Figure 2.1 summarizes this trend, based on data from the New York Stock Exchange.

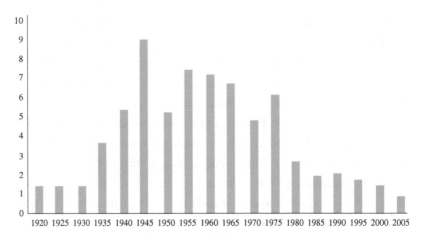

Figure 2.1   Average Holding Period, Stocks
Source: New York Stock Exchange.

Why has this changed? There are several contributing reasons. With the widespread availability of the Internet, it has become cheap and easy to move in and out of stocks as frequently as desired, and unlike the past when people relied on stockbrokers, most individuals trade online and enter their own orders.

Key Point

A few decades ago, investors held onto their stocks for years. Today, it is more typical to see holding periods measured in months and even in weeks.

Another cause is a widespread perception that buy and hold is not a wise move. Many people have seen their long-term portfolios lose value or fail to keep pace with inflation. This is due in part to selection of stocks that have not always been the best choices; but it explains why so many investors opt for much shorter holding periods than in the past. So a combination of price, access, and impatience contributes to the demise of buy and hold.

In the past, buy and hold was known as the conservative way to invest. It might still be true, depending on which companies are included in the portfolio. But today more traders favor fast profits and rapid movement of money from one company's stock to another.

Example

Living in the past: You remember your parents and how they invested, buying shares of stock and holding onto them for years. Your father recently complained that "these kids today" are impatient and buy and sell in a matter of weeks, even days. You see his point, and then you remember some of the companies he bought and held forever, such as General Motors and Kodak.

Another part of the problem is that some powerful and successful companies of the past have either fallen out of favor or gone out of business. In the 1970s the strongest blue-chip companies included General Motors and Eastman Kodak.

These companies, once held in high esteem, fell victim to competition, unsustainable retirement benefits, or changing technology. Kodak was late to recognize that digital cameras were replacing film, for example, and that led to the company's bankruptcy and plunging stock valuation.

Key Point

Today's strongest and most powerful large companies may fall from grace in the future, and some will not even exist.

The point is that companies once thought to be so strong they would dominate forever can easily become obsolete and give way to stronger companies and even to new market sectors. In 1970, for example, digital photography did not exist, and neither did entire industries that dominate today's market. These include everything connected to the computer industry, online service companies like Google, Yahoo!, eBay, and, of course, the computer giants, like Microsoft and Apple. The industries associated with online activity (computers, search engines, social media) did not exist only a few decades ago.

This explains why 40-year buy-and-hold investing is probably more dangerous than other methods. Change beyond imagination makes buy and hold a risky venture even for the strongest, best-capitalized companies.

The reliability of financial statements is only a starting point in the critical analysis of companies as potential investments, whether long-term or short-term. In 1970, anyone reviewing the financial statements of General Motors or Eastman Kodak would not have seen any warning of the demise of these corporate giants. So even while analysis of the fundamentals is crucial for picking investments today, everyone should remember that the fundamentals rely on past trends to anticipate the future. But the numbers are not the whole story.

They are a beginning, however. So a study of financial statements is a sound way to compare companies and to pick likely investments based on capital strength, working capital, and profitability.

The next chapter begins this quest with a study of the balance sheet, the listing of assets, liabilities, and shareholders' net worth.

CHAPTER 3
BALANCE SHEET RATIOS—TESTING WORKING CAPITAL

The almighty dollar, that great object of universal devotion.
——Washington Irving, *Wolfert's Roost*, 1855

Fundamental analysis is widely misunderstood. It reveals many trends concerning financial strength or weakness; but it cannot serve *directly* as the means for picking stocks. The financial statements are a starting point for understanding a company's working capital, profitability, and cash management levels. The analysis of all of this has to be comparative (from year to year for one company and between different companies or sectors).

Any investor who tries to pick a company as a sound investment based only on published financial statements has overlooked the point: You may begin with a review of financial statements, but you need to then make a comparative analysis to be able to judge whether a company has the financial strength to maintain its growth and competitive position.

This process begins with the balance sheet.

footnotes

a section of the annual report providing explanations of many of the line items of the financial statements, disclosing off-balance sheet items, and showing how estimates were developed.

accumulated depreciation

the total of each year's depreciation deduction written off as current-year expense each year; the sum of these deductions (accumulated depreciation) is deducted from the basis price of capital assets to arrive at the net asset value.

Key Point

Sound fundamental analysis relies on using a *comparative* analysis; no financial statements can represent all that you need to know.

THE BALANCE SHEET IN REVIEW

The balance sheet is a one-page summary of the balances of assets, liabilities, and net worth as of a specific, fixed date.

This date is the end of a fiscal quarter or fiscal year. The standard reporting format includes current balances as well as at least one prior period. Some quarterly balance sheets will include the same information for the three prior quarters. For most publicly listed companies, the results are reported in millions of dollars; this means you have to add six zeroes to the reported results to find actual, full dollar values. For example, if an account balance for inventories is 113.10, it means the true dollar amount is $113,100,000, or $113.10 million.

current assets

all assets in the form of cash or convertible to cash within one year (inventories, accounts receivable, and securities owned).

Example

It's a year, fiscally speaking: You expected to see an annual balance sheet and income statement for a company on December 31. It didn't show up, and you discovered it would not be prepared until March 31. At first, this puzzled you, until you realized the company's fiscal year ended on that date. The only published statement you would find on December 31 would be for the third quarter of the fiscal year.

Key Point

Balance sheets often are presented in an abbreviated format. When you observe the note "$ mil" or "in millions" it means you need to add six zeroes to determine the full dollar amount.

Because the balance sheet is highly summarized, you will need to look into *footnotes* to find more details of what one-line totals really mean. For example, the capital asset accounts (property, plant, and equipment) are likely to be reported as "net," meaning the single total of all assets as basis price, minus *accumulated depreciation*.

The balance sheet is intended as a summary of the asset, liability, and net worth accounts. The total values of all liabilities and shareholders' equity (net worth) will be equal to the sum of all assets. These accounts are further broken down into widely agreed-upon categories. On the asset side, these include: *current assets*, *fixed or long-term assets*, *intangible assets*, and *deferred or prepaid assets*.

On the liability side of the balance sheet, classifications include *current liabilities*, *long-term liabilities*, and *deferred credits*.

For an example of the balance sheet, McDonald's published its quarterly report showing the current quarter, as well as quarter-end values for three previous periods. This is summarized in Table 3.1.

fixed or long-term assets

the plant, equipment, real estate, and other capital assets owned by the company, less accumulated depreciation.

Table 3.1 McDonald's Balance Sheet

Assets	9/30/2013	6/30/2013	3/31/2013	12/31/2012
Cash and Short-Term Investments	2,544.30	2,278.40	1,869.30	2,336.10
Receivables—Total	1,285.30	1,301.90	1,230.00	1,375.30
Inventories—Total	113.10	107.80	105.20	121.70
Total Current Assets	4,734.10	4,632.10	4,191.20	4,922.10
Net Property, Plant, and Equipment	25,081.50	24,280.40	24,290.10	24,677.20
Total Assets	35,551.30	34,453.40	34,123.80	35,386.50
Liabilities				
Accounts Payable	3,822.30	2,805.00	3,017.10	3,403.10
Debt in Current Liabilities	NA	NA	NA	NA
Total Current Liabilities	3,822.30	2,805.00	3,017.10	3,403.10
Long-Term Debt	13,487.80	13,369.80	12,797.90	13,632.50
Total Liabilities	20,386.40	19,282.70	18,895.60	20,092.90

(continued)

Table 3.1 (Continued)

Stockholder's Equity	9/30/2013	6/30/2013	3/31/2013	12/31/2012
Minority Interest	NA	NA	NA	NA
Preferred Stock	0.00	0.00	0.00	NA
Common Stock	16.60	16.60	16.60	16.60
Retained Earnings	40,354.60	40,402.40	39,776.40	39,278.00
Treasury Stock	−31,685.50	−31,198.10	−30,811.30	−30,576.30
Total Stockholders' Equity	15,164.90	15,170.70	15,228.20	15,293.60
Total Liabilities and Stockholders' Equity	35,551.30	34,453.40	34,123.80	35,386.50

Source: NASDAQ, MCD annual statement.

These distinctions are essential because specific balance sheet ratios require an understanding of current versus long-term, applied both to assets and to liabilities.

Example

Comparing apples to apples: You are reviewing the financial statements of a company (e.g., Apple). You notice four columns, one for the current quarter and one for each of the preceding quarters. It seems like a lot of busy work, until you realize that in studying these dollar values, you can see how balances have risen or fallen from one period to the next.

intangible assets

all assets with value but lacking physical attributes; these include goodwill, brand names, and covenants, none of which have physical value but do have worth. The value of intangible assets may be estimated or assigned at a point of merger or acquisition.

FLAWS IN THE BALANCE SHEET

Since the balance sheet reports values of accounts as of a fixed date, its immediate value is limited. The real value in the balance sheet is in identifying trends over a period of time, from one balance sheet to another, and in the study of balance sheet ratios.

Key Point

Balance sheets represent account values as of a specific and fixed date. This is a quarter-end or year-end. The statement is good for spotting trends, but one period's balances do not reveal much by themselves.

Even with these limited purposes in mind, the balance sheet also contains some serious flaws and shortcomings. For example, *reserves* are set up for bad debts, and the reserve balance is deducted from the balance of money due from customers. However, the reserve is always an estimate; so based on whether the corporation was aggressive in setting its reserve, or very cautious, the outcome is affected, not only for the total value of assets and net worth but also for total current assets.

Valuation is also a factor for the value of inventory. Any corporation with large inventory balances is going to value that inventory according to one of many methods. These include actual cost basis or adjusted current value, which might be significantly higher or lower than original cost. Some portion of inventory might be lost due to damage, obsolescence, or theft.

Yet another problem with the balance sheet is that the *book value* of some accounts is far from the true current value.

Capital assets, including real estate, equipment, vehicles, and other assets with a lifetime utility beyond one year, are set up as fixed or long-term assets and then depreciated over a specific *recovery period*. This is the number of years of depreciation allowed by Internal Revenue Service guidelines. Some assets can be depreciated over longer time periods, and elections to use these are limited.

For example, a company spends money to buy the current year office supplies. This is an expense and is recognized in the current year, meaning the entire amount is written off against revenues, and reduces the amount of net income. However, in that same year, the company also spends money to buy a fleet of new trucks. These are capital assets and must be set up as long-term assets, and then depreciated over several years.

Vehicles are normally written off over five years, using a system called *accelerated depreciation*. This means that more depreciation is allowed in the earlier years and less is allowed later. This is an alternative to *straight-line depreciation*, in which the same amount is written off each

deferred or prepaid assets

the value of any cost or expense properly belonging in a future fiscal year; when cash is paid in advance of the proper period for recognizing that transaction, it may be classified as a deferred asset or as a prepaid asset. For example, when a company pays three years of insurance premiums in the current year, two of those years are properly classified as prepaid, and listed as assets to be recognized in the proper later fiscal year.

current liabilities

debts payable within 12 months, including all accounts payable, accrued taxes, and 12 months of payments due on long-term debts.

long-term liabilities

all debts due after the next 12 months, including long-term notes and bonds payable.

deferred credits

nonliability credits for revenue received that will not be
(continued)

year. The mandated schedule actually takes six years because the first year recognizes only part-year depreciation. So according to the IRS tables, the schedule for depreciation is as follows:

Year	%
1	20.00%
2	32.00
3	19.20
4	11.52
5	11.52
6	5.76

Source: Internal Revenue Service, Publication 946, "How to Depreciate Property," www.irs.gov.

This is where the valuation problems begin. Some assets become more valuable over time. These may include vehicles and airplanes, for example, or real estate. If a company buys its own building and takes depreciation over 39 years, it will eventually write the value down to zero. (The value of land is not depreciated at all, and is always carried at original cost.)

Key Point

The stated net value of assets on the balance sheet might be extremely different than the true market value of the same asset.

However, that land and building might have appreciated in value, in some cases significantly. So a real estate investment that has been entirely reduced to zero for the building and original cost for the land will be a very low-value asset. However, current market value could be substantially higher.

Example

Worthless real estate: You are reviewing the balance sheet of a company that owns a lot of real estate and has for many decades. You are puzzled to see that the value of improvements (all real estate except land) is zero on the balance sheet. How can this be? Then you research and discover that all of the buildings have been depreciated down to zero. The balance sheet fails to account for the current market value of its assets.

This means that the value of total assets is understated, as is the real value of shareholders' equity. Under GAAP rules, all capital assets are reported at original basis, minus depreciation. So any number of assets with market value will be reported after the depreciation recovery period as being worth zero.

Key Point

GAAP sets standards and rules for accounting, but it does nothing to ensure that asset values are realistic in today's market; all values are based on original cost, minus accumulated depreciation—no matter what that asset is really worth.

GAAP rules make balance sheet valuation very inaccurate. The GAAP system might be replaced in the near future with the International Financial Reporting Standards (IFRS), which allow companies to adjust capital assets based on current market value. This valuation method includes adjusting depreciated assets to current market value based on independent appraisals; while this could be abused to inflate asset value, careful safeguards should also be included to ensure a reasonable book value adjustment.

The timing of changing over to IFRS is not clear. The Securities and Exchange Commission (SEC) has extended its original deadline, and as of 2014 no clear new deadline has been set.

THE IMPORTANCE OF FOOTNOTES

Financial statements, especially those included in the formal annual report, are accompanied by a complex series of footnotes. These often

earned until a future fiscal year; because this income is not properly booked as revenue in the current fiscal year, it is set up under the liability section of the balance sheet and scheduled to be reversed and booked as revenue in the fiscal year in which it will be earned.

reserves

adjustments made to estimate losses or valuation of certain balance sheet accounts, including reserves for bad debts deducted from the balance of accounts receivable; the level of reserve affects the net value of accounts.

book value

the dollar value of assets as reported on the balance sheet, usually consisting of the original cost of a capital asset, minus accumulated depreciation.

recovery period

the number of years provided to write off a capital asset, with the correct period dictated by Internal Revenue Service tables and subject to limited elections.

accelerated depreciation

a method of writing off capital assets based on
(continued)

run up to 100 pages or more and can easily make up more than half of the overall volume of the annual report.

Many of these footnotes involve technical accounting issues, such as the method used for inventory valuation, calculation of foreign exchange profit or loss, or extensive explanations of *contingent liabilities* and other items not shown on the balance sheet.

Many other footnotes are simply explanations of how the company has set up reserves, accounting methods used to price inventories, and nonrecurring items (extraordinary items), such as write-offs for exceptionally large losses.

Footnotes are also used to expand highly summarized accounts into greater detail. For example, the balance sheet might provide one line for net property, plant, and equipment (capital assets). The footnote expands this by breaking down all of the subcategories (real estate, equipment, vehicles, furniture, etc.) and showing accumulated depreciation for each.

Key Point

The type of footnote most investors will find useful is one that expands on and provides more details for the highly summarized values on the balance sheet.

Most traders should be able to tell which footnotes provide good insight into the balance sheet, and which ones are too technical or do not add any additional information needed to decide whether to buy (or sell) shares. It can take time to make your way through dozens of pages of footnotes, but with practice, you can develop a sense of what you need to know. Without an accounting degree, most investors will be interested in very few of the footnotes, but those are worth reading.

THE KEY BALANCE SHEET RATIOS

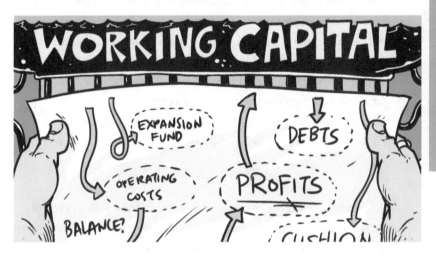

Most balance sheet ratios are tests of working capital—the level of cash available to fund the immediate and long-term operations of the organization. This is crucial because if a company does not have adequate working capital, it is difficult to expand operations, pay current debts, and create a cushion for times when cash is not available (e.g., when customers take longer than usual to pay their bills).

Example

Current might not be accurate: You have always liked the current ratio because it is simple and easy to follow. But you have been surprised to see that even when a company has a big loss one year, its current ratio does not seem to change. How can this be? If you lose money, you reason, your working capital should suffer. Then you realize that some companies offset poor performing years by incurring more long-term debt. That solves this year's ratio but could cause a lot of problems in the distant future.

There are several ways to calculate working capital, and each adds value to the overall analysis of a corporation's working capital strength (or weakness). The most popular method is called *current ratio*. This is a comparison between current assets (cash and other assets convertible

higher write-off allowed in earlier years, and lower amounts in later years; this is allowed for specific recovery periods as an alternative to straight-line depreciation, or writing off the same amount each year.

straight-line depreciation

a method of calculating depreciation in which the same amount is deducted each year; the total basis of capital assets is divided by the number of years in the recovery period to find the annual deduction (with less allowed in the first year based on when the asset was placed in service).

contingent liabilities

Estimated
dollar values
of potential
debts—that
is, what might
become debts in
the future; these
often include
the estimated
dollar amount
of lawsuits filed
against the
corporation but
not yet settled
or determined.
They are not
yet liabilities
but have to
be disclosed
because their
impact on the
valuation of the
company could
be substantial.

current ratio

a test of
working capital,
consisting of
dividing current
assets by current
liabilities, and
expressing
(continued)

to cash within one year) and current liabilities (debts due and payable within the next 12 months).

The current ratio is calculated by dividing current assets by current liabilities. As a general observation, the current ratio is expected to reside between 1 and 2. It is a simple calculation that shows whether current assets are high enough to pay current debts, and observations of this ratio should be made over a series of years. When you see the current ratio beginning to slip downward (especially if it falls lower than 1) it could be a warning that working capital is going to suffer in the near future. This might result in difficulties paying current debts.

For example, McDonald's reported (in Table 3.1) current assets of $4,734.1 and current liabilities of $3,822.3. The current ratio was:

$$4,734.1 \div 3,822.3 = 1.2$$

One problem with the current ratio is that it doesn't always tell the whole story. It can be affected by unusually high balances in inventory or accounts receivable, so that there could be an artificially high result in the calculation, even though in practice those current assets might not be as easily convertible as cash.

Key Point

The current ratio is well known because it is simple; but when accounts receivable and inventory change quickly or are growing each year, the current ratio is not a reliable long-term indicator.

For companies with unusually large inventories or with a tendency to experience wide swings in inventory values on a seasonal basis, an alternative to the current ratio is the *quick ratio*, which is the current ratio excluding inventory. This is also called quick assets ratio or the acid test.

The calculation has two parts. First, the book value of inventory is deducted from current assets. Second, the net is divided by current liabilities. This, along with the current ratio, is a key test of working capital for the next 12 months.

The McDonald's cash ratio includes the values in the current ratio but has to be adjusted by the value of inventory, $113.1. The quick ratio in this case was identical to the current ratio because the inventory value was too small to change the outcome:

$$(4,734.1 - 113.1) \div 3,822.3 = 1.2$$

Another version of working capital testing is called the *cash ratio*. This is more conservative than the current ratio or quick ratio, because it excludes both inventory and accounts receivable. The cash ratio tests a company's ability to pay current debts with the most liquid of its current assets—namely, cash.

Here is the cash ratio for McDonald's adjusted current ratio not only for the $113.1 inventory but also for $1,285.3 for accounts receivable:

$$(4,734.1 - 113.10 - 1,285.3) \div 3,822.3 = 0.9$$

the answer as a single digit without percentage signs.

The test of working capital may be limited to current assets and liabilities in one of these three forms (current ratio, quick ratio, and cash ratio). But in practice, working capital is managed and planned over many years. Another test, the *debt ratio*, might be the most important balance sheet ratio of all. This compares long-term debt to *total capitalization*.

The debt ratio is calculated by dividing long-term debt by total capitalization. This produces a percentage, although the ratio is expressed as a single value without percentage signs, usually to one decimal.

The balance sheet for McDonald's reported long-term liabilities at $13,487.80 and shareholders' equity at $15,164.90. So the debt ratio was:

$$13,487.8 \div (13,487.8 + 15,164.9) = 47.1$$

The debt ratio is one of the most important tests of working capital, and control over debt is tested on two levels. First, the corporate debt ratio should be compared with the debt ratio of a company's competitors. Each sector is likely to experience a "normal" range of long-term debt, based on the type of product or service it markets. The second test is the trend over many years. If the debt is level or declining, it is a positive indicator; but if the long-term debt is rising, it is a negative indicator.

quick ratio

a test of working capital excluding inventory values; the total of current assets excluding inventory, divided by current liabilities.

Example

Slowly going out of business: A lot of long-term debt might not seem like a big problem. However, if debt keeps increasing, it ultimately requires more and more interest to keep up. If the debt ratio goes over 100 percent it means there is no tangible equity left. When GM filed bankruptcy, its debt ratio was over 200 percent, and that didn't happen overnight. It grew and was shown in year-to-year trends.

cash ratio

a conservative test of working capital.

debt ratio

a test of long-term working capital for a company; the ratio is a comparison between long-term debt and total capitalization (long-term debt plus shareholders' equity).

Key Point

The term "debt ratio" describes a number of different calculations. The most reliable is the one used in this book, comparing long-term debt to total capitalization (long-term debt plus shareholders' equity).

total capitalization

the complete source of capital for an organization, consisting of long-term debt and shareholders' equity.

The higher the long-term debt, the more future profits have to be used up for debt service. This means having not only to repay the debt but also to pay interest on that debt. If a company's long-term debt keeps rising each year, more and more of the future profits will be absorbed by that debt, and less will remain to fund future growth or pay dividends.

If long-term debt begins to approach 100 (meaning 100 percent of total capitalization consisting of debt), less remains for net equity capitalization. If a company's debt ratio moves above 100 (100 percent), it means there is no net equity remaining. So if the debt ratio is 115, it means that equity is at *minus* 15 percent compared with long-term debt of 115 percent.

The debt ratio has several different calculation methods. The foregoing is based on total capitalization; but debt ratio or debt-to-equity ratio is also used to describe long-term debt divided by assets, or as a comparison between debt and equity. Using total capitalization makes the most sense because its trend reveals gradual tendencies to increase or decrease a company's reliance on debt versus growth in equity over many years.

The next chapter examines the formatting and ratios of the income statement.

BUT THOSE TRENDS AND RATIOS *COME FROM* THE BALANCE SHEET.

WITHOUT THAT, THERE ARE *NO* RATIOS, RIGHT?

I THINK THE BALANCE SHEET IS KIND OF *BORING*.

IT'S *JUST* A LIST OF NUMBERS AND TOTALS.

BUT THOSE NUMBERS CAN BE *BOILED DOWN* INTO *VALUABLE* INFORMATION.

JUST LIKE WHAT YOU FIND IN THE *FOOTNOTES*.

4

INCOME STATEMENT RATIOS—TRENDS AND PROFITS

Good people are good business because they've come to wisdom through failure.
We get very little wisdom from success, you know.
—William Saroyan, *New York Journal-American*,
August 23, 1961

The second financial statement is the income statement (also called the Profit and Loss Statement). Unlike the balance sheet, which reports balances as of a fixed date, the income statement summarizes transactions over a period of time. This usually is a fiscal quarter or a fiscal year.

The income statement's period ends on the same date that the balance sheet summarizes balances of assets, liabilities, and stockholders' equity. For example, if the income statement summarizes all transactions from January 1 through December 31, the corresponding balance sheet is dated December 31.

revenue

the top line of the income statement, representing earned income of the company, and including cash receipts as well as income earned and not yet received.

cost of goods sold

costs directly associated with the generation of revenue, including merchandise purchased, adjustments for changes in inventory levels, direct labor, and other specific costs.

Key Point

The income statement summarizes transactions over a period of time; its ending date is the same date that the corresponding balance sheet reports balances of assets, liabilities, and equity accounts.

The income statement has several parts. At the very top is *revenue* (or income); deducted from this is the *cost of goods sold*, resulting in *gross profit*. After this, *operating expenses* are deducted to arrive at *operating profit*. Next, a series of *nonoperating income and expense* items are adjusted. (These include currency exchange, interest income or expense, capital gains or losses, and any other items not belonging to the operations of the company.) This adjustment results in *pretax income*. Taxes are then deducted to arrive at the *net profit*.

The income statement is a series of transactions, reduced by categories described earlier to end up with net profit. These categorical distinctions are critically important because they provide the basis for many ratios:

Revenue – Cost of goods sold = Gross profit – General expenses

= Net operating profit + Other income – Other expenses

= Pretax profit – taxes

= Net income

THE INCOME STATEMENT IN REVIEW

The income statement is a summary of transactions over a specific period of time, a fiscal quarter or year. The categories begin with the top line (revenue), and categories are subtracted all the way to the bottom line, net income.

These categories are the keys to income statement ratio analysis and an understanding of trends. The comparative value of trends observed over many years is the core of fundamental analysis.

Key Point

The various categories on the income statement are used to calculate ratios and spot trends over time.

gross profit

the net difference between revenues and the cost of goods sold, representing pre-expense profits.

The income statement's transactions include not only the cash moving in and out of the company but also a series of accruals. These are adjustments made to the cash transactions of the company to move everything into the proper period of recognition. For example, income is earned in the current year but will not be collected until next year. In this case, an accrual is made to recognize income and set up the amount under the current asset, Accounts Receivable. When income is received, the receivable is reversed and cash is increased.

On the cost and expense side, a company owes bills at the end of the period, but will not pay them until the following month. So an accrual is set up to post the expense to the proper income statement account, and offset that with the current liability, Accounts Payable. When the bill is paid, the reduction in cash is offset by a removal of the bill from accounts payable.

operating expenses

general and administrative expenses and selling expenses, appearing on the income statement as reductions of gross profit to arrive at the operating profit.

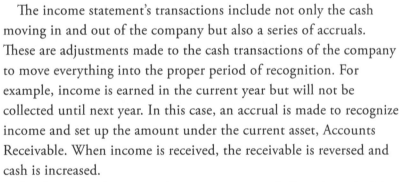

operating profit

the remaining profit after operating expenses are deducted from gross profit, representing the profit from operations, but excluding nonoperating adjustments for other income or expenses, and for taxes.

Nonoperating income and expenses

all items outside of operating profit, including currency exchange adjustments, interest income or expenses, nonrecurring and nonoperating items, and other items.

The accrual system allows the company to move transactions into the proper period. Without this system in place, a cash-only set of trades would be very inaccurate because items of revenue, costs, and expenses could appear in the wrong fiscal quarter or year. This would make the results inaccurate. With the accrual system, a company is able to create accurate results year after year, helping ensure that trends and the ratios that are developed from trends will be as accurate as possible.

Another attribute of the income statement is that it usually is prepared on a comparative basis. This means the current fiscal quarter is compared to the same quarter in the previous year, or that a series of the last four quarters are shown side by side. The fiscal year would be shown with the current year and the previous fiscal year side by side.

The *comparative statement* allows anyone reviewing the income statement to see how this year looks next to last year. Comparative income statements disclose a lot of useful information that would not be gleaned from a statement for the current year only.

The income statement may also employ both dollar values and percentages as one form of analysis. This is especially useful when reviewing comparative statements. The percentages help to quickly spot important changes from one period to the next, when dollar values might not be as obvious on a comparative basis.

Key Point

The use of dollar values as well as percentages is a good way to spot ratios quickly. Percentages are more easily comprehended in context than dollar amounts.

Table 4.1 summarizes a comparative income statement for McDonald's for four quarterly results, with all dollar values in the millions. This means to get the true dollar value, six zeroes have to be added to what the statement shows.

This is a comparative statement for four fiscal quarters. It could be modified to add percentages. For example, a comparative statement for the last two quarters, with percentages, would look like the statement in Table 4.2.

Table 4.1 McDonald's Income Statement

	9/30/2013	6/30/2013	3/31/2013	12/31/2012
Total Revenues (Net Sales)	7,323.40	7,083.80	6,605.30	6,952.10
Cost of Goods Sold	4,412.80	4,318.60	4,121.20	4,223.80
Selling and Administrative Expenses	493.90	567.50	534.60	522.50
Operating Income	− 2,416.70	2,197.70	1,949.50	2,197.80
Interest Expense	130.50	129.80	128.10	129.60
Pretax Income	2,272.60	2,059.90	1,816.80	2,068.00
Other Income	− 13.60	− 8.00	− 4.60	− 0.20
Net Income	1,522.20	1,396.50	1,270.20	1,396.10

Source: NASDAQ, MCD Annual Statement.

Table 4.2 McDonald's Income Statement

	9/30/2013	%	6/30/2013	%
Total Revenues (Net Sales)	7,323.40	100.0	7,083.80	100.0
Cost of Goods Sold	4,412.80		4,318.60	
Gross Profit	2,910.60	39.7	2,765.20	39.0
Selling and Administrative Expenses	493.90		567.50	
Operating Income	2,416.70	33.0	2,197.70	31.0
Interest Expense	130.50		129.80	
Other Expense	13.60		8.00	
Pretax Income	2,272.60	31.0	2,059.90	29.1
Other Adjustments	750.40		663.40	
Net Income	1,522.20	20.8	1,396.50	19.7

Source: Derived from NASDAQ, MCD Annual Statement.

These adjustments point out a few problems in how financial results are reported. The highly summarized first version excludes "other adjustments" between pretax income and net income, so these have to be calculated to make the math work out. This is a normal practice when the purpose of the summarized report is to reveal highlights of the financial results, rather than to present a mathematically complete picture.

In order to make the percentage breakdown work correctly, the missing elements have been put back into the comparative statement. Another line, gross profit, was added to the percentage-based statement. The change in gross profit is a very important item on the income statement and should be included in the percentage breakdown.

pretax income

operating profit plus other income or less other expenses, representing the profit from operations before deducting the federal or foreign income tax liability (state and local taxes are deducted as part of operating expenses).

net profit

the overall profit from all operating and nonoperating activities and taxes; the bottom line used to calculate net return.

comparative statement

an income statement reporting the current quarter and previous quarters in the same fiscal year, or the same fiscal quarter in the previous fiscal year; or reporting the full current fiscal year and the previous full fiscal year.

Key Point

Revenue is always represented as 100 percent for the purpose of ratio analysis. Every other line on the income statement is compared to revenue.

In the percentage system, revenue (top line) is always 100 percent, and each item under that reduces the total until the bottom line, the net return. To analyze this statement, some observations can be made:

1. Gross profit was 0.7 percent higher in the most recent quarter, an improvement over the previous period.
2. Operating income was a full 2 percent better in the most recent quarter, a substantial positive change.
3. Pretax income was 2.9 percent better than the previous quarter.
4. Net income was 1.1 percent better than the prior quarter. So the net return of 20.8 percent reflects a positive change.

Example

The percentage game: Your analysis was made much easier by observing the percentages instead of dollar amounts. Percentages, you discovered, are much easier to comprehend in comparative form. Dollar values cannot be as easily appreciated in terms of the trend they represent. The net profit trend of 5, 7.5, and 8.25 percent is quite clear, but net profits of $5,000, $7,500, and $8,250 are not as clear, and are not as easy to track.

FLAWS IN THE INCOME STATEMENT

Like the balance sheet, the income statement contains some serious flaws. The first of these is found in the way that operating and nonoperating items are combined into the one statement.

For example, the income statement lists one-time and extraordinary items. These are listed below operating net profit, but they remain a part of the income statement. Some examples include big gains or losses on currency exchange (and today, a growing number of companies operate internationally, so currency exchange could play a big role in net profits, even though this is not an operating item); capital gains from selling assets; changes in the way that inventory is valued; write-off of large assets due to mergers or acquisitions; and costs of acquiring or disposing of subsidiary companies.

> **Key Point**
>
> The typical income statement is designed to isolate nonoperating profit or loss from operating results, so that operating profit can be compared year after year without being distorted by nonrecurring adjustments.

A rationale for including these on the income statement is that they have to be reported somewhere, and they do represent a part of overall operations. This is true. However, when investors compare two companies in the same sector, the inclusion of large nonoperating profit or loss could make the comparison less than reliable. It could even distort outcome so no meaningful comparison is even possible.

A solution to this problem is found, at least partially, in an adjustment invented by Standard & Poor's, known as *core earnings* adjustments.

A comparison among companies in the same industry reveals the importance of core earnings adjustments for fundamental tests applied not only on the income statement but also on the balance sheet. The greater the core earnings adjustments, the greater the distortion of all financial ratios.

For example, compare two retail companies, JC Penney and Walmart. While these are vastly different in capital level and revenues, the core earnings adjustments reveal how much difference these adjustments make (Table 4.3).

core earnings

the adjusted net earnings of a company after all noncore profit or loss has been removed; developed by S&P, core earnings adjustments remove one-time and nonoperating items from the income statement. The core earnings number is found on the S&P Stock Reports provided to clients of most online brokerage services.

Table 4.3 Net Earnings and Core Earnings, JC Penney

Year	$ Millions		
	Net Earnings	**Core Earnings**	**Difference**
2009	567	258	309
2010	249	396	−147
2011	378	464	−86
2012	−152	−194	42
2013	−985	−1,074	89

Source: S&P Stock Reports.

JC Penney reported substantial changes between net earnings and core earnings, even though the dollar values were small compared to Walmart's earnings levels. But in 2009, core earnings sliced reported net earnings by more than half, a considerable change.

Walmart is one of those companies with almost no core earnings adjustments (Table 4.4).

Table 4.4 Net Earnings and Core Earnings, Walmart

	$ Millions		
Year	**Net Earnings**	**Core Earnings**	**Difference**
2009	13,254	13,505	−251
2010	14,414	14,414	0
2011	15,355	15,355	0
2012	15,766	15,766	0
2013	16,999	16,999	0

Source: S&P Stock Reports.

Few companies can report such consistent comparisons between net and core earnings. In a different industry, a comparison between DuPont and Dow Chemical demonstrates how core earnings adjustments can be substantial, so that a like-kind comparison between companies based on net earnings is difficult if not impossible (Table 4.5).

Table 4.5 Net Earnings and Core Earnings, DuPont

	$ Millions		
Year	**Net Earnings**	**Core Earnings**	**Difference**
2009	1,755	1,543	212
2010	3,031	3,112	−81
2011	3,474	3,090	384
2012	2,468	2,730	−262
2013	2,849	3,115	−266

Source: S&P Stock Reports.

These adjustments can be either way, as this table reveals. However, in the case of Dow Chemical, the change between net earnings and core net is even more pronounced (Table 4.6).

In this instance, net earnings were higher than core earnings in four of the five years; so in this case, adjustments were especially severe, especially in 2013, when nearly 31 percent of reported earnings fell into the noncore category. This has a big impact on most income statement ratios, including net return, P/E, and more.

Table 4.6 Net Earnings and Core Earnings, Dow Chemical

Year	$ Millions		
	Net Earnings	Core Earnings	Difference
2009	538	–312	850
2010	2,321	2,024	297
2011	2,784	2,265	519
2012	1,182	1,248	–66
2013	4,787	3,310	1,477

Source: S&P Stock Reports.

Yet another potential inaccuracy on the income statement is the possibility that some items don't get reported. These may include operations not reported anywhere on the financial statements, which, while deceptive, may also be illegal. This was one of the practices that landed Enron in trouble; undisclosed operations were set up to absorb losses while the reported income statement listed inflated profits.

Example

The core of the apple: You were interested in a particular company whose earnings have been consistent at 8 percent, and whose revenues have been rising steadily over many years. However, when you reviewed the net expressed as core earnings, you found big adjustments. Core earnings have been gradually declining from year to year. Because many of the noncore items were accounting adjustments and sales of capital assets, you realize that the reported net earnings will not continue, and that the initial report did not provide a true and complete picture of the company's earnings.

Key Point

The income statement should report *all* items. If anything is excluded, it distorts the overall picture of profitability for the company.

Other forms of inaccurate reporting may include any of the several methods for distorting revenue and net earnings in the current fiscal year: booking revenue in the wrong year, capitalizing expenses, setting up accruals to create added income, and deferring income to future periods in order to set up unofficial reserves for following years.

THE IMPORTANCE OF FOOTNOTES AND MANAGEMENT'S COMMENTARY

In the annual report, two sections accompany the financial statements and provide valuable insights about what the statements reveal, what they mean, and how to read them.

First is the largest section of the annual report, the footnotes. This section explains many of the items on both the balance sheet and income statement. There may be dozens of footnotes in an annual statement, but some of the most important are the following:

1. Significant accounting policies and practices, explaining accounting policies and judgments used in setting valuation and making accounting decisions
2. Pension plans and retirement programs, explaining how asset values, costs, and income or loss within these programs were calculated, and the level at which retirement plans are overfunded or underfunded by the company
3. Stock options, explaining the rights provided to officers and employees allowing them to buy shares of stock at a fixed price and by a specified date, and how exercise affects stock valuation
4. Income taxes, explaining how the company calculated current and deferred tax liabilities; these include federal, state, local, and foreign tax liabilities.

Many additional footnotes will be included to explain key elements both on and off the financial statements. Many affect both the balance sheet and the income statement. For example, a contingent liability (e.g., the potential cost involved in a pending lawsuit) affects future liabilities, but also has a direct impact on future net profits.

Key Point

Footnotes might appear as overly technical additions to the financial statements. However, disclosures included in footnotes are essential in judging the company's operating results.

The footnotes have to be reviewed, not on a technical accounting basis but to determine what information you need to know beyond what you find on the financial statements.

Another section of the annual report that may provide great insight is called "Management's Discussion and Analysis of Financial Condition and Results of Operations" (MD&A). This is management's explanation of how they read the financial statements and what the results mean. The discussion involves interpretations of what you see on the statements, as well as matters not shown on the financial statements but, from management's point of view, what you should know. The MD&A also includes a discussion of what management considers the key ratios and trends based on the published reports. In fact, under Securities and Exchange Commission (SEC) rules, management is required to disclose anything about trends that could have a significant impact on the company's financial health and profitability.

THE KEY INCOME STATEMENT RATIOS

The income statement is divided as it is to set apart those costs and expenses with specific attributes. For example, *direct costs* are assigned to the cost of goods sold because these costs—such as merchandise purchased and direct labor—are necessary to generate revenue. In comparison, all levels of expense are essential but are not directly related to generation of revenue.

direct costs

costs directly related to the generation of revenue, as compared to expenses, which are not directly related; direct costs include merchandise purchase and direct labor.

Example

The cost of doing business: You have noticed that a particular company's direct costs have been growing each year as a percentage of revenue. This initially looks like a big negative (even though net profits have remained consistent). But upon researching the question, you discover that the company has been expanding its product lines, including a very profitable new line with a higher than average cost to manufacture. Based on this variable, you realize that what first seemed like out-of-control costs actually were a symptom of growth.

gross margin

the percentage that gross costs represent in relation to revenue, calculated by dividing gross costs by revenue; this is a key income statement ratio.

The level of direct costs and the cost of goods sold define how carefully a company manages its gross profit. Cost of goods sold includes adjustments for changes in inventory as well as direct costs. The net of cost of goods sold includes:

Beginning inventory
+ Merchandise purchased
+ Direct labor
+ Other direct costs
– Ending inventory

The net direct costs are subtracted from revenue to arrive at gross profit; when gross profit is divided by revenue, the resulting percentage is call *gross margin*.

For example, McDonald's reported the following gross profit and gross margin for four quarters (Table 4.7).

Table 4.7 McDonald's Gross Profit and Gross Margin

	$ Millions			
	9/30/2013	**6/30/2013**	**3/31/2013**	**12/31/2012**
Revenue	7,323.40	7,083.80	6,605.30	6,952.10
Costs	4,412.80	4,318.60	4,121.20	4,223.80
Gross Profit	2,910.60	2,765.20	2,484.10	2,728.30
Gross Margin	39.7%	39.0%	37.7%	39.2%

Source: Derived from NASDAQ, MCD Annual Statement.

The results demonstrate a one-year trend in gross margin. For the three most recent quarters, the margin rose. However, this could be caused partly by seasonal factors, so without a more extensive analysis, it is not possible to draw absolute conclusions from this. However, it could be significant that a full 2 percent change in gross margin occurred between the March quarter and the September quarter.

To calculate gross margin, divide gross profit by revenues. For example, the 9/30/2013 calculation is:

$$2,910.60 \div 7,323.40 = 39.7\%$$

Another key income statement ratio is *operating margin*. This is the percentage of operating profit compared to revenue. Table 4.8 shows the dollar values and resulting operating margin for four quarters.

operating margin

the percentage of operating profit compared to revenue, the level of profits from operations and before calculation of nonoperating income or expense or taxes.

Table 4.8 McDonald's Operating Profit and Operating Margin

	$ Millions			
	9/30/2013	**6/30/2013**	**3/31/2013**	**12/31/2012**
Revenue	7,323.40	7,083.80	6,605.30	6,952.10
Costs	4,412.80	4,318.60	4,121.20	4,223.80
Expenses	493.90	567.50	534.60	530.50
Operating Profit	2,416.70	2,197.70	1,949.50	2,197.80
Operating Margin	33.0%	31.0%	29.5%	31.6%

Source: Derived from NASDAQ, MCD Annual Statement.

The operating margin varied between these four quarters, approximately to the same degree as the gross margin. The level of expenses was quite low in dollar values compared to revenue, so the effect of expenses was minimal.

To calculate operating margin, divide operating profit by revenues. For example, the 9/30/2013 calculation is:

$$2,416.70 \div 7,323.40 = 33\%$$

After operating profit, the other income and expenses are adjusted to arrive at the *pretax margin*. These other items include nonoperating transactions, including currency exchanges, write-offs, capital gains and losses, and any other form of profit or loss outside of the operating profit.

The calculation of pretax margin involves dividing operating profit by revenue. Table 4.9 shows four quarters of McDonald's results leading to pretax profit and pretax margin.

pretax margin

the percentage of profit remaining after adjusting operating margin for other income and expenses.

Table 4.9 McDonald's Pretax Profit and Pretax Margin

	$ Millions			
	9/30/2013	**6/30/2013**	**3/31/2013**	**12/31/2012**
Revenue	7,323.40	7,083.80	6,605.30	6,952.10
Costs	4,412.80	4,318.60	4,121.20	4,223.80
Expenses	493.90	567.50	534.60	530.50
Other items	144.10	137.80	132.70	129.80
Pretax Profit	2,272.60	2,059.90	1,816.80	2,068.00
Pretax Margin	31.0%	29.1%	27.5%	29.7%

Source: Derived from NASDAQ, MCD Annual Statement.

This summary conforms to the previous trends, with pretax margin reflecting relatively small adjustments in both expenses and other items. Pretax margin is viewed by many analysts as a true picture of a company's results, especially considering that multinational companies (like McDonald's) operate in many different counties and are subject to many different tax rates.

Example

An international puzzle: In comparing pretax margin for several different companies in the same sector, you noticed that there was little consistency. In fact, pretax margin varied by quite a lot. You discovered that this was due to different levels of costs for

(continued)

product lines. However, you also realized that pretax margins for each company should be well controlled from year to year. In this case, comparisons between companies are not always accurate due to the many differences in product mix.

To calculate pretax margin, divide pretax profit by revenues. For example, the 9/30/13 calculation is:

$$2,272.60 \div 7,323.40 = 31\%$$

After pretax profit, the tax liability is deducted to arrive at the last number on the income statement: net profit. When this is divided by revenue, one of the most widely used ratios, net return, is revealed. In Table 4.10 four quarters of results for McDonald's show dollar values and net return, net profit divided by revenue.

Table 4.10 McDonald's Net Profit and Net Return

	$ Millions			
	9/30/2013	**6/30/2013**	**3/31/2013**	**12/31/2012**
Revenue	7,323.40	7,083.80	6,605.30	6,952.10
Costs	4,412.80	4,318.60	4,121.20	4,223.80
Expenses	493.90	567.50	534.60	530.50
Other items	144.10	137.80	132.70	129.80
Taxes	750.40	663.40	546.60	671.90
Net Profit	1,522.20	1,396.50	1,270.20	1,396.10
Net Return	20.8%	19.7%	19.2%	20.1%

Source: Derived from NASDAQ, MCD Annual Statement.

The net return is fairly close for each quarter. This is typical of how the bottom line ends up with its net return. This is a positive trend because net return is not declining; in a well-managed company, you expect to see consistency in net return, but it is not realistic to expect it to rise every year.

Key Point

The average value of shareholders' equity should be calculated accurately, and based on how much it has changed and when changes occurred during the year.

Net return is the best-known and most widely used ratio derived from the income statement. To calculate net return, divide net profit by revenues. For example, the 9/30/13 calculation is:

$$2,272.60 \div 7,323.40 = 31\%$$

A final set of calculations from the income statement are based on net return on shareholders' equity rather than on revenues. The equity side of the equation excludes preferred stock, and combines common stock with retained earnings.

The level of equity often changes during the year. This occurs not only because net profits are added to retained earnings, but also because new shares might be issued or outstanding shares retired. In both cases, net shareholders' equity is different at the beginning and end of the year.

To find the average, a simplified method is to add the equity amount at the beginning and end of the year, and divide by two. However, if the change occurs closer to the beginning or end of the year, this is not accurate. For example, if equity occurs at the beginning of the fourth fiscal month, the accurate method would be to add the beginning equity (in effect for three months) to three times the ending equity (representing nine months of the year), and then divide the result by four (representing the four segments or quarters).

If changes have not been substantial from the beginning to the end of the year, the simplified method should be adequate to derive return on shareholders' equity.

Two calculations are used to find return on equity (ROE): the *pretax ROE*, which is the calculation before taxes, and *after-tax ROE*, or ROE based on net income.

The calculation in the case of McDonald's can be based on the 9/30/13 quarter:

Pretax income	2,272.60
After-tax profit (net return)	1,522.20

The four quarterly dollar values of shareholders' equity were reported as:

9/30/13	15,164.90
6/30/13	15.170.70
3/31/13	15,228.20
12/31/12	15,293.60

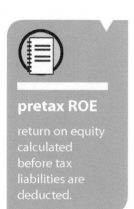

pretax ROE

return on equity calculated before tax liabilities are deducted.

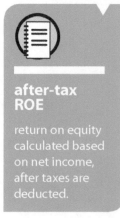

after-tax ROE

return on equity calculated based on net income, after taxes are deducted.

Because the levels of equity changed very little, the average can be calculated using the latest and the earliest values, and dividing by 2:

$$(15,164.90 + 15,293.60) \div 2 = 15,229.25$$

To calculate each version of ROE:

Pretax ROE: $2,272.60 \div 15,229.25 = 14.9\%$
After-tax ROE: $1,522.20 \div 15,229.25 = 10.0\%$

This enables you to see what the ROE was on the basis on pretax and after-tax profits, and it provides a valuable comparison that can be applied to each quarter or fiscal year.

Example

Inconsistent results: You have noticed that the after-tax results for companies in the same industry often are quite different. It first seemed that they should all be identical, until you uncovered the most critical variable: Some companies derive most of their profits overseas, so a variety of effective corporate tax rates make the after-tax results quite different among companies in the same sector.

The income statement reveals many useful values that, when applied in ratio form, begin to form trends. Studied over many years, the trends in turn reveal how effectively management has been able to create revenues and earnings.

The next chapter describes the five key trends that every investor needs, at least as a starting point in developing your fundamental analysis program for picking stocks.

5

FIVE KEY TRENDS EVERY INVESTOR NEEDS

Never invest your money in anything that eats or needs repainting.
—Billy Rose, *New York Post*, October 26, 1957

This chapter examines and compares five key fundamental indicators—
the P/E ratio, dividend yield, dividend history, revenue and earnings,
and the debt ratio.

Fundamental indicators are best studied as part of a trend. This
chapter provides a 10-year trend for each of these indicators. They are
also best studied on a comparative basis, so analysis is offered for three
companies: McDonald's (MCD), DuPont (DD), and Dow Chemical
(DOW) for fiscal years 2004 through 2013.

The format and length of this trend analysis enable you to see how
trends move over time, and whether they are positive or negative. Some
of the changes in trends are subtle and others are obvious.

Before embarking on the study of fundamental trends, every trader
needs to appreciate the nature of the indicator and what it reveals. It is
not enough to know whether a trend is positive, negative, or neutral.

Key Point

Trends are not always purely positive or negative, but may provide subtle clues about how to identify fundamental strength or weakness.

Each indicator contains subtle but considerable aspects that affect the decision-making process.

For example, the P/E ratio compares a technical value (price per share) to a fundamental value (earnings per share). This makes P/E an oddity. Most forms of analysis are restricted to the fundamental or technical side. P/E is compared to a broadly assumed medium of "good," which is between 10 and 25 by most analysts' calculation. But beyond that, there is disagreement about the positive or negative of both high and low P/E ratios and ranges.

Dividend yield is the percentage of the dividend per share compared to the current value per share. As the price of the stock declines, the yield rises; conversely, as the price rises, the yield declines. This is one of the aspects of dividend yield to keep in mind. A second issue is the dividend per share. This book emphasizes the number of years that dividends are raised. When a company raises dividends for 10 years or more, it is called a *dividend achiever* and is considered an exceptional condition. However, a second test is the *payout ratio*. This is the percentage of earnings paid out in dividends. This ratio is not included among the fundamental tests in this book, because the raised dividends are more important; however, if the payout ratio were to begin to decline over time, that would be a negative trend. So it is one more thing to observe in the overall testing of dividends declared and paid.

Revenue and earnings also contain subtle but essential fine points worth knowing. For example, while it is desirable to see the dollar level of both revenue and earnings increase every year, it is just as important to compare year-to-year net returns. The net return (net earnings divided by revenue) should remain at a consistent level each year, unless the mix of business changes (e.g., due to mergers or acquisitions that change the nature of overall products or services marketed). If both revenue and earnings grow, but the net return slips, that is a sign that costs and expenses are outpacing the growth curve, and that is a negative. In addition, all trends tend to level out over time, so it is not

dividend yield

the percentage of dividend earned, calculated by dividing dividend per share by the original basis in stock.

realistic to expect revenue and earnings to grow indefinitely at the same rate. That curve will plateau.

Example

Indefinite statistical success: You invested in a company whose revenue and net profit rose every year, but the year after you invested, both flattened out. This didn't make sense until you looked into the matter. Revenue, you concluded, could not rise indefinitely because the company had reached saturation of its market share. Earnings were also capped because it is not realistic to assume indefinite growth. The bottom line: When the trends seem overly positive, they could be occurring during a growth period, but you should not expect them to continue forever. They never do.

Key Point

A statistical principle that applies to trends is how numerical values change over time. No trends continue at the same level forever; they tend to level out over time.

The debt ratio also has to be reviewed with an appreciation for the subtle meanings underlying it. Of course, the lower the level of long-term debt, the more positive the indicator. However, there are situations in which a company will prefer to capitalize its operations with debt rather than with equity. If the interest rate on bonds is lower than the dividend yield, for example, debt could be a preferred method for funding growth. For example, if the company wants to acquire a competitor, it may fund the acquisition through a new bond issue. If the expected profits would more than cover the debt service, higher debt could make sense. The debt ratio also needs to be evaluated not only for its long-term trend (with increases in debt examined and understood) but also in relation to other companies in the same sector. What is the typical debt ratio and how does the subject company compare?

A reasonable conclusion about all fundamental analysis is that any trend may be positive or negative depending on how the reasons for change are

dividend achiever

a company whose declared and paid dividends have increased every year for at least the past 10 years, a distinction indicating highest quality among dividend-paying companies.

payout ratio

the percentage of earnings paid in dividends, computed by dividing dividends per share by earnings per share.

understood; how those changes affect or do not affect profits; and whether the trend itself indicates a stronger or a weaker capital structure.

TREND #1: THE PRICE/EARNINGS RATIO (P/E)

The P/E ratio often is misunderstood in the market. It compares the current price to the most recently reported earnings per share. This means the time period involved is not the same for each side. Current price is today's known price, but earnings may be weeks or months out of date. Price per share is a technical signal, and the value of earnings per share is fundamental.

Key Point

The P/E ratio is an oddity. It combines a technical value (price) with a fundamental value (earnings), and each side applies to a different time period.

Because of these factors, the P/E is a hybrid indicator, combining both types of analysis. As a general rule, the P/E is considered moderate when it is found between 10 and 25. Below that, there may be a lack of interest among investors; above that, the stock might be overpriced. But this is a general guideline and P/E is controversial. Proponents of both low and high P/E make this case in favor of a different level than the 25/10 range within a year.

A low P/E could point to not just a lack of interest but a real bargain-priced stock. High P/E is not always an overpriced stock but could be one that has greater than average potential for future growth.

Because P/E combines two different sides, one technical and the other fundamental, it is necessary to perform analysis of the *range* of a P/E from high to low for each fiscal year, and to compare this range over a period of time. A single P/E does not reveal much about the trend over time, and cannot be relied upon for any accurate conclusions.

P/E is computed by dividing the current price per share by the most recent earnings per share. For example, if yesterday's closing price was $50.25 and earnings reported for the most recent quarter were $2.34 per share, the current P/E is:

$$\$50.25 \div \$2.34 = 21.5$$

The result, 21.5, is called the *multiple*. This is the number of years of earnings reflected in the current price. This explains why the P/E is such an important indicator. The P/E is an abbreviated reflection of how the stock price per share compares with earnings. So if P/E is under 10, it does often mean there is a lack of market interest in the company; if it is sky-high—for example, 95—that means the stock is overpriced. The current price is the equivalent of 95 years of earnings at current levels.

The P/E is based on today's price and the most recently known earnings. A variation on this is called *forward P/E*. This is based on an estimate of future earnings per share.

The problem with using estimates is that the result lacks reliability. Although the standard P/E also has the flaw of different periods for each side of the equation, it is based on known results. The forward P/E provides some benefit for analysts, but the conclusions drawn depend on whose earnings estimate is used.

forward P/E

an estimate of the P/E based not on historical earnings but on estimated future earnings; the calculation involves dividing current price per share by expected earnings per share, usually over the next 12 months.

Example

A glowing estimate for the future: You have been using forward P/E to identify companies with positive growth potential. But in the past two years, you were disappointed to discover that the actual outcome never ended up as good as the forward P/E. Your acquired wisdom from this revealed the problem: Although fundamentals may be out of date, the numbers are realistic. Forward P/E and other forecasts are not as reliable.

Key Point

Forward P/E is useful in some forecasting applications, but because it is an estimate, it can also be used to create a desired outcome.

The P/E ratio is best analyzed for its annual range from high to low, and over a period of years. Table 5.1 summarizes this for the three companies in this chapter's analysis.

Table 5.1 P/E Ratio Comparative Analysis

	McDonald's		DuPont		Dow Chemical	
Year	**High**	**Low**	**High**	**Low**	**High**	**Low**
2004	18	14	26	23	18	12
2005	17	13	27	18	12	9
2006	19	14	15	11	12	9
2007	33	22	17	13	16	13
2008	18	12	24	10	70	24
2009	16	12	19	8	—	—
2010	18	13	15	10	20	13
2011	19	14	16	10	21	10
2012	19	16	22	18	52	39
2013	19	16	21	15	12	8

Source: S&P Stock Reports and annual reports.

These outcomes can be more effectively understood and compared by converting them to graphs. Figure 5.1 summarizes the annual range of P/E for McDonald's (MCD).

The P/E trend for MCD has been very consistent, with the exception of 2007. Because this spike is one-time and does not recur, it should be removed from the analysis of the long-term trend. This is a statistical concept. Because spikes are exceptions, they distort the true picture for averaging or trend tracking. Without 2007, MCD's P/E has been between 16 and 19 (high) and 12 and 16 (low). This is a very small range, indicating consistent and predictable P/E trends over time.

The story is not as clear with DuPont (DD), whose 10-year P/E is summarized in Figure 5.2.

In this case, P/E has generally remained in the broadly defined mid-range between 25 and 10, with some exceptions. And the range itself has declined over the 10 years. But unlike MCD, with its very narrow year-to-year range

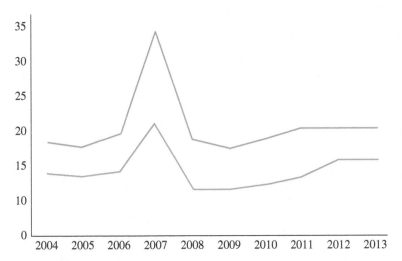

Figure 5.1 McDonald's P/E Ratio
Source: S&P Stock Reports.

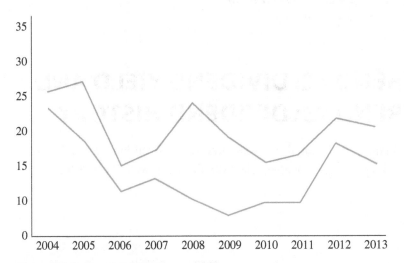

Figure 5.2 DuPont's P/E Ratio
Source: S&P Stock Reports.

from high to low, DD's P/E has shown far more volatility. The range itself is half of the analysis; the distance between high and low is the other half, and greater volatility is a negative aspect of the P/E ratio (Figure 5.3).

The third company, Dow Chemical (DOW), was the most volatile of all. The gap in the trend for 2009 occurred because the income picture was drastically low compared to other years. The year before had spiked up to a range of 70 and 24, a huge distortion off the typical range. In 2012, the range spiked again. In this case, the spikes cannot be removed from the analysis, because they recur and also because for DOW, typical P/E is not easily defined.

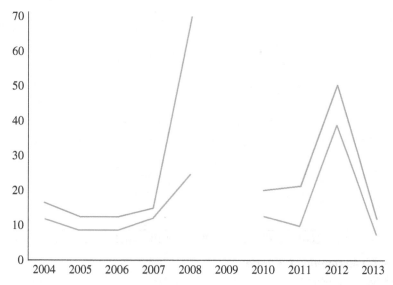

Figure 5.3 Dow Chemical's P/E Ratio
Source: S&P Stock Reports.

TREND #2: DIVIDEND YIELD AND TREND #3: DIVIDEND HISTORY

Dividend yield is not always well understood. Intuition tells us that as a stock's price rises, dividend yield should rise as well; but this is not

the case. The yield is reported as the percentage of dividend per share compared to the current price.

For example, you paid $42 per share for 100 shares of stock. The stated dividend is $1.25 per share. Dividend yield is:

$$\$1.25 \div \$42 = 3.0\%$$

The yield increases if the stock price declines:

$$\$1.25 \div \$40 = 3.1\%$$
$$\$1.25 \div \$38 = 3.3\%$$
$$\$1.25 \div \$36 = 3.5\%$$

The yield decreases if the stock price rises:

$$\$1.25 \div \$44 = 2.8\%$$
$$\$1.25 \div \$46 = 2.7\%$$
$$\$1.25 \div \$48 = 2.6\%$$

Another point about dividend yield often overlooked by investors: The effective yield you earn is based on the price you pay and the yield in effect at that price. This does not change even if the stock price moves substantially up or down, but remains fixed. This is true until the dividend per share is changed; even then, the accurate calculation of the new yield should be based on the new dividend per share, divided by the price you paid for stock.

Key Point

Your dividend yield is based on the price you paid for shares, and not on the current price level.

Dividend yield should serve as one of the core indicators in selecting a company as a potential investment. Companies paying higher than average dividends may represent the strongest potential investment candidates, as long as the yield has been offered consistently over time. But just looking for the highest possible yield could mislead you as well.

For example, if a company is in serious trouble and its share price plummets, dividend yield will increase, at times dramatically. So buying shares of this company could expose you to loss, potentially a very large loss, if the only criterion used is dividend yield. To pick a true high-quality company based on dividend yield, you also need to analyze dividend history.

Example

The dividend trap: You have been trying to find companies yielding 4 percent or more in annual dividends. One company currently is yielding 4.25 percent, so you are considering buying shares. You also noticed that only a few months ago, dividend yield was nearly one point lower. Further analysis revealed that at that time, share price was $33 per share, so the $1 per share annual dividend was 3 percent. Today's share price is at $25, accounting for the $1 per share, or 4 percent dividend. The higher yield is not positive, given the eight-point drop in share price. Before investing, you decide to investigate the reasons that the company dropped nearly one-fourth of its share price value.

This is simply the record of dividends per share that have been paid year after year. If you limit your stock selection to those companies that meet the definition of dividend achiever (increasing dividends per share every year for at least 10 years), you are likely to end up with a list of very high-quality companies.

Two cautionary points about this, however. First, also check the payout ratio to make sure that the annual increases are consistent as percentages of earnings. Second, if you find a company that has increased dividends in 9 or 8 of the past 10 years, you could expand your search to include these. For example, DuPont increased its dividend in only 6 out of the past 10 years; but the other 4 years were flat (dividend did not decline). This means the trend was not negative, although it was not as strong as McDonald's, which grew its dividend consistently every year, from 0.55 per share in 2004 up to 3.12 per share in 2013. Table 5.2 summarizes dividend per share for the three subject companies.

These results are better understood and compared when the trend is presented visually. Figure 5.4 shows the dividend per share for McDonald's over a 10-year period.

The consistent increase in dividends per share each year is easily seen. The dramatic rise each year is also visible in Figure 5.4.

Table 5.2 Dividends per Share Comparative Analysis

Year	McDonald's MCD	DuPont DD	Dow Chemical DOW
2004	0.55	1.40	1.34
2005	0.67	1.46	1.34
2006	1.00	1.48	1.50
2007	1.50	1.52	1.64
2008	1.63	1.64	1.68
2009	2.05	1.64	0.60
2010	2.26	1.64	0.60
2011	2.53	1.64	0.80
2012	2.87	1.70	1.53
2013	3.12	1.78	1.28

Source: S&P Stock Reports and annual reports.

The trend for DuPont, shown in Figure 5.5, was also generally on the increase, but the rate of growth was not as dramatic. The four years from 2008 to 2011 were flat.

Dow Chemical was very volatile in terms of dividend per share during the same 10-year period. Not only did the dividend decline

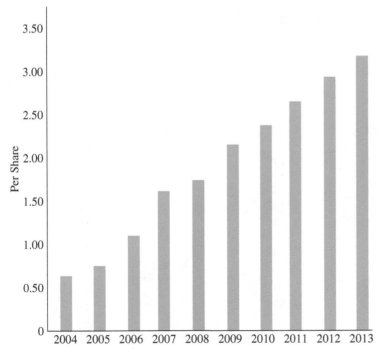

Figure 5.4 McDonald's Dividend History
Source: S&P Stock Reports.

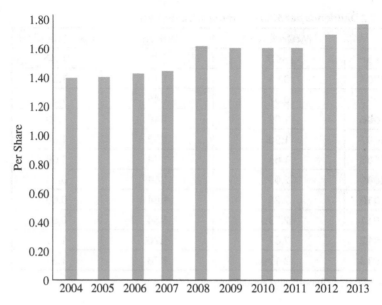

Figure 5.5 DuPont's Dividend History
Source: S&P Stock Reports.

dramatically in 2009, but when it again increased in 2012, the dividend was lower than the 2007–2008 levels. And for 2013, the dividend decreased. This volatile history makes it difficult to predict the future of dividends for the company (Figure 5.6).

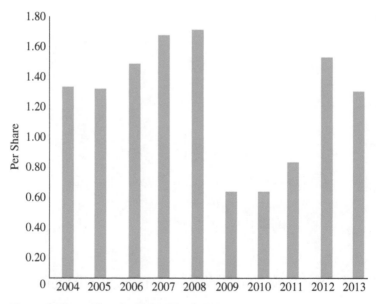

Figure 5.6 Dow Chemical's Dividend History
Source: S&P Stock Reports.

Dividend history is a useful fundamental indicator because it reveals so much about the company and its working capital. The funds must be available to pay a higher dividend, or the dividend has to be fixed or decreased. So dividend growth is a symptom of the profitability trend, as well as the level of yield the company approves.

Key Point

Growth in dividends paid is a symptom of growth, with strong increases indicating effective working capital controls *and* profits.

The volatility for DOW is further seen in the payout ratio, which swung wildly from zero up to 271 percent in 2008. The more stable years reported a payout ratio between 29 and 55 percent, a wide range but somewhat more predictable. In comparison, DD reported a declining payout ratio from 79 percent in 2004 down to 59 percent in 2013, with a lot of volatility in between. The most reliable of all was MCD, whose payout ratio moved from 31 percent in 2004 up to 56 percent in 2013, with a spike to 78 percent in 2007.

TREND #4: REVENUE AND EARNINGS

The analysis of revenue and earnings may be the most difficult to understand. Many analysts believe it to be an easy test, based on the desire to see ever higher numbers on both sides.

However, all trends tend to plateau and the rate of change tends to decrease over time. The subtle changes in net return are also crucial to understanding whether a change is positive. A reasonable outcome is for net return to remain consistent year after year. Settling for increasing revenue and earnings is not enough if, at the same time, the net return is declining.

Key Point

If net return declines even while revenue and earnings increase, it is a negative trend. Net return should remain consistent or grow over time.

The trend should be observed over several years. However, no universal standard should be applied because net return varies by industry. So a comparison among the same companies in each sector may be appropriate, but ultimately the trend for the subject company is what matters the most.

Table 5.3 summarizes revenue for the three companies in this analysis. McDonald's revenue rose in 9 of 10 years; DuPont rose overall with volatility within the 10-year range; and Dow Chemical's revenue level rose in 8 of the 10 years.

Table 5.3 Revenue Comparative Analysis

	Revenue ($ millions)		
	McDonald's	**DuPont**	**Dow Chemical**
Year	**MCD**	**DD**	**DOW**
2004	19,065	27,340	40,161
2005	20,460	26,639	46,307
2006	21,586	27,421	49,124
2007	22,787	29,376	53,515
2008	23,522	30,529	57,514
2009	22,475	26,109	44,875
2010	24,075	31,505	53,674
2011	27,006	37,961	59,985
2012	27,567	34,812	56,786
2013	28,106	35,935	57,080

Source: S&P Stock Reports and annual reports.

Earnings do not always tell the same story as revenue trends. Table 5.4 summarizes the dollar values (in millions of dollars) for the three companies.

Table 5.4 Earnings Comparative Analysis

	Earnings ($ millions)		
	McDonald's	DuPont	Dow Chemical
Year	MCD	DD	DOW
2004	2,279	1,780	2,797
2005	2,602	2,053	4,535
2006	2,873	3,148	3,724
2007	2,335	2,988	2,887
2008	4,313	2,007	579
2009	4,551	1,755	538
2010	4,946	3,031	2,321
2011	5,503	3,474	2,784
2012	5,465	2,468	1,182
2013	5,586	2,849	4,787

Source: S&P Stock Reports and annual reports.

To appreciate the meaning of revenue and earnings, they should be studied together. For this purpose, a series of graphs shows the more complete story. Figure 5.7 summarizes revenue and earnings for MCD.

Earnings tracked revenues on the same curve, which is a very positive indication. MCD showed very little variation from the positive two-part trend.

The case for DuPont's revenue and earnings trend is shown in Figure 5.8.

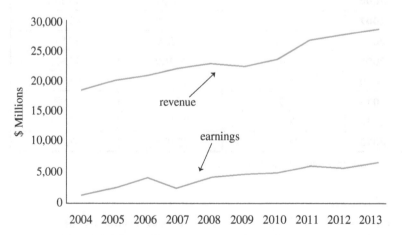

Figure 5.7 McDonald's Revenue and Earnings
Source: S&P Stock Reports.

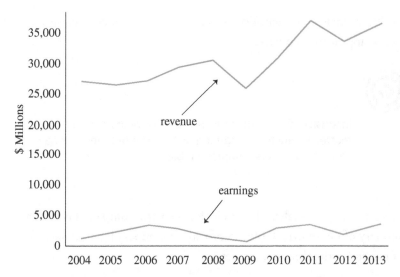

Figure 5.8 DuPont's Revenue and Earnings
Source: S&P Stock Reports.

This is a different situation. Revenue did not rise in a steady trend, but revealed two years of decline (2009 and 2012). Earnings did not track well but remained quite low and, compared to the revenue trend, were very flat. Compared to MCD, the DD trend was not positive.

The trend for Dow Chemical is shown in Figure 5.9.

This trend is very similar to the DuPont trend. Revenue did not climb consistently over the period, but rose and fell over this period.

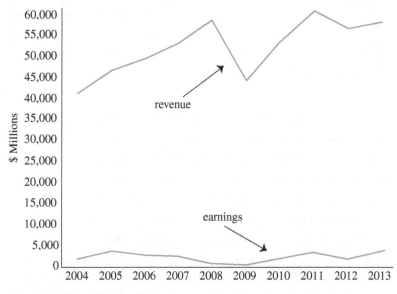

Figure 5.9 Dow Chemical's Revenue and Earnings
Source: S&P Stock Reports.

Earnings were low and flat. Even though overall revenues rose, earnings did not appear to keep pace.

Key Point

Inconsistent growth in revenue and earnings does not matter as much as a bigger question: Did net return remain consistent, or was it unpredictable?

Another way to analyze the results for the three companies is with a summary of net return. Table 5.5 provides a comparative summary of net return for the three companies.

Table 5.5 Net Return Comparative Analysis

	McDonald's	DuPont	Dow Chemical
Year	MCD	DD	DOW
2004	12.0%	6.5%	7.0%
2005	12.7	7.7	9.8
2006	13.3	11.5	7.6
2007	10.2	10.2	5.4
2008	18.3	6.6	1.0
2009	20.0	6.7	1.2
2010	20.5	9.6	4.3
2011	20.4	9.2	4.6
2012	19.8	7.1	2.1
2013	19.9	7.9	8.4

This comparison provides good insight into the relative changes in revenue and earnings. MCD's net return grew during the 10-year period, even with the two most recent years lower than the previous three. The change is small compared with the growth in dollar values.

DuPont had a more mixed history. Removing the 2005 and 2006 spikes, net return grew only slightly over the 10-year period. And the two most recent years were lower than the previous two.

Dow Chemical was the most volatile of the three, and growth over 10 years was slight, with 2013 only 1.4 percent above 2004. And the most recent result appears high compared to the previous five years, so there is no guarantee that the 8.4 percent level will hold up in future fiscal years.

This type of analysis points out not only the degree of volatility in change for net return, but also levels of reliability in the outcome. It appears that MCD has established an exceptionally strong growth curve based on net return; but both DD and DOW are unpredictable, so an astute investor cannot know where the next entry in the trend is likely to occur. It seems reasonable to assume that MCD's next net return will be somewhere between 18 and 20 percent. But DD and DOW cannot be accurately predicted based on recent outcomes.

Example

Consistency is reassuring: You have been studying return for several different companies. You find yourself drawn to the company with consistent returns over many years. And when you check other fundamentals, you also discover that they are just as positive and consistent. This one factor—consistency—is a sign of strong management.

retained earnings

part of total shareholders' equity on the balance sheet, the accumulated balances of all historical profits; each year's profit is added to retained earnings (or losses deducted from it).

TREND #5: DEBT RATIO

The debt ratio is a reflection of the relationship between two forms of capitalization, debt and equity. The equity side represents shareholders' equity plus the accumulated *retained earnings* (profits for each year), and is also the net difference between total assets and total liabilities. The debt side of the equation is all long-term debts, including bonds and long-term notes.

The debt ratio summarizes the degree of total capitalization represented by borrowing rather than investing. Because a company can capitalize its operations in both ways, the balance between equity and debt is a major consideration in the selection of one investment over another.

There are times when using debt rather than equity makes sense. For example, a company may issue bonds or borrow in the form of long-term notes to finance a major acquisition. As long as the return on revenues for the newly acquired company is greater than the interest cost on borrowed funds, debt capitalization makes sense. It may also be justified by arranging borrowings with an interest rate below the effective dividend yield. For example, if a company can borrow money at 2 percent but dividends are 4 percent, it makes sense to fund expanded operations with debt.

Key Point

rising debt is usually interpreted as a negative trend. However, if rising net returns outpace rising debt, the overall trend is a positive one.

Even with this reality in mind, analysts generally like to see a lower debt ratio rather than a higher one, or to see the percentage of debt declining over time and not increasing. The more a company relies on debt capitalization, the less money will be available from future profits to pay dividends or to fund more expansion.

The debt ratio trend is one of the most overlooked of all balance sheet ratios. But it should be included in the basic fundamental program because it reveals a trend of great importance to every investor. The total long-term debt is divided by total capitalization (long-term debt plus shareholders'

equity) to arrive at the percentage represented by debt. This is expressed as a number to one decimal place and without percentage signs.

The debt ratios for the three sample companies are presented in Table 5.6.

Table 5.6 Debt Ratio Comparative Analysis

	McDonald's	DuPont	Dow Chemical
Year	MCD	DD	DOW
2004	35.8	29.2	47.4
2005	35.7	39.1	37.4
2006	33.7	37.2	30.4
2007	31.0	32.5	25.9
2008	41.6	49.8	35.2
2009	—	55.5	46.3
2010	44.0	51.0	45.0
2011	—	55.2	40.1
2012	47.1	47.7	46.9
2013	46.9	37.4	36.9

Source: S&P Stock Reports and annual reports.

The two years of MCD's debt ratio with no values reported are years when debt was not a significant value or when it was zero. Note that MCD's debt has been rising over the 10-year period. However, during this time, the company was also expanding, especially in its international operations. This is a good example of how a company can rely on debt to expand its market share. Looking back to revenue and earnings in this same period, the growth curve was substantial. And while long-term debt increased from 35.8 to 46.9 (a 31 percent increase in the level of debt), net return grew from 12.0 percent to 19.9 percent (growth of 66 percent).

Key Point

Higher debt makes sense when debt capital is used to expand markets and create higher earnings and consistent or higher net return.

This change and the growth of debt are summarized in Figure 5.10. This visual summary helps analysts to appreciate the level of change within the debt ratio trend.

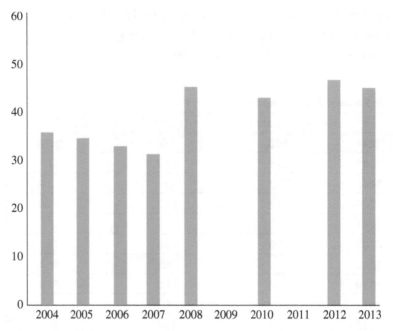

Figure 5.10 McDonald's Debt Ratio
Source: S&P Stock Reports.

In the case of DuPont, the debt ratio rose and peaked in 2009 and then declined. The net return for the same period mirrored the rise and fall of these levels, providing little insight into the future trend for this company. The debt ratio trend is summarized in Figure 5.11.

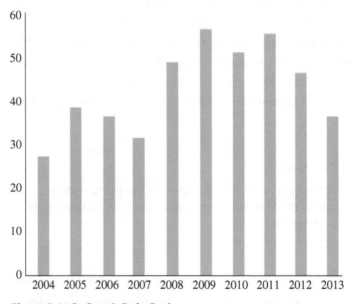

Figure 5.11 DuPont's Debt Ratio
Source: S&P Stock Reports.

One problem in the collective trend for DD has been that even while revenues rose, earnings have not kept pace. Over the 10-year period, net return rose 22 percent while debt ratio rose 28 percent. Compared to McDonald's, whose profits rose twice as much as debt, the trend for DD is disappointing.

How should an investor view this comparison? If the decision is to buy one company's stock or the other, it is clear that MCD has stronger fundamentals and a more successful series of fundamental trends over 10 years. This does not mean that DD would not be a sound investment; it does mean that if the decision is to be based on the study of revenue/earnings and debt trends, MCD has a stronger track record.

Example

Coke or Pepsi?: It makes good sense to select companies as investment candidates based on a strong track record of fundamentals. For example, do you prefer Coke or Pepsi? Or does it even matter? A personal preference for one product, or dislike of another, is a personal issue and not a sensible basis for picking an investment. Even so, many investors pick stocks impulsively or emotionally, which might explain why they do not always experience strong profits.

Key Point

Making comparisons of fundamental trends among several companies allows investors to see how strong or weak companies are in relation to one another. However, to draw accurate conclusions, the underlying reasons also have to be studied and quantified.

Dow Chemical presents a different picture altogether. MCD and DD could be compared based on the rise of debt versus the rise of net return, indicating a relationship between the use of debt and improvement in net profits. DOW presents a more typical outcome expected by analysts, in which debt declines while net return improves.

The debt ratio is summarized for Dow Chemical in Figure 5.12. The debt level fell strongly through 2007 and then rose again. However, overall debt fell 22 percent from 47.4 in 2004 down to 36.9 in 2013. This was a decline of 22 percent. During the same period, net return rose from 7.0 percent to 8.4 percent, an improvement of 20%.

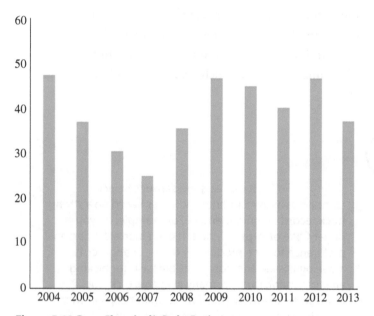

Figure 5.12 Dow Chemical's Debt Ratio
Source: S&P Stock Reports.

This is the strongest of outcomes among the three companies in one respect: Debt fell while net return rose. Even though the McDonald's overall fundamentals were the strongest (including justification for higher debt with each higher net return), the Dow Chemical results are clearly positive, but in a different way.

For all investors, the lesson of this chapter is clear: All ratios and trends contain subtle nuances and underlying reasoning that make it impossible to apply a single standard to all situations. Each ratio has to be not only understood in context but also applied collectively. It provides greater insight when two or more indicators are compared side by side, such as growth in net return versus changes in the debt ratio.

This is an advanced way of studying trends. Unfortunately, a lot of trend analysis looks at each ratio and trend as a separate indicator, and does not go further in attempting to develop an understanding of what change really means. In the case of MCD, higher debt was part of the process for creating greater revenue and earnings and higher net return. DD presented an uncertain result. And DOW reported lower debt with higher net return.

Example

What does the company sell?: A key question for anyone trying to find the best investment is, what does the company sell? This is a starting point of fundamental trend analysis. So when a friend tells you to buy shares of a company, ask them what the company sells. You will probably find that in half of the cases your friend does not know the answer.

All three cases were different and presented data that is not necessarily comparable. It does help to make fundamental comparisons among several companies, just to develop insight about the long-term trends and how they work together. But comparisons have to be made with other trends in mind as well. The relationships between net return and long-term debt, between revenue/earnings growth and net return, and between P/E range and year-to-year change make this point.

The next chapter moves beyond these specific trends and examines the contents of the annual report. This report contains not only the standard financial statements and footnotes but also useful narrative sections.

I'VE *HEARD* OF DEBT RATIO. PRETTY *OBSCURE* STUFF.

NOT REALLY. IF THE RATIO IS *TOO HIGH*, IT SPELLS *TROUBLE* FOR THE FUTURE.

JUST LIKE YOU CAN SPOT THE *WINNER* IN CHESS SEVERAL MOVES *BEFORE* THE CHECKMATE.

YES, AS YOU *PROVED* TO ME TODAY.

YEAH, SINDI *ALWAYS* WINS!

THAT'S BECAUSE SHE *KNOWS* HOW TO *READ* THE TREND.

THE ANNUAL REPORT AND WHAT IT REVEALS

CHAPTER **6**

Ours is the age of substitutes; instead of language, we have jargon; instead of principles, slogans; instead of genuine ideas, bright ideas.
—Eric Bentley, *The Dramatic Event*, 1954

A company's annual report is based on published and audited financial statements and much more. It is presented as a financial overview of the last fiscal year, but in fact it is both a financial and a public relations document.

The annual report is distributed to all of the stakeholders: customers, employees, investors, and regulators. A very similar financial report is also sent to the Securities and Exchange Commission (SEC), and is called a 10-K. (A similar quarterly version, the 10-Q, is also published but often without the final outcome of a fully audited statement.)

> ### Key Point
> The annual report is not only for investors; it goes to many different stakeholders, including federal and state regulators.

Besides the full year's financial statements, the annual report includes forecast changes for the next year, and management's interpretation and explanation of what the latest results show. It is inevitable that even when results are negative, management is likely to try to put a positive spin on the outcome. Many years ago, a small company issued its annual report with net losses that were higher than the net losses for the past four years. Management's explanation of this was, "The reduction in the rate of increase in net losses underscores our move toward profitability." In other words, we lost more money this year, but at a lower rate than before—good news. But actually, just more bad news.

This document is usually a full-color document with many dazzling photos printed on glossy paper, all extolling the high quality of the company, its cultural ethics, and the positive outcomes of its product sales. As great as the pictures and slogans might be, it's important to focus on what the numbers reveal. The positive imagery may, in fact, obscure what comes down to a weak year and bad news, not the opposite.

Key Point

If you're looking for a balanced and complete summary of both the good and the bad, the annual report—as a glossy presentation—is not the right document for you.

For example, General Motors filed one of the largest bankruptcy actions in U.S. history in 2009. At the time, its total assets were $82.29 billion and total debts were more than twice as much, at $172.81 billion.[1]

---

[1] Linda Sandler et al., "GM Files Bankruptcy to Spin Off More Competitive Firm," Bloomberg.com, June 1, 2009.

Could this have been anticipated by reviewing the annual report? Yes, if you looked at the numbers alone, but not if you looked at the glossy pictures and read the endless clichés in the annual report published for fiscal year 2004, five years before the bankruptcy. These clichés included:

Hands on the wheel. Eyes on the road.

We're on the right road.

Experience prestige.

A work of art.

Delight the senses.

Driven to excite.

Bring it on.

Power and style.

Breakthrough technology.

Peace of mind.

Fresh thinking.

Drive one company further.

No borders, no boundaries.

Global tool box.

Drive more dreams to reality.

Families first.

Drive to a bright new future.

Witness the evolution.

Touching lives.[2]

Example

The best slogans: How do you pick a company? Do you read the annual report? If so, do slogans sway you in any way? Or do they have no effect on you? Here's a good test: Read the slogan and then ask yourself, "What does this mean in terms of quality?" Does the slogan define a solid investment, or is it just a series of words? So to be critical about this, remember to keep an eye on the ball, build your own destiny, and develop your fundamental tool chest. (Get it?)

These were all in one annual report of 108 pages, which features page after page of attractive pictures of GM autos. But nowhere in the report do you find the disclosure, "We are going broke."

---

[2] General Motors, annual report 2004.

Annual reports do a great disservice to a company's stakeholders when the situation is dire but rather than honestly reporting it, the company resorts to dazzling photos and clichés meant to paint a positive and exciting picture. But as long as the numbers are correct and certified by an independent audit, a company can say whatever it wants in its annual statement.

SECTIONS OF THE ANNUAL REPORT

The annual report contains several different sections, and anyone reading the report should understand which ones are financial, and which ones are public relations.

Key Point

Both financial and promotional sections are mixed together in the annual report, and it is difficult at times to separate them from one another.

The line is often blurry. While the purpose of the annual report is to summarize annual performance and capital strength, management wants to report in the best possible light. So even while discussing the audited financial results, there will be some public relations effort mixed in. However, because the format for publicly listed companies is reasonably standard, reading more than one annual report becomes easier as you gain familiarity with that format.

The usual sections of the report are as follows:

1. **The letter to stockholders** (also called the letter from the chairman of the board, message to stockholders, letter to stakeholders, or letter from the CEO) is a fairly common

feature of the annual report, usually appearing near the front of the report. The purpose of this letter is to present management's view of the past year and also of future changes, goals and strategies, or improvements. If results for the year have been poor, management often provides a rationale for (1) why it happened and (2) how the following year will be better.

Key Point

A letter to stockholders seems like a friendly discussion from executive management; but it is one of the primary promotional sections of the annual report.

While General Motors is by no means the only company to spin its results, it is a good example. In the fiscal 2012 stockholder's letter, a number of highlighted themes included "a year of significant progress," "creating a sustainable competitive advantage," and "building the most robust business model."[3]

However, the financial results tell a different story. Compare total revenue and earnings for three years of GM outcomes, as shown in Table 6.1.

Table 6.1 General Motors' Financial Results

Year	$ Millions		Net Return
	Revenue	Earnings	
2011	$150,276	$9,190	6.1%
2012	152,256	6,188	4.1
2013	155,427	5,346	3.4

Source: S&P Stock Reports.

This brief summary reveals something far more disturbing than "significant progress" or a "competitive advantage." In fact, as revenues rose during this period, earnings fell, and the net return declined dramatically. During the same period, the debt ratio went from 6.6 to 11.8, an increase in long-term debt of nearly 79 percent.

---

[3] General Motors, 2012 annual report.

Key Point

Expect to find emphasis in the annual report on good news, with any negative aspects left out. The numbers disclose the results, but the annual report does not draw attention to anything negative.

So in reading the letter at the beginning of an annual report, be aware of how certain financial highlights are selected to cast the best light on the situation, and how the platitudes included in the letter do not have any real meaning. A review of the actual financial results and application of key ratios tell the real story.

2. **Products and markets** is a section that is purely public relations. This section includes numerous photos of products and describes markets and marketing strategy. Although this section does include important information about which products and markets contribute the most to overall revenue and earnings, the purpose of this section is to emphasize the positive attributes of products through pictures and graphs, and not to dig into the numbers in too much detail.

3. **Financial highlights** usually includes only a brief overview of revenues, earnings, and earnings per share. This might be broken down by segment or region, and is likely to include some very attractive graphs and charts. Anyone who wants a quick overview can easily get it from this section, but this does not provide explanations of the positive or negative results found in the more detailed numbers.

By this point, you are likely to be on page 20 to 25 of the annual report, out of a total running from 95 to 150 pages. Many people will stop here without any doubt, trusting the letter to shareholders and financial highlights to tell the whole story. But there is much more, and these early sections are meant to provide a brief and highly optimistic view of the past year and even more optimistic projections of what is yet to come.

4. **Management's discussion** is one of the most critical and revealing sections of the annual report. It should be studied carefully. In this section, management has to use the real numbers and disclose what they mean, so (finally) the

annual report gets down to the results and what they mean. This section is likely to also explain significant accounting decisions and policies. This means that the company values inventory, elects to use specific accounting methods, and establishes reserves for bad debts, among other decisions. While this will get more technical than most investors like, the section has many important disclosures.

Key Point

Management's discussion includes disclosures of how certain accounting decisions were made; even the technical explanations are useful, and this is one of the most revealing sections of the report.

5. **The opinion letter** is a letter provided to the company from its independent auditing firm. The letter explains whether, in the opinion of the auditing firm, the financial statements are accurate and complete, and whether this opinion is qualified in any way. As a general rule, an unqualified opinion is the best available evidence that you can trust the financial statements. In fact, the numbers are likely to be far more reliable than the multicolored pie charts and graphs, or the letter to the stockholders; but to know that you can trust the numbers, you also need to have the auditing firm's opinion letter.

6. **Consolidated financial statements** are the real results that everyone wants and needs. These statements include the balance sheet, income statement, statement of cash flows, and supplementary reports (such as diluted earnings per share). These also are prepared on a comparative basis, showing the current year and one or more prior years.

7. **Footnotes** take up more space than any other. For example, GM's 2012 annual statement takes up 182 pages, and 56 percent, or 102 pages, is devoted to footnotes. Some of these are required due to technical accounting rules, while others are supplementary schedules for the more summarized financial statements. Among the most interesting are the explanations in footnotes for items not on the balance sheet, such as obligations for long-term contracts (liabilities that are not shown anywhere) or

potentially large contingent liabilities. These are possible obligations. For example, if lawsuits have been filed against the company, a contingent liability is what the company would have to pay if it loses the lawsuit.

Key Point

Footnotes take up more space than any other section. You probably can't read them all, but some do give you insight not found in the financial statements.

Example

The complex is better, right?: Some footnotes are quite clear as to what they disclose. But others are highly technical, and a few just make no sense and appear to obscure the issue. For example, when you read that "profits were actuarially adjusted to reflect estimated restatements based on past experience and future projections with more optimistic assumptions," what does it mean? If you don't know, you're not alone.

Some footnotes are intended as explanations for the numbers themselves or how they were developed. For example, in GM's 2012 annual report, Note 2 ("Basis of Presentation") explains:

Use of Estimates in the Preparation of the Financial Statements

The consolidated financial statements are prepared in conformity with U.S. GAAP, which requires the use of estimates, judgments, and assumptions that affect the amounts of assets and liabilities at the reporting date and the amounts of revenue and expenses in the periods presented. We believe that the accounting estimates employed are appropriate and the resulting balances are reasonable; however, due to the inherent uncertainties in making estimates actual results could differ from the original estimates, requiring adjustments to these balances in future periods.[4]

---

[4] General Motors 2012 annual report, p. 75.

Some further disclosures get quite technical, such as an explanation of how securities listed on the balance sheet are valued:

Note 7. Marketable Securities

We measure the fair value of our marketable securities using a market approach where identical or comparable prices are available and an income approach in other cases. We obtain the majority of the prices used in this valuation from a pricing service. Our pricing service utilizes industry standard pricing models that consider various inputs, including benchmark yields, reported trades, broker/dealer quotes, issuer spreads and benchmark securities as well as other relevant economic measures. We conduct an annual review of valuations provided by our pricing service, which includes discussion and analysis of the inputs used by the pricing service to provide prices for the types of securities we hold. These inputs include prices for comparable securities, bid/ask quotes, interest rate yields and prepayment spreads. Based on our review we believe the prices received from our pricing service are a reliable representation of exit prices.[5]

The highly technical nature of these footnotes is typical. Much of the explanations involve accounting disclaimers and disclosures, so for any nonaccountants, these are overly complex and difficult to interpret. However, a read of these two footnotes can be simplified. Note 2 simply states that the financial statements were prepared according to the rules and requirements of Generally Accepted Accounting Principles (GAAP), including methods used for setting estimates. And Note 7 reveals that marketable securities are valued based on fair market value, and then explains how that is determined. However, it takes 143 words to say all of that.

8. **Stock price** is a history of movement in the stock price over time. You would expect to see a rising stock price corresponding to rising revenues and earnings, and the opposite as well, a falling price with declining revenues and earnings. However, this is not always the case. Companies rarely include other indicators in their annual reports.

---

[5] General Motors 2012 annual report, p. 96.

The debt ratio, dividend yield, and net return would be valuable additions. Considering the large size of most annual reports, adding one or two pages of key ratios would not be space-consuming, and investors and other stakeholders would gain much better insights.

Key Point

Not every company highlights its stock price history. This, like most ratios, is often excluded from the annual report.

9. **Names and addresses** include the corporate offices, both headquarters and major centers around the country and the world. It also has contact information for those interested in direct discussions with company representatives. The names of the highest corporate officers and board members are also provided, although it is rare for their email or other contact information to be provided.

THE ANNUAL REPORT AS A MARKETING DOCUMENT

There is a legitimate purpose to the annual report beyond the financial statements and footnotes. In fact, the annual report is one of the primary promotional tools available to publicly listed companies.

Example

The big promo: You have questions about some of the statements about products, markets, and the future as reported in the annual statement. When you call stockholder services, you are told that no one can answer your questions because the report was not prepared internally. It was drafted by an outside advertising firm and no one in the company knows what it all means. Of course, the financial data has to be supported; but the promotional stuff is questionable. Why did you call in the first place? You were hoping for a more extended explanation of why last year's net loss was seen to "pave the way to a dynamic future growth curve and higher share price in an exciting future."

All companies subject to oversight by the SEC and state regulators have to operate within specific disclosure and reporting guidelines. This applies to the 10-K and 10-Q reports filed with the SEC (and containing the same financial information as the annual report). However, in the annual report, management has many opportunities to spin their results and to highlight what they want investors to know. These opportunities are found in management's discussion, financial highlights (derived from the statements), and even the footnotes.

Key Point

The annual report is more a marketing and promotional document than a financial report. The financial information is greatly summarized. The annual report is a good overview, but does not go into a lot of detail in the numbers.

However, because it is a marketing document, you cannot expect companies to highlight negative information. For example GM's 2012 annual report made quite a fanfare about its revenues rising from 2011 ($150,276 in $ millions) to 2012 ($152,256). Nowhere did the report mention the decline in net earnings (from $9,190 in 2011 to $6,188 in 2012), or the large drop in net return, from 6.1 percent down to 4.1 percent.[6]

So management has an advantage in how they design and format their annual reports. They can focus on specific aspects of the results and also on the always bright future, and they can ignore some of the disappointing outcomes. However, they cannot hide the facts. The rules of disclosure are specific, but you probably need to crunch your own numbers to find ratios like net return. And you will also have to draw your own conclusions about a company's viability as a promising investment candidate. The annual report provides you with the tools but not the specifics.

HOW TO USE THE ANNUAL REPORT

How you use the annual report is going to be determined by what you are looking for. It's probably the best source for finding out what a company makes and markets. All annual reports spend time

---

[6] S&P Stock Reports for General Motors.

emphasizing their great products and explaining how they market to specific regions or countries. GM is a good example of this. You learn that GM is not just making and selling cars but also involved in parts, service, and financing of auto sales. It's a diverse company.

Key Point

If you want to follow 10-year trends, don't rely on the annual report. This is best used to learn what the company markets and where it operates.

You probably cannot get enough detail in the annual report to perform a range of long-term trend analyses that you definitely need to make decisions based on the fundamentals. The financial information in the annual report is greatly summarized. Although some expansion is found in the footnotes, it is a difficult document for trying to piece together a detailed analysis. In addition, the time periods are limited, usually to two or three years (sometimes five years). Trends are best when the period is longer, and a 10-year study of trends is better than a lesser period.

For more detailed information about a company's financial and technical performance, you can find a 10-year summary with the S&P Stock Reports. These also provide narrative descriptions of the business, as well as ratings and price targets, comparisons to competitors in the same sectors, and industry definitions and summaries.

Valuable Resource

The S&P Stock Reports are provided free to subscribers of many of the best-known online brokerage firms. This is a useful tool for identifying the fundamental status of companies and for making comparisons.

The main advantage of annual reports is as a promotional tool, which also includes highly summarized financial results. It is not practical for in-depth trend analysis. So the annual report is a worthy starting point for finding out what a company offers to its customers, and for supplementing the financial statements with detailed (and often technical) footnotes. These provide expansions of the numbers, disclosures, and projections of future changes in the financial statements.

The next chapter examines the fundamental signals not found on the financial statement. These may provide guidance for picking companies and considering the indicators you need to make a fully informed decision.

7

FUNDAMENTALS NOT ON THE STATEMENT

A criminal is a person with predatory instincts who has not sufficient capital to form a corporation.
—Howard Scott, *The New Dictionary of Thought*, 1957

Investors new to the world of the markets may tend to assume that all of the information they need to pick stocks is found in the financial statements and footnotes. These reports, prepared by the company and its auditors, filed with the SEC and carefully documented with dozens of pages of footnotes, do paint the large picture; but there is much more that never shows up on those statements.

There is nothing illegal or deceptive about the existence of off-financial statement fundamentals. Statements are rigid in their formats and are not designed for estimates or even for reporting anything outside of the two major financial statement concerns: working capital and profitability.

This chapter examines additional fundamental indicators of interest to investors trying to identify safe and profitable companies, and explains how to study and interpret them.

DIVIDEND YIELD, PAYOUT RATIO, AND HISTORY

Dividends are often overlooked in the larger scheme of decisions investors make. The tendency is to think of a dividend as a small dollar amount that is not especially important; it appears in the account four times per year and may be under $100.

Key Point

Dividends are easily overlooked, but they represent a significant portion of total returns from investing in stocks.

Even though the dollar amount may be small, dividends should be considered as a major factor in which company's stock you pick. The dividend yield is a good means for comparison among two or more companies in the same industry. This yield may also represent a major portion of overall income from investing in a dividend-paying company.

Example

Bank pays you dividend of $50: You are comparing three stocks in the same sector. Fundamentally, you consider all of them to be of equal value, so how do you make your decision? In addition to exhaustively comparing all of the indicators you can think of, you also check the dividend. You notice that two of the companies yield about 2 to 3 percent, but the third one is over 4 percent. Not only that, but also the dividend has been raised every year for the past 10 years. This makes your choice much easier.

A long-term study revealed that profits from earnings growth are only slightly greater than profits from dividends. Between 1926 and 2006, dividend yield accounted for about 44 percent of total returns from stock investments.[1]

Dividends are expressed as the amount per share and also the annual percentage of return. For example, if a dividend is expressed as 2.50 percent and dividend per share is 0.67, that means that the annual return (when four quarterly dividends are added together) is 2.50 percent based on the current stock price. If the stock price per share is $107.20, the calculation of yield is based on the dividend per share and that price. So 0.67 per share, paid every quarter, is an annual payment of $268:

$$\$268 \div \$107.20 = 2.50\%$$

The yield is always based on the price per share at the moment. So if you pay $107.20 per share, your dividend yield will be 2.50 percent for as long as you own shares. It does not matter how much the stated dividend yield rises or falls; the yield you earn is based on your original cost per share.

As the stock price rises, yield declines, and as the price declines, yield rises. This occurs because the calculation is based on the currently fixed dividend per share versus the ever-changing price per share. An example of this is shown in Table 7.1.

Table 7.1 Dividend Yield with Changing Stock Prices

Price per Share	Dividend per Share	Yield
Rising price		
$107.20	$0.67 \times 4 = \$268$	$268 \div 107.20 = 2.50\%$
109.20	$0.67 \times 4 = \$268$	$268 \div 109.20 = 2.45$
111.20	$0.67 \times 4 = \$268$	$268 \div 111.20 = 2.41$
113.20	$0.67 \times 4 = \$268$	$268 \div 113.20 = 2.37$
Falling price		
$107.20	$0.67 \times 4 = \$268$	$268 \div 107.20 = 2.50\%$
105.20	$0.67 \times 4 = \$268$	$268 \div 105.20 = 2.55$
103.20	$0.67 \times 4 = \$268$	$268 \div 103.20 = 2.60$
101.20	$0.67 \times 4 = \$268$	$268 \div 101.20 = 2.65$
99.20	$0.67 \times 4 = \$268$	$268 \div 99.20 = 2.70$

[1] "Ibbotson Stocks, Bonds, Bills and Inflation Classic Yearbook," *Morningstar*, 2011.

This exercise makes an important point:

A higher dividend yield is not always a good indicator for a worthy investment. For example, if the stock in the foregoing example fell in one day by 11 points, down to $96.20 per share, dividend yield would be 2.79 percent, far higher than the previous 2.50 percent. But why did the stock fall 11 points?

> **Key Point**
>
> An increasing dividend yield might be good news, or it might be a danger signal of negative changes in the company.

If the company is on the verge of declaring bankruptcy, it would probably not be a good time to buy shares. That greatly increased yield looks positive at first glance, but when you discover the reason for a decline in the stock price, it might indicate a big negative for the company.

record date

the date on which the stockholder is acknowledged as being eligible for the current dividend; this date occurs two days after the ex-dividend date.

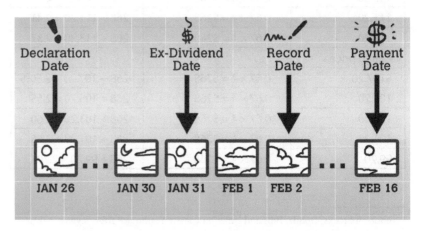

The dates can be confusing unless their rationale is explained. Because it takes three days to settle a stock trade, a purchase has to be made by the day before ex-dividend. Thus, *record date* is two days after *ex-dividend date* (the day before ex-dividend plus three days). The *payment date* varies because it is set by the company, and may take up to one month.

> **Example**
>
> **Making the dates work for you:** You bought shares of stock one day before ex-dividend date, meaning you earned the dividend. You then sold shares on the ex-dividend date. As long as you owned shares the day before, you will be the shareholder of record and the dividend is yours. As long as you don't lose on the stock trade, this fast in-and-out method is profitable because you get a quarterly dividend for owning the stock only one or two days.

ex-dividend date

the date on which dividends are no longer earned; to earn a current dividend, shares must be bought at least one day before ex-dividend date.

The relationship between the last day to place an order to buy shares, the ex-dividend date, and the record date is shown in Figure 7.1.

An annual yield (such as 2.50 percent in the previous example) can be turned into a *compound rate of return* quite easily. This is accomplished through *reinvestment of dividends*, a choice you make when you place an order to buy shares of stock.

payment date

the date on which dividends are paid to stockholders of record, usually several weeks after the record date.

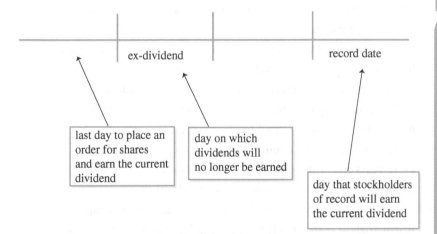

compound rate of return

a return calculated with partial-year returns rather than the annual stated or nominal yield.

Figure 7.1 Important Dividend Dates

reinvestment of dividends

a choice made at the time shares are purchased, to use earned dividends to buy additional partial shares of stock, as opposed to receiving a cash payment.

A compound rate is based on the nominal rate and the frequency of payment. For example, a quarterly dividend is paid out four times per year. A 2.50 percent yield is equal to 0.625 percent per quarter. To compound, add 1 to the quarterly yield in decimal form, and multiply by 1 added to the initial quarterly yield:

1st quarter:	.00625
2nd quarter:	$1.00625 \times 1.00625 = 1.01254$
3rd quarter:	$1.01254 \times 1.00625 = 1.01887$
4th quarter:	$1.01887 \times 1.00625 = 1.02524$

In this case, the nominal yield of 2.50 percent is compounded over four quarters to an annual yield of 2.524 percent. So reinvesting dividends yields slightly higher annual return than just taking cash.

Key Point

Compounding dividends looks like a small difference in the yield, but over time it can add up to a nice level of additional income.

It could make more sense to take the cash dividend, as long as it can be reinvested elsewhere at a higher rate than the yield on the stock. However, for many investors who have picked companies yielding higher than average dividends, the reinvestment route makes the most sense. It adds no risk to the position of owning stock and picking up quarterly dividends, and it provides a compound rate of return.

In comparing dividend yield among several different companies, one important selection is to seek companies whose dividend has been increased every year. When dividends are increased without exception for 10 years or more, these companies are called dividend achievers.

Selecting companies for investment based on a 20-year history of dividends is a sound method for narrowing down your list. It may be flexible; for example, if your target company increased dividends in 8 or more years out of the past 10, you could consider this company, as well as companies meeting the strict 10-year definition.

In studying the history of dividends per share, an accompanying ratio worth analysis is the dividend payout ratio. This is the percentage of earnings paid out each year in the form of dividends.

Valuable Resource

Mergent is the company that developed the concept of dividend achievers. Today, many index funds are based on the dividend achiever benchmark. Mergent also markets subscriptions to its annual dividend achiever book at **www.mergent.com**.

The payout ratio may vary from one year to the next, so a good way to study it is to remove unusual spikes in the percentage and look for the overall 10-year trend. A 10-year summary for three companies in the same industry is shown in Table 7.2.

Table 7.2 Dividends per Share (DPS) and Payout Ratio (PR), 10 Years

Company	Caterpillar		Deere		Cummins	
Year	DPS	PR	DPS	PR	DPS	PR
2004	0.78	27%	0.53	19%	0.30	16%
2005	0.91	23%	0.61	21%	0.30	11%
2006	1.10	21%	0.78	22%	0.33	9%
2007	1.32	25%	0.91	23%	0.43	12%
2008	1.68	30%	1.06	23%	0.60	15%
2009	1.68	117%	1.12	54%	0.70	32%
2010	2.16	52%	1.16	27%	0.88	17%
2011	1.80	24%	1.52	23%	1.33	14%
2012	1.96	23%	1.79	23%	1.80	21%
2013	1.72	30%	1.99	22%	2.25	28%

Source: S&P Stock Reports.

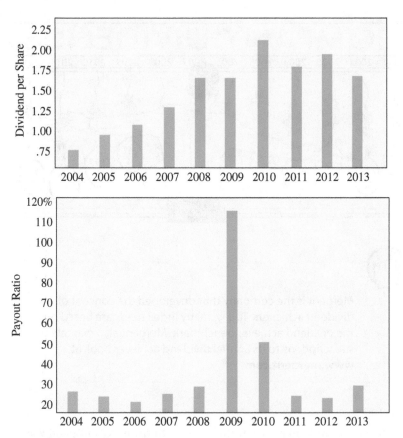

Figure 7.2 Caterpillar—Dividend per Share and Payout Ratio
Source: Based on data from S&P Stock Reports.

These have also been transferred into graph form. Caterpillar's dividend per share and payout ratio are shown in Figure 7.2.

Figure 7.2 allows you to see how the trend moved over the one-year period. The dividend per share rose in the first few years and then leveled out. The payout ratio for CAT was quite low for most of the period, meaning that the company was paying dividends with only a small portion of its total earnings.

Deere's dividend per share and payout ratio are summarized in Figure 7.3.

In this company's 10-year history, dividend per share rose steadily throughout the period. However, except for the one-year spike, the payout ratio remained well below 50 percent of earnings. Payout has been primarily flat during this period.

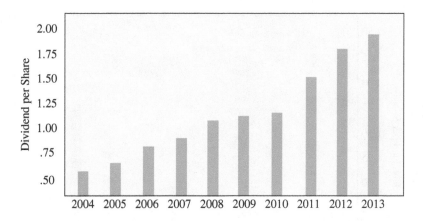

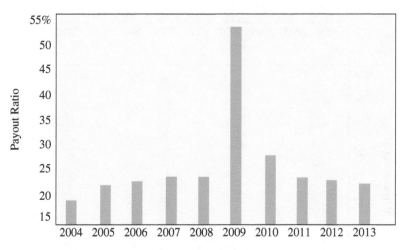

Figure 7.3 Deere—Dividend per Share and Payout Ratio
Source: Based on data from S&P Stock Reports.

Example

Which rate to watch?: You own shares in a company whose dividend is average. But in looking at shares of one of its competitors, you see that the dividend has been increasing steadily every year. Both companies had growth, but it seems the dividend for the competitor is outpacing your company. The difference might be found in the trend for the payout ratio, an indicator that often is overlooked.

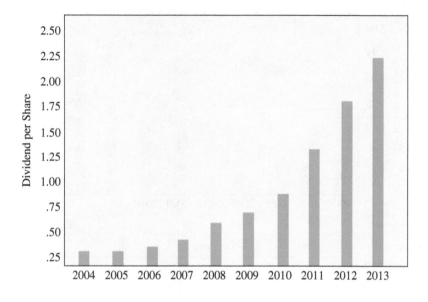

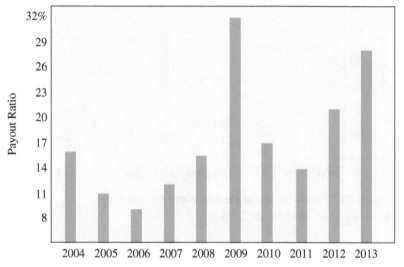

Figure 7.4 Cummins—Dividend per Share and Payout Ratio
Source: Based on data from S&P Stock Reports.

The final example for Cummins is summarized in Figure 7.4.

The outcome for 10 years of CMI showed a dramatic increase in dividends per share throughout this period. Likewise, the payout ratio gradually increased from 16 percent in 2004 to a total of 28 percent in 2013.

This comparative analysis of dividends per share and payout ratio reveals a lot about a company's dividend policies. Remembering that dividends represent on average 44% of total returns from stock investing, this analysis is a crucial one. However, dividend information is not included on the financial statements.[2]

MARKET CAP

Also not included on the summaries of the balance sheet or income statement is the *market capitalization* of a company (abbreviated to market cap). This is the value of a share of stock multiplied by the number of shares outstanding.

Market cap does not appear on the financial statements, but it often is confused by investors with shareholders' equity. The total equity is the initial par value of shares when issued, and this does not change. Equity is increased by annual profits or decreased by losses.

In comparison, market cap varies based on the price per share. As the price rises, so does market cap. Actual ownership of a company is not held by the company itself, but by all of its investors. This group includes institutional and individual investors. These may include corporate officers who acquire shares on their own or are granted stock options, which can be exercised to buy shares.

market capitalization

also abbreviated market cap, the value of a company based on multiplying price per share by the number of shares outstanding.

Key Point

Market cap is not the same thing as shareholders' equity. Since shares are owned by investors and not the company, market cap changes with the stock's price. Equity changes with the addition of profits.

As a general rule, the greater the dollar value of market cap, the more stability and less risk is involved with owning shares. The definition of what constitutes *large cap* varies, however. Some define it as total dollar value of $5 billion or more, and others use the value of $10 billion.

A *mid cap* company has less dollar value in its shares, and a *small cap* is the smallest.

---

[2] The study referenced earlier in this chapter noted an average of 10 percent returns, including 4.4 percent from dividend yield. So of the total, 44 percent is attributed to dividends.

large cap

companies with the largest dollar value of market capitalization, which may be either $5 billion or more or $10 billion or more.

The distinctions between these capitalization ranges are a matter of opinion, and the two major divisions are as follows:

	Capitalization Level #1	**Capitalization Level # 2**
Small cap	under $1 billion	under $2 billion
Mid cap	$1 billion–$5 billion	$2 billion–$10 billion
Large cap	over $5 billion	over $10 billion

The #2 level often is even more finely divided to include *mega cap*, *micro cap*, and *nano cap* categories.

The key issue about capitalization is that the larger the number (price per shares multiplied by shares outstanding), the more stability you are likely to find in the investment.

mid cap

companies with medium dollar levels of capitalization, either between $1 and $5 billion, or between $2 and $10 billion.

Example

Stability with low volume: Many investors like larger cap companies because they are safe. But you have come to a realization: There is a trade-off between safety and growth. Larger companies tend to grow slowly because they are so large, and smaller companies can yield fast profits due to their smaller market cap. By the way, losses can also happen faster.

small cap

a company with the lowest range of total capitalization, defined as under $1 billion or under $2 billion.

Outstanding shares, which are multiplied by price per share to determine capitalization, may change in two ways. First, the company may issue new shares, creating a likely reduction in price per share to either account for the new numbers or to dilute the value of older shares. The second way of changing shares is yet another key fundamental not showing up on the balance sheet: retiring of stock.

Stock can be retired when the company has enough cash to buy its own shares on the market, paying the current price per share. When a company decides to spend money to buy its own shares, the general belief is that management must consider the price a bargain level. Otherwise, why spend money to buy shares?

mega cap

a company with more than $200 billion of capitalization.

Key Point

A company retires stock through buying when two conditions prevail. First, it has to have the cash. Second, it has to believe it makes more profit buying its stock than it would in other ways.

Any shares the company buys are retired. This means they are permanently deducted from net worth and called *treasury stock*. When companies have a share amount of cash available and they believe their best investment is to retire shares, this is a positive signal for the market. You might not find a line item for treasury stock in the shareholders' equity portion of the balance sheet, and this might be explained only in a footnote.

When a company retires stock in this manner, the total of declared dividends to be paid is also reduced. This explains why a company would be willing to give up cash and retire part of its equity value. For example, if operations yield an average of 2 percent per year but

micro cap

a company with capitalization, defined between $50 million and $250 million.

nano cap

a company with capitalization below $50 million.

Treasury stock

the value of stock purchased and retired by the company, and permanently deducted from the shareholders' equity value.

dividends are at 3.5 percent at the current price level, retiring shares is a better return on investment than expanding operations.

CONTINGENT LIABILITIES AND OTHER LIABILITIES

The dollar value of contingent liabilities cannot be known. It depends on the outcome of the underlying matter. For example, Merck (MRK) agreed to pay $100 million in February 2014 to settle lawsuits going back more than five years. This was regarding its birth control product NuvaRing and included more than 3,800 plaintiffs.[3]

Until this settlement was announced (and subject to approval by at least 95 percent of the plaintiffs), Merck had to treat this as a contingent liability since the outcome of the lawsuit could not be known.

Many large companies, especially pharmaceutical companies, carry contingent liabilities, often for many years, due to the complexity of the issues involved and the time required for the matters to work their way through the courts.

Key Point

Contingent liabilities are left off the balance sheet because the amount cannot be known until the matter has been decided, and that could take years.

---

[3] Jef Feeley and David Voreacos, "Merck to Pay $100 Million NuvaRing Pact if Women Join," *Bloomberg News*, February 7, 2014.

Contingent liabilities may be carried for other matters as well, such as potential costs of collective bargaining discussions with unions.

Beyond contingent liabilities, some forms of debt are going to show up only in the footnotes because GAAP rules exclude them from recognition as actual liabilities. The exclusion of liabilities may lead to mischief if exclusion is intentional. For example, Enron left off many liabilities by placing debts in offshore companies while using capital to expand operations. In this way, debts were stated below the actual long-term debt level, but the company was able to put borrowed funds to good use in its operations.

MARKET VALUE OF LONG-TERM ASSETS

One of the glaring exclusions in the balance sheet is the reported value of capital assets. These have to be carried at net book value, according to the GAAP rules.[4]

Example

What is your building worth?: A company owns real estate it bought 50 years ago, at an original cost of $14 million ($12 million building and $2 million land). Today, the building has been depreciated fully. The book value of this asset is now $2 million (land cannot be depreciated). However, the true market value of this building has grown over the past 50 years and is now worth an estimated $300 million. But book value remains at the net depreciated value of $2 million, and any differences between book value and market value are assigned to the footnotes. Meanwhile, assets and net worth remain well under the realistic levels of value.

---

[4] Under IFRS, adjustments can be made to report currently owned capital assets at fair market value, subject to specific standards, such as appraisals, to set those values.

🎯 **Key Point**

One of the big flaws in GAAP is in undervaluing of capital assets. This not only fails to report the true value of a company but also could lead to a takeover well below the full market value of assets.

This has become a problem in the past, especially in setting the value of companies that became buyout targets. In 1986, Lucky Stores was carrying more stores than rivals Safeway and Kroger, and the book value of its real estate was $300 million. But a takeover offer was made by American Stores for $2.5 billion in cash, with full knowledge that the true market value of Lucky's real estate was far higher than the reported $300 million. Had the company been able to carry the true market value of real estate on its balance sheet, both the asset value and shareholders' equity would have been substantially higher.[5]

As long as the GAAP rules continue to apply, long-term assets are going to be carried at original basis, minus depreciation. This is the case even when the true value of the asset rises over time, especially for assets like real estate.

---

[5] Nancy Yoshihara, "Lucky's Stock Rises on Reports That It Is Buyout Target," *Los Angeles Times*, September 18, 1986.

INSIDER TRADING

One fundamental that does not show up anywhere, expect possibly the footnotes of the annual statement, is the level of trading in company stock by insiders (e.g., corporate executives, major shareholders, or members of the Board of Directors).

Insider trading is completely legal and subject to strict oversight. Regulators like the SEC have an interest in ensuring that such trades are not made with any insider information not known to the general public. Assuming that decisions to buy or sell are made for reasons not involving insider information (like pending new product announcements, approval or denial of approval of new products by regulators, or pending mergers or acquisitions), the level of trading may provide good fundamental information.

insider trading

any buy or sell of company stock on the part of key corporate executives, management, or board members.

Just like the act of the company buying and retiring its own stock, executives have a keen interest in the value per share of stock each of them holds in their own portfolio. As long as they know the same level of information as the general public, there may be any number of reasons to buy or sell stock.

Key Point

Insider trading is legal and describes buy or sell decisions by key executives or stockholders. In comparison, trading on inside information is illegal because that information is not known to the public.

An executive might believe in the long-term value of the company and projections of growth, and want to own shares. If an executive is planning to retire in the near future, selling shares could occur strictly as a personal planning decision. So there may be dozens of possible reasons for trading in company stock, including exercising stock options or selling all holdings as part of a retirement plan.

With this in mind, it is not possible to apply a blanket set of assumptions for reasons that stock is either bought or sold by an insider. However, it does make sense to be aware of trends and to keep an eye on them. This is especially the case when many executives buy or sell their shares in a short period of time.

THE VALUE OF GOOD MANAGEMENT

Most investors who observe how a company is managed will agree that exceptional management makes all the difference. The leadership of Chrysler under Lee Iacocca (1980–1992) and the leadership of General Motors under Jack Welch (1981–2001) were inspiring stories of exceptional management and of how those companies were turned around.

Often overlooked in the analysis of a company as a potential investment is the value of its management. A new and untried CEO cannot make promises based on past performance, and is an unknown factor. But an executive who has succeeded in past leadership roles adds greatly to the prospects for the future growth of a company.

Key Point

Exceptional management often makes all the difference between profit and loss, success and failure, and solvency and bankruptcy.

This is an intangible feature, of course. But few can dispute the key factor of exceptional management. Steve Jobs ran Apple Computer from its first days in 1976 through 1985, when he was forced out. A decade later, Apple was in trouble and from 1996 to 1998 Jobs returned as an advisor, saving the company from the brink of insolvency. From 1998 to 2011 he was CEO once again, and during that tenure he transformed Apple into the most valuable publicly traded company.

None of the factors in Jobs' exceptional leadership and vision could be found on the company's balance sheet, even though the benefits of his leadership did show up in the numbers.[6]

Example

Leadership qualities: Some publicly traded companies rely on the reputation, skill, and talent of one individual. This is a highly positive aspect to the company and should affect investment decisions. However, a single individual adds vulnerability as well. What happens when that person moves on or expires?

The complete study of fundamentals must begin with the balance sheet and income statement. However, much more is discovered in the footnotes, as well as through factors not found on the financial statements: Dividends, market cap, contingent liabilities, market value of long-term assets, *insider trading*, and the value of good management all add to the fundamental value of a corporation.

This chapter concludes the fundamental section of this book. The next chapter begins the technical section with an explanation of three major theories about stock prices: the Dow Theory, efficient market hypothesis, and random walk hypothesis.

---

[6] Michael Hiltzik, "Steve Jobs: More Than a Turnaround Artist," *Los Angeles Times*, October 5, 2011.

THEORIES AND WHAT THEY MEAN

People prefer theory to practice because it involves them in no more real responsibility than a game of checkers, while it permits them to feel they're doing something serious and important.

—Leo Stein, *Journey into the Self*, 1950

Many theories have been developed to explain not only how the market works but also how investors behave. These are useful for developing a set of beliefs and observations about how prices change; but you also should remember that theories are not enough. They serve as a starting point only, and cannot act as a substitute for good judgment, awareness of risk, and smart decisions.

The ultimate theory of the market is invariably based on the idea that you enter a position in the belief that you will generate a profit. So if you buy shares, you expect prices to rise. But one broad assumption worth always remembering is that your entry price is part of an everchanging price within an auction marketplace. Some investors believe prices will rise, so their unconscious belief is that their entry price is the "zero price." From that price, only a higher price is likely, possible, or even inevitable; so if prices fall, this zero price assumption results in disappointment.

Key Point

Your entry price for stock is not a starting point but part of a continuous series of price moves, both up and down.

Realistically, you have to view the purchase price of shares not as zero but as part of a continuous struggle between buyers and sellers to move the price in the desired direction. This is where the study of technical analysis becomes valuable; it helps identify the likely indicators that cause prices to rise or to fall.

Even when you understand some of the causes of price change, all of those beliefs begin with observation of price and investor behavior. And that behavior is studied under a series of beliefs or theories about the market.

Dow Theory

a set of beliefs about stock price behavior based on the writings of Charles Dow, serving as the foundation for modern technical analysis.

THE DOW THEORY

The starting point for modern technical analysis is the *Dow Theory*. This is a set of beliefs based on the writings of Charles Dow, who, with Edward Jones, founded the company Dow Jones, publisher of the *Wall Street Journal* and developer of the famous Dow Jones Industrial Average (DJIA) and other market averages. Of particular importance besides the DJIA are the Dow Jones Utilities Average and Transportation Average.

Charles Dow developed a simple index to track prices in a few companies. He did not call this the Dow Theory; the name came about after his death and was formalized by his successors at Dow Jones. However, at the end of the nineteenth century, Dow observed that stock prices tended to act in a particular manner and that collectively there was an element of predictability in those price trends.

Example

What is your market theory?: You have been studying the technical side of the market, and especially the work of Charles Dow. You realize that he was a pioneer in identifying and tracking trends, but the application of his theories actually took off after his lifetime. You speculate: What would the markets look like today without the index culture on which we depend?

A number of rules or tenets are applied under the Dow Theory to observe price movement in the markets:

1. **There are three different types of price movements in the market.** These are primary, medium, and short movements or trends. A *primary trend* lasts from a year or less, up to several years in total. It may be a *bull trend* or a *bear trend*.

    The primary trend (or main movement) is described as a market-wide one, so that a bull market or a bear market is the current direction in which market prices are moving.

    A *secondary trend* (or medium swing) moves in the direction opposite the prevailing primary trend, and retraces a portion of price movements in the primary trend.

    The *minor trend*, or short swing, may last for only a matter of hours, or up to a few days. It is the least predicable of all trends and often involves only minor price changes.

primary trend

described by the Dow Theory, the longest-term trend in the market, lasting from under a year to several years in duration.

bull trend

a trend characterized by generally rising prices.

2. **There are three phases to all market trends.**

    The Dow Theory observes three distinct phases to price trends. The first of these is the *accumulation phase*. During this time, experienced investors buy (in a bull market) before most investors.

    The accumulation phase assumes that a small body of investors are more astute than the market as a whole, and tend to act before most investors recognize the opportunity.

    This section of the Dow Theory conforms to the contrarian theory of investing (see more about this later in

bear trend

a trend characterized by generally falling prices.

secondary trend

a trend, either bullish or bearish, that lasts from a matter of several days up to several months, which tends to contradict movement of the primary trend.

minor trend

the changes in price lasting from only a few hours up to a few days, representing the most chaotic and difficult to predict of all market trends.

this chapter). The idea here is that most investors follow the crowd, buying when others buy and selling when others sell, and that the majority who act in these ways often time their decisions poorly. The accumulation phase is controlled by a small group of investors with insights more accurate than average, based on experience and knowledge of market behavior.

Key Point

Contrarians don't just do the opposite of most traders. They are contrary because they trade based on analysis instead of on emotion.

The second phase is called the *big move phase* or a type of catch-up phase, in which the market as a whole recognizes what the minority knew during the accumulation phase. At this point, the majority then follows suit.

In this second phase the crowd mentality of the market is in control. This means that the tendency is to follow the majority, even though history shows that the majority is often poor at timing its decisions.

Example

Are you part of the market's mob mentality?: You have noticed that at certain times, either greed or panic takes over the markets, and the crowd seems to all move in the same direction. You resist. But you have also discovered that it is very difficult to resist mob mentality. When you don't go along, you're an outsider. And what if the rest of them are right and you're the only one who isn't?

The third and final phase is called the *excess phase*. This phase is characterized by a high volume of speculation and high confidence. However, this ultimately ends up being ill-timed.

The excess and characteristic speculation seen during this phase eventually leads to a *distribution phase*, which is the same as the accumulation phase, but characterized by a minority of knowledgeable investors selling instead of buying.

Once the distribution phase begins, the three phases repeat in a bearish fashion, dominated by selling activity rather buying. The three phases recur in both bull and bear markets. The excess phase is then referred to as a despair phase, in which optimism about rising price is replaced by pessimism or even panic concerning falling prices.

accumulation phase

the first of three trend phases under the Dow Theory, during which knowledgeable investors begin to buy shares even though the larger market does not recognize the opportunity.

3. The market discounts all news.

This part of the theory assumes that all stock prices include adjustments for all publicly known information, as soon as that information is made public. Some investors assume that this theory supports the efficient market hypothesis (see more on this later in this chapter). However, it does not logically lead to that conclusion.

big move phase

the second of three phases under the Dow Theory, in which the majority of traders follow the trend set by a minority, and trade into a stock.

Key Point

Discounting news does not make a market efficient; it only creates a fast response, which at times can be exaggerated and thus very inefficient.

In an *efficient* market, the fast adjustment in prices would accurately adjust for news. But in reality, these adjustments often are exaggerated. For example, a disappointing earnings surprise may lead to a big drop in stock price on the day of the announcement, only to reverse and recapture some or all of the decline in the sessions that follow.

excess phase

the third of three phases under the Dow Theory, in which traders follow the trend and begin to speculate, often at the wrong time in the price cycle; in a bear market, "excess" is replaced with "despair."

distribution phase

the conclusion to the excess phase under the Dow Theory, in which a minority of astute investors begin selling shares before the larger market recognizes that the cycle has turned; this is the same as the accumulation phase, but with selling in place of buying.

So discounting all news may occur rapidly, but the reaction itself is often far from efficient. When reaction, whether positive or negative, exceeds a rational level of change, it leads to great inefficiency. This phenomenon is witnessed repeatedly. Any time a surprise becomes known (such as better than expected earnings or worse than expected earnings), an excessive level of price change commonly occurs, with corrections taking anywhere from a few hours to a few days.

4. Market averages must confirm each other to identify a new trend.

The three primary averages include industrials, utilities, and transportation stocks. Under the Dow Theory, a new primary trend occurs not merely when the apparent long-term direction occurs, but also when at least one of the other averages changes direction in the same way as the industrials.

Because the industrials are the average tracked for a primary trend, this confirmation from the other averages is required before a new primary trend can be declared. However, this is by no means settled science. It's a matter of opinion. Because the duration of a primary and secondary trend can vary, a confirming change in direction can be called a new primary trend or just part of a secondary reaction. Only in hindsight (at times requiring years) does the real timing of a trend become obvious.

At the beginning of the twentieth century, when the Dow Theory was being fine-tuned, a great volume of manufacturing was occurring domestically and shipment of goods usually took place by rail. So the transportation average was seen as a primary indicator of the health of the economy. The transportation average was viewed originally as a benchmark for manufacturing and industrial activity.

Today, with much less reliance on rail transport (due to most manufacturing taking place overseas), the transportation average has evolved. It still includes railroads as well as trucking lines, but also includes airlines and other modes of transportation, both for industry and for other purposes.

Key Point

The original purpose for including transportations in analysis of market trends was based on heavy reliance on railroads when manufacturing activity was high. Today, manufacturing has declined and rails share the burden with trucking companies and airlines.

In its original set of assumptions, a change in direction of industrials has to be confirmed by the transportation average, because of its crucial relationship to industry. Even though the original logic no longer applies to the same degree, Dow Theory watchers still expect to see industrial moves confirmed by the transportation or utility average. Once one of these two also changes direction, the likelihood of a new primary trend increases.

Example

Have you considered the source?: You have wondered why Dow expected industrial trends to be confirmed by transportation. But then you realize the world has changed. In Dow's time, all goods were moved by train; so if the industrials reversed and then transportation reversed as well, it had to be a significant event. Today, you realize, confirmation can come in several forms. But Dow's original concept of confirmation continues to work today.

5. Trends must be confirmed by trading volume.

The Dow Theory assumes that all trends are confirmed by volume, with strong changes in trend direction accompanied by high volume. Swing traders see this in the short term, knowing that a one-day volume spike often signals a change in direction. This three- to five-day signal also applies for longer-term trends.

Under the Dow Theory, a change in price direction accompanied with high trading volume reflects the true sentiments of the market at that time. High volume can be caused by strong buying pressure or selling pressure, so the broader assumption also is based on the belief that when a trend is confirmed with volume it is due to the activity of buyers (for new bullish trends) or sellers (for new bearish trends).

6. Trends will continue until new signals evolve, marking a reversal and change in direction.

Short-term price movement is likely to be chaotic, with many retracements in the form of short-term downward movement during bullish markets, or upward movement in bearish markets.

A retracement usually does not last long, and when it ends the prevailing price direction resumes. At the moment it is difficult to tell the difference between a retracement and a reversal, the latter signaling the end of the prevailing trend. However, for that to occur, you would expect to see new signals indicating a reversal and the end of the current trend.

These signals naturally include a change in direction of one of the Dow market averages, confirmed by movement in a second one. However, these changes do not occur at the same time. Because of the uncertainty of timing, when price does change, it creates uncertainty. Beyond the Dow Theory, you need to rely on other technical signals to determine whether the move is a retracement or the beginning of a new, opposite trend. Many of the tools you need to improve timing and to recognize price movement (whether primary trend or short-term price swings) are included in coming chapters.

Dow Theory Assumptions

The Dow Theory is based on the foregoing six tenets or rules. However, it also relies on a series of assumptions:

1. A primary trend cannot be controlled or manipulated.

The first assumption refers to manipulation. Some large investors, such as institutions, high-frequency traders (HFTs), or day traders, might have an incentive to try to manipulate the market, but this is not possible according to the Dow Theory.

Key Point

A lot of market activity is based on the assumption that primary trends can be influenced in some way, and this is not the case.

Prices can be manipulated with a large volume of speculation. While secondary trends and short-term price trends can be influenced by activity in the market, primary trends are set over the long term and are not as impacted.

The prices of shares in one company can also be manipulated by traders with large holdings in the company, takeover rumors, pending mergers and acquisitions, and earnings surprises. But these are isolated to individual companies and are not influential on primary trends.

2. Market averages discount the entire market.

Assuming that all available information is discounted into prices of every stock, the same observation is applied to the averages (which consist of a number of stocks, and thus the discount also applies to averages). This discounting effect is also assumed to affect the averages in the same manner as individual stocks, but the actual known information often is opposite among a series of stocks. Some may be discounted by disappointing earnings announcements, while others are inflated by better than expected earnings surprises.

The discounts that you observe in individual stocks certainly influence the larger averages, notably when a weighted average is heavily influenced by only a handful of stocks.[1]

If heavy influence by a few stocks affects (discounts) the market in the same manner, it means that the discount affects the entire market. However, this is likely to be a momentary factor rather than a permanent influence.

3. The Dow Theory provides guidance but not definitive answers.

Like all theories, the Dow Theory consists of a set of generalizations about the markets, investor behavior, and price movement. However, they do not apply in all cases. These tenets provide market guidance and are not absolute rules.

Key Point

The Dow Theory, like all theories, offers a set of general statements and observations. But it never applies 100 percent of the time. Smart traders realize that exceptions do occur.

---

[1] For example, the Dow Jones Industrial Average as of April 10, 2014, included 30 stocks. However, four stocks (Visa, IBM, Goldman Sachs, and 3M) accounted for 27.28 percent, more than one-fourth of the total.

With this in mind, traders may observe the technical value of the Dow Theory, but also be open to exceptions and to other theories, especially when it comes to the behavior of investors. The tendency for the majority is to buy as bull markets begin to peak, and to sell when bear markets reach the extent of a decline. In other words, the old adage, "Buy low and sell high," should be expanded with a second part: "Instead of the other way around."

Example

Gut reactions to the markets: Are you a "typical" trader or a free thinker? The typical trader does, indeed, gut-react to markets, meaning he or she ends up buying high and selling low. The advice to do the opposite appears simplistic, but actually it's quite profound.

Many theories can be found and studied, but the Dow Theory is the foundation for most trend analysis and for the range of technical analysis in use today.

EFFICIENT MARKET HYPOTHESIS (EMH)

Among the theories concerning market behavior, and especially price predictability, is the *efficient market hypothesis (EMH)*. This is the belief that the current prices of stocks have taken into account all known information about that company—in other words, the price itself acts efficiently.

efficient market hypothesis (EMH)

a market theory stating that the market acts efficiently, and that stock prices reflect all known information at each moment.

The fact that short-term prices very clearly act chaotically creates a problem for this hypothesis. Anyone who has observed price behavior following an earnings surprise has seen exaggerated movement of price, followed by a correction to fix that overreaction. This is hardly efficient.

Supporters of EMH have developed a rationale for this short-term chaos in stock prices. They explain that the market is *informationally efficient*. This means that even in cases where price acts inefficiently, information is efficiently taken into account.

The problem with EMH, even adjusted to an informationally efficient model, is that the market is not at all efficient. Under EMH, the conclusion that must be drawn is that it's impossible to consistently earn a return better than the market average. In other words, since all prices are right based on current information, there are no systems available to outperform the market.

This belief is cynical because it claims that traders will perform at the market average over time. That may be comforting to anyone who has not been able to beat the average market return (including most mutual funds). However, it can clearly be proven to be wrong, especially with some key technical indicators.

**information-
ally efficient**

descriptive of
the efficient
market
hypothesis
(EMH) as an
explanation for
the short-term
price chaos of
the market;
under this
explanation,
information is
taken into price
in an efficient
manner even
if the price
movement
or reaction is
chaotic.

Key Point

The efficient market hypothesis attempts to explain that markets are price-efficient or informationally efficient; in fact, the market is neither.

These technical indicators can be tracked over time and shown to predict price strength or weakness, if traders will only observe them. In coming chapters, many of these indicators are explained. For example, if you track price momentum, you soon discover that when prices are overbought, the usual response is a price decline; when that price is oversold, the next most likely step is a price increase. Momentum is one of many indicators that can be measured reliably. It does not provide a 100 percent guarantee that price will move in the direction indicated, but it will improve timing of entry and exit from positions.

Momentum is only one of many indicators that can be used to anticipate price movement, especially price reversals. However, under the EMH approach, it does not matter. All current prices are fair and accurate because all known information has already been rolled into that price.

There are three degrees of efficiency under EMH—weak, semi-strong, and strong. A *weak form EMH* assumes that only past information is included in the current price of stock.

The *semi-strong form EMH* expands on weak form with the belief that current prices also have taken into account all publicly known information about a company, and that prices change immediately based on that information.

The final variation, *strong form EMH*, adds information not known to the public—in other words, includes insider information—and is based on the belief that the current price reflects this, as well as information known publicly.

The entire range of EMH and its variation assumes that the stock market is a *rational market*. This would mean that the markets are always fair and reasonable, and this is reflected in the price. Evidence contradicts this assumption, however.

Example

Is the market rational? Or quite insane?: Do you believe that the market and its traders are rational? If you operate on that assumption, then you're part of the crowd and its mentality. Sadly, this means you could be wrong more often than right. In a practical sense, you need to make decisions for rational reasons, and not emotional ones.

weak form EMH

efficient market hypothesis based on the belief that current prices have taken past information into account, but not necessarily current information.

semi-strong form EMH

a variation of the efficient market hypothesis that assumes current stock prices include past publicly known information as well as current information about a company, and that prices change immediately as a result.

Anyone who observes price behavior is continually perplexed at how prices actually move. This includes overreaction to news; failure to react as expected to news, rumors, or dividend announcements; and price movement without any identifiable cause. In other words, the market is an *auction market* in which buyers offer competitive bids against sellers' competitive ask prices, and orders are executed only when the two prices coincide (unless a trader places a *market order*, meaning the current price becomes the trading price).

There are many underlying reasons for prices to rise or fall. A big part of this is the volume of interest among buyers and sellers, for rational as well as irrational reasons. Adding to this is the level of rumor or news, such as earnings announcements, pending announcements and expectations, takeover rumors, or expected mergers or acquisitions.

In this array of causes for prices to rise or fall, efficiency is not likely to be the result. While some aspects of prices may be efficient in the long term, trading opportunities occur in the short term, where prices are not at all efficient.

Key Point

A distinction has to be made between long-term market efficiency (which is practical) and short-term efficiency, which is not remotely likely. Short-term price movement is chaotic and unpredictable.

strong form EMH

a version of the efficient market hypothesis (EMF) in which all information, regardless of whether it is known publicly, is immediately reflected in the current price of stock.

Some market scholars have made a point that the market is micro-efficient but not macro-efficient. This refers to a belief that EMH is applicable to individual stocks, but not for the larger market and its primary trends. Even this assumption is questioned by David Dreman, who has observed that immediate responses in stock prices are not necessarily efficient, but that longer-term price behavior is more efficient in comparison.[2]

Even with evidence to the contrary, EMH has remained a favorite theory, notably in academia. However, among active traders, it is highly doubted as a useful belief for trading. If it were accepted, it would not matter what stocks were picked because all prices would be fair. So a cyclical economic change in one sector would not be a factor in the

---

[2] David Dreman, *Contrarian Investment Strategy: The Next Generation* (New York: Simon & Schuster, 1998).

timing of investments, although most investors understand how cycles cause sectors to move in and out of favor.

Accompanying the elusive rational market is a similar concept describing the behavior of traders. This *rational expectation* is based on a belief that when information is known to the market as a whole, traders will agree on a rational or logical course of action.

This is clearly not the case; traders are more likely to act in concert and follow the crowd mentality even when the majority is wrong. So buying high and selling low commonly occurs due to the behavior of the majority. The efficient market hypothesis rests on the assumption that people hold onto rational expectation in how they trade. Evidence points to the opposite truth, in which a minority of contrarian investors act based on rational analysis rather than just following the majority.

rational market

a type of market that behaves in a rational and logical manner; for example, efficient market hypothesis assumes the market is rational because it reflects all known information in the current price.

Example

Resisting your impulses: You have noticed lately that the market is on a downturn—at least the market for the stocks you own. Is this permanent? You are thinking about selling shares and waiting out this bad news, and then getting back in. And then you remember the advice to remain calm and make rational decisions. You decide to remain calm and wait things out. Eventually, markets will turn and come back. But if you sell at the bottom, you will miss out on the swing.

Those who support EMH will argue that some investors overreact and others underreact, but that the range of reactions conforms to what statisticians call a normal distribution, with

auction market

a market such as the exchange market for listed stocks, in which a buyer's bid price is matched to the seller's asked price; execution occurs when these prices agree.

some outperforming and others underperforming the market. But on average, EMH claims that price movement cannot be used to outperform the market over time—in spite of what technicians observe with the use of well-constructed technical analysis to include indicators and confirmation.

So in spite of what proponents of EMH claim, the market as a whole is not always right. It is more likely to be wrong, presenting opportunities for contrarians, but not for those believing in EMH.

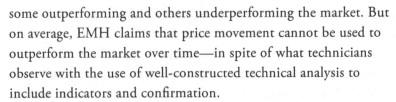

Key Point

Perhaps the biggest surprise to proponents of any efficiency model is the realization that the markets as a broadly defined force are *not* always right.

EMH has been challenged on the basis of the theory's flaws as well as through behavioral economics. This is the study of how traders act and react, and it attributes imperfect market price behavior to a series of practical causes and effects. These include bias, such as overconfidence, brand loyalty, and selective information tendencies. Humans are flawed in how they analyze facts and process information, and the range of possible outcomes because of this tendency draws EMH into question—not only as a theory but also as part of the flawed market culture.

market order

an order to buy or sell based not on a stated price but on the current available bid price (to buy) or asked price (to sell) for that security.

For example, many studies have concluded that low-P/E stocks yield better long-term returns than high-P/E stocks. Even so, investors tend to ignore low-P/E stocks because these are viewed as out of favor among investors; they may prefer overpriced stocks due to high interest in the stock, even though the price is way too high.[3]

RANDOM WALK HYPOTHESIS (RWH)

A theory with many similar attributes to EMH is the *random walk hypothesis (RWH)*, a belief that all price movement is unpredictable and random; based on the theory, it would be impossible to outperform the

---

[3] David Dreman and Michael Berry, "Overreaction, Underreaction, and the Low-P/E Effect," *Financial Analysts Journal* 51, no. 4 (1995): 21–30.

averages of the market. Like the rule of roulette, it is the same 50/50 bet as black versus red.[4]

The random walk is very similar to EMH in the sense that it is based on the assumption that the beginning price is accurate, and that is not always the case. Any short-term chaos leading to exaggerated price reaction makes this point, and this occurs regularly in the market.

Key Point

If you assume beginning prices are right but price movement is random, the entire assumption base for the RWH falls apart.

rational expectation

a belief that, given full information about a stock's price, most people will behave in a rational and predictable manner; this belief is required in order to accept the efficient market hypothesis (EMH).

The argument for the random walk is usually traced back to Eugene Fama and his published work in 1965. The theory has been tested in many ways, but every investor and trader can observe situations in which price movement has been excessive and would be expected to self-correct within a few trading days. This tendency is far from random, and is caused by a variety of distortions in supply and demand,

---

[4] Actually, the red versus black bet in roulette is not even 50/50. Because half of the numbers from 1 to 36 are black and the other half red, it appears to be 50/50. But two additional values, 0 and 00, make the odds somewhat lower than 50/50, favoring the house over time.

random walk hypothesis (RWH)

a theory stating that the market averages cannot be beaten because all movement, up or down, is entirely random and unpredictable.

allowing astute traders to time trades to exploit exaggerated price movement. Even so, proponents of this theory prefer to believe that stock price movement is random and that market behavior is based on the 50/50 nature of trading.[5]

Countering those who subscribe to the RWH are many analysts and economists who think the market is somewhat predictable. Virtually every technical analyst subscribes to this idea; otherwise, there would be no point in performing analysis at all. Some analysts believe prices can be predicted based on past pricing trends and movements; others believe that current indicators for reversal (based on price, volume, and momentum) can be used to forecast coming price changes, either reversals or continuation patterns. When these are confirmed by a second indicator forecasting the same future movement, confidence can and should be quite high.

Example

Believing in a rational market (or wishful thinking): Is the market rational? Does it react logically to news, and is price change predictable? You ask yourself these questions, but then you observe how markets act. Then you realize it is not rational, at least in the short term. Is this a problem or an opportunity?

Among those who have written on the topic of the RWH and its flaws are two professors (Lo and Mackinley), who based their book on extensive tests, demonstrating that market trends make price movement predictable and far from random.[6]

OTHER THEORIES

Contrarian investing often is misunderstood to mean investing opposite of the majority. This is not what the term means. While most traders tend to make buy or sell decisions impulsively and based on emotions (greed during up markets, panic in down markets), contrarians tend to base timing and decisions on cold, rational analysis rather than on emotion.

---

[5] Eugene Fama, "The Behavior of Stock Market Prices," *Journal of Business* 38 (1965): 34–105.

[6] Andrew W. Lo and Archie Craig Mackinlay, *A Non-random Walk down Wall Street*, 5th ed. (Princeton, NJ: Princeton University Press, 2002), 4–47.

Key Point

A contrarian is not going to do the opposite of the majority for no good reason. This trader tends to rely on cold, hard analysis and to resist responding emotionally to price movement.

To understand what contrarian investing means, remember the market adage, "Bulls and bears can make a profit, while pigs and chickens get slaughtered."

A contrarian may favor a bullish move in the market as a whole or in an individual stock, based on a thorough study of fundamental indicators and technical indicators. The fundamentals reveal the strongest and safest companies, and the technical signals help to improve timing of entry and exit.

Another theory is called the *50 percent principle*. This refers to the likelihood that a short-term trend will experience opposite-moving price changes as a natural event.

This is a *general* principle, when in practice a *retracement* may be more or less than 50 percent of the noted gain. In addition, the rule applies to short-term price movement and less so to longer-term trends.

Such retracements are to be expected as a natural part of a trend. It may be caused by investors taking profits or closing positions to minimize losses, for example. Another generalization is that if the retracement exceeds 50 percent, it could mean the trend has ended and a reversal is underway. However, this theory should be confirmed by independent indicators.

Closely related to the short-term retracement idea is the *Fibonacci retracement theory*. This is based on a numerical sequence believed to recur in nature, and to provide specific percentages of retracement that should be expected during a trend.

50 percent principle

a market theory stating that trends undergo price corrections averaging 50 percent of the gains; for example, a trend that has moved up 20 percent is expected to experience a 10 percent downward retracement, and a trend moving down 30 percent should expect an upward retracement of 15 percent.

The sequence is named for thirteenth-century mathematician Leonardo Fibonacci. He developed the sequence, observing that it recurs often in art, architecture, and nature. The sequence consists of adding the previous two numbers together:

0, 1, 1, 2, 3, 5, 8, 13, 21, 34, 55, 88, 144, 233, 377 . . .

Note that every digit is the sum of the previous two digits $(13 + 8 = 21)$. This sequence is used to estimate the degree of retracement and to also determine when an apparent retracement actually represents a reversal.

retracement

a temporary price movement in the direction opposite the current trend.

Example

Magical numbers: Some traders are dubious about the value of the Fibonacci series. However, a close study of it reveals that the relationships between values in the sequence often correspond to the levels of price retracements. It isn't magic, but it could provide one (of many) useful technical tools for timing trades.

Fibonacci retracement theory

a belief that a specific sequence of numbers can be used to develop numerals for identifying likely degrees of retracement within a trend.

Three ratios are key to this form of analysis:

23.6 is derived by dividing any number in the sequence by the number occurring three places beyond. For example: $55 \div 233 = 23.6$. This level would represent a shallow retracement and is most likely to be interpreted as what technicians call a *flag*.

The second ratio is 38.2, derived by dividing any number in the sequence by the number found two places after. For example, $55 \div 144 = 38.2$. This is termed a moderate retracement.

Third is the most important ratio, 61.8. To compute, divide any number in the sequence by the number immediately before—for example, 55 ÷ 34 = 1.618 (after removing the full number value "1," the 61.8 remains). This is the ratio recurring often in nature and art; it is called the *golden ratio*.

The calculations are used to estimate how far a retracement will move. For example, U.S. Steel (X) saw its stock rise from $24.00 to $28.50 in November 2013, a move of 4.5 points. A downward retracement occurred shortly after. Applying the strong retracement level, the stock price is expected to decline by 2.71 points (4.5 × .618 = 2.71 points).

In fact, the stock price declined to $25.75, or 2.75 points before the uptrend resumed.

The Fibonacci retracement is an interesting and useful guideline for *likely* retracement levels. But it is not a universal rule, and it does not always apply with reliability. It is one of many technical tools useful for estimating the degree of retracement.

With no shortage of theories about market and investor behavior, it may be difficult to begin to decide which ones to accept or reject. A good rule of thumb is that technical signals work if used cautiously and with thorough analysis. Before acting on any signal, it also makes sense to find confirmation of what one indicator forecasts, with a different indicator forecasting the same likely price movement and direction.

This process begins with the study of price charts, where any number of valuable indicators are found. The next chapter introduces the subject of charting and how it is done.

flag

a price pattern with a moving rectangular shape like a flag, with a mast on either side, usually representing a short-term minor retracement within the current trend.

golden ratio

the strongest ratio in the Fibonacci sequence, also called *Phi*, indicating the most likely point for retracement to occur.

182

9 CHARTING AND ITS VALUE

*There are two classes of people who tell what is going to happen in the future:
Those who don't know, and those who don't know they don't know.*
—John Kenneth Galbraith, *Washington Post*,
February 28, 1988

The price chart is a summary of trading prices over a period of time. Traders want to know (1) opening and closing prices, (2) trading range during each session, (3) volume of trading, (4) momentum for either buyers or sellers, and (5) specific indicators forecasting price movement and direction.

This is a lot to expect from a single price chart, but in fact that is precisely what the *chartist* studies and uses.

For many investors new to technical analysis, the value of charting can easily be questioned. How can you tell how prices will move in the future? If markets are either efficient or random (see the previous chapter), prediction has no value whatsoever. If you believe that markets can be predicted, is charting the way to make such predictions?

chartist

a technical analyst who relies on price charts to spot signals for price movement, including strength or weakness in a current trend, and signs that a trend is likely to continue or reverse.

Key Point

The value of charting relies on how much you think prediction of price movement is possible.

In fact, many signals have been shown in the past to provide reliable information about future price direction. Nothing works all of the time, so traders need to seek independent confirmation for one signal with at least one additional signal pointing to the same likely change yet to come. Even then, a crucial point to keep in mind is this: Even the strongest signals, confirmed by multiple other signals, can fail. No signals work all of the time. For this reason, traders need to keep trades to a minimum dollar amount and to avoid placing too much risk on any one trade. Charts are useful for improving the timing of entry and exit in trades, but they do not remove all market risk; nothing does.

A starting point in developing a risk-aware technical program is to become familiar with the price chart in its various forms.

Edward Jones
& Charles Dow
1883

TYPES OF CHARTS

Stock charts have evolved since widespread use of the Internet. In the past, investors had to construct their own charts manually or rely on expensive charting services. Today numerous online free charting sites are available, and you can choose from among many that provide dozens of indicators beyond just tracking the price.

Key Point

Charting used to be time-consuming and expensive. With the Internet, it is free, easy, and fast to find a chart.

In this book, charts from www.StockCharts.com are used, which is a free service that provides great flexibility in the type of chart you pick, and which indicators you want included.

Valuable Resource
Flexible charting services are available online. A search will reveal many useful and easy to use services. This book uses charts provided by **www.StockCharts.com**.

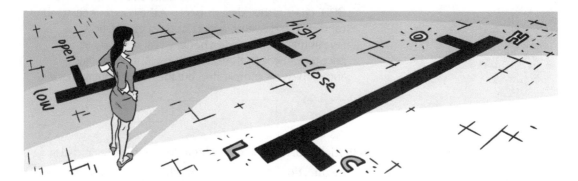

Among the many kinds of charts, a once popular type was the *OHLC chart*. This stands for "open, high, low, close."

The OHLC daily entry consists of a vertical line stretching from the high to the low price of the day, a short horizontal line extending to the left for the opening price, and another horizontal line extending to the right for the closing price. This formation is shown in Figure 9.1.

OHLC chart

a stock price chart reporting the open, high, low, and closing price for each session.

Key Point
The OHLC chart used to be the norm, but it is not visually complete, and today it has become obsolete compared to more visual charting systems, like candlesticks.

OHLC Line

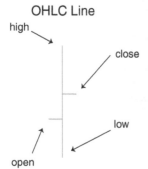

Figure 9.1 OHLC Line

The OHLC chart has minimal value because it is not easy to spot trends over a series of sessions. Even though this form of chart is visual, a better and more useful chart is the *candlestick*. A candlestick is a variety of the OHLC that contains the same information and more.

Example
Relying on past systems: Some traders have chosen the OHLC chart as their default, because they don't understand candlesticks. However, a short study of candlesticks reveals that they provide a better visual summary of price movement. By the same argument, modern-day automobiles are complicated, but they tend to outlive horses.

The candlestick provides the open, high, low, and close, and also summarizes the direction of movement. A white or clear candlestick appears in a session when the price moves higher, and a black candlestick occurs when the price moves lower in the session.

The candlestick and its attributes are shown in Figure 9.2.

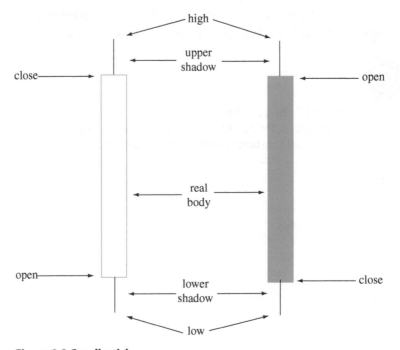

Figure 9.2 Candlestick

The array of information on the candlestick is easier to comprehend that the more primitive OHLC chart.

Key Point

A key benefit to the candlestick chart is its highly visual summary of price range, open and close, and direction of movement for each session.

Other charting formats include a variety of line charts, based on opening prices, closing prices, or both. But compared to the candlestick, these alternatives are not practical.

To compare candlestick charts to other forms, review the chart of U.S. Steel in different formats. Figure 9.3 shows a six-month line chart.

Figure 9.3 U.S. Steel—Line Chart
Source: Chart courtesy of StockCharts.com.

Figure 9.3 provides very basic information about the movement of the company's stock price. However, it does not provide detailed visual information. Somewhat better than the line chart is the OHLC version of the same data. Figure 9.4 reveals this outcome for the same company and period of time.

The best visual representation of stock price movement is found in the candlestick chart, which is shown in Figure 9.5.

Figure 9.4 U.S. Steel—OHLC Chart
Source: Chart courtesy of StockCharts.com.

Figure 9.5 U.S. Steel—Candlestick Chart
Source: Chart courtesy of StockCharts.com.

In coming chapters, this candlestick chart format is used to show many of the technical signals, and how they are used in conjunction with price. The foregoing charts are limited to only price information; however, these can be modified to include volume, momentum, and many more indicators chartists use.

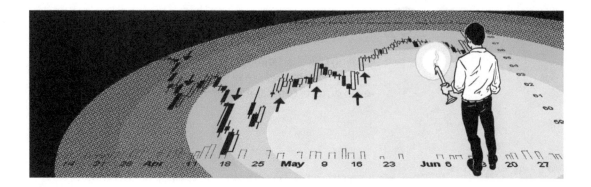

The remaining sections of this chapter deal with the attributes of candlestick indicators and charts, and how this format has become the standard for technical analysis.

SCALING OF CHART VALUES

In comparing data of stock charts, the *scaling* has to be kept in mind, because not all charts use the same scale. The scale is set automatically so that the range of prices appear for the selected period without exception.

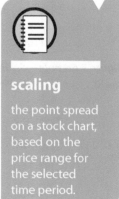

scaling

the point spread on a stock chart, based on the price range for the selected time period.

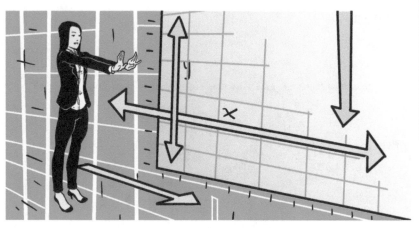

For example, on a three-month chart, the chart for Apple (AAPL) requires five-point increments and 14 levels of price, as shown in Figure 9.6.

The five-point spread in price increments is spread over 14 different price levels, shown in the scale at the right. In comparison, Yahoo! requires only eight price increments and uses a one-point price spread, shown in Figure 9.7.

Key Point

Scaling of a chart defines how volatile price appears. A more in-depth study may reveal that scaling affects and even distorts comparative analysis.

Figure 9.6 Apple—Scaling Five Points
Source: Chart courtesy of StockCharts.com.

Figure 9.7 Yahoo—Scaling One Point
Source: Chart courtesy of StockCharts.com.

The difference here is essential to accurately reading charts. It would be easy to compare these two companies based on vastly different scales over the same period of time. But just looking at the level of price movement, it appears at first that both stocks are approximately the same in terms of *volatility*. In fact, however, they are quite different. Because Yahoo!'s prices moved only in one-point increments, it involved far greater volatility than Apple.

volatility

the degree of movement in price over time, reflecting relative degrees of market risk.

Example
Earning scale: A trader started out comparing different stocks by looking for volatility in chart patterns. However, it soon became apparent that this was not a reliable system. Why? Because with different scaling between companies, the patterns in one chart do not have the same significance as those in another. It all depends on the scaling.

As a measurement of market risk, or the risk of price moving more or less than you expect, Yahoo!'s price spread showed a 21 percent change from high to low, or seven points:

$$(40 - 33) \div 33 = 21\%$$

Apple moved many more points, but volatility was lower based on a price spread over three months of 75 points:

$$(555 - 480) \div 480 = 16\%$$

This analysis demonstrates that volatility cannot be measured or compared on the basis of the number of points that price moves. It is relative. Although Apple moved in a range of 75 points over three months, it was less volatile than the much lower-priced Yahoo!. In this case, volatility is reflected in the spread of prices on the chart using the same three-month period for both of these stocks.

Whenever charts are compared between two or more companies, price range movement is the test to decide whether a company is more or less volatile. On a technical (price-based) level, selection of one company over another for trading should be based on many factors, including market risk, and volatility measures this accurately.

Because the prices of these two stocks are quite different, it seems rational to think of Apple as higher-risk because of the higher point spread. However, when the two stocks are compared on the same basis, this argument no longer makes sense.

Key Point

Analyzing volatility with scaling in mind provides more insight than the appearance of price movement over the chart's period.

For example, if you bought 100 shares of Apple and paid the latest price on the chart, it would cost $51,900 plus trading costs. If instead you bought 1,428 shares of Yahoo!, it would cost the same, approximately $51,900. When you compare investing the same dollar amount, you have made both possible candidates the same in terms of dollar risk. Now the difference between Apple's volatility (16 percent) and Yahoo!'s volatility (21 percent) becomes clearer. Yahoo has greater market risk in terms of its price volatility.

Scaling of charts can easily distort what appears to be a level of volatility. In the preceding example, the price range of Apple, covering 75 points, makes the stock appear more volatile than the lower-priced Yahoo! spread of only seven points. But when the dollar amounts are equalized, the calculated price spread volatility becomes clear.

CANDLESTICK BASICS

If you keep price volatility in mind as you study price charts, you will be able to more clearly evaluate and judge market risk for stock, even when comparing two companies with vastly different price levels and chart scales.

So with scaling in mind, the next step is to begin studying how to read the price chart. Today, the standard of charting is the candlestick chart, for good reasons. The candlestick reveals a wealth of information about the degree of price movement (high to low), opening and closing price (top and bottom of the rectangle), and direction (white or black). Compared to any other charting method, candlesticks are the most informative type of chart.

Here are some observations about charting that are crucial in how price patterns are interpreted:

1. *Indicators are most important close to resistance and support.* The most important locations in a price chart are *resistance* and *support.* These are the borders of the trading range. When reversal patterns appear close to either of these, the reversal is much stronger than anywhere else. When a reversal indicator occurs as price moves above resistance or below support, it increases the chances for reversal.

2. *Scaling defines volatility; not all chart patterns are equal.* You cannot identify degrees of volatility just by observing the swing from high to low in the chart. Scaling of that chart may be only fractions of a point, or many points. So the price volatility is relative, but it also represents price movement within the scale. To understand how volatile the price range is, traders need to compare charts among several stocks.

3. *Patterns apply on all time levels, whether daily, hourly, or by the minute.* The daily chart (used throughout this book) is the most popular trading level used today. However, many traders prefer hourly charts or even charts that represent minutes rather than hours or days. However, all candlestick (and other) price patterns apply to all time increments.

resistance

the highest price level in the current trading range, representing the highest price at which traders are willing to buy and sell; price should not easily break through resistance and remain above without reversing.

support

the lowest price level in the current trading range, representing the lowest price at which traders are willing to buy and sell; price should not easily break through support and remain below without reversing.

reversal

an indicator forecasting a change in the current price trend, to movement in the opposite direction.

4. *No pattern is going to be reliable 100 percent of the time. Even with strong confirmation, be prepared for a degree of failure in timing.* Every pattern will mislead some portion of the time. Before entering a trade, every reversal indicator has to be subjected to independent *confirmation*. This is a separate indicator that forecasts the same reversal; without confirmation, the reversal should not be acted upon, even for the strongest of candlestick indicators. Many candlesticks are unreliable on their own because they lead to reversal half the time, and do not the other half. Others are reliable up to 80 percent of the time.[1]

Confirmation
The location of a second indicator that provides the same forecast as the first; this may be in the form of a candlestick pattern, price gap, volume spike, momentum oscillator, or other technical signal.

Example
Does your signal confirm?: A trader has located a very strong reversal signal on the current chart of a company being tracked. But when seeking confirmation, the trader found only signals contradicting reversal, and showing likely continuation—or no signals at all. Without confirmation, is it safe to make a trade? A wise decision is to take no action when the signals contradict one another.

5. *Reversal can occur only if there is a current trend to reverse. A reversal* requires a change in the existing trend. So a bearish reversal requires an existing *uptrend*, and a bullish reversal requires an existing *downtrend*. A bullish reversal found within an uptrend is a *continuation* and not a reversal.

SINGLE-SESSION INDICATORS

Several candlesticks involve only one session. Even though the information from a one-session indicator is limited, the reversal or continuation forecast can be quite strong.

---

[1] Thomas Bulkowski, *Encyclopedia of Candlestick Charts* (Hoboken, NJ: John Wiley & Sons, 2008), 8–9.

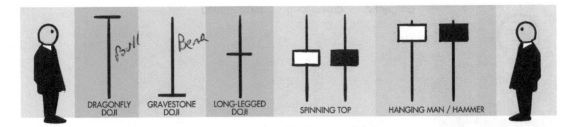

The two most prominent among single-session candlesticks are the *doji* and the *long candlestick.*

Among doji sessions, several specific types may appear. These include the *dragonfly doji*, which is a bullish indicator. It is likely to be found at the bottom of a downtrend. The long lower *shadow* reveals an attempt among traders to move prices lower, which failed. The *real body* of the candlestick is replaced by the doji body, a short horizontal line.

Another doji formation is *gravestone doji*, which is the opposite of a dragonfly. It is a bearish signal with the horizontal line at the bottom.

While the dragonfly and gravestone are opposite types of doji sessions, another can be either bullish or bearish. The *long-legged doji* has exceptionally long upper *and* lower shadows, with a horizontal line in the middle. Generally, when this appears during an uptrend, it signals a reversal to the downside; when it is found in a downtrend, it could work as a bullish reversal. However, as an uncertain indicator, the long-legged doji is most useful as a confirmation signal of other reversal indicators.

uptrend

a current trend involving a series of progressively higher price levels, also called a bullish price movement or a bull trend.

downtrend

a current trend involving a series of progressively lower price levels, also called a bearish price movement or a bear trend.

Example

A long-legged dilemma: You have been looking for reliable confirmation signals. The long-legged doji seems like a strong signal because it is characterized by exceptionally long upper and lower shadows. But because it relies on where it shows up and can mean bullish or bearish trends, you soon discover that you need more confirmation than just this one signal.

The doji can be found very often in a price chart, and may have great variety. It is rarely perfect in the three general forms of dragonfly, gravestone, or long-legged.

The three primary classifications of doji are shown in Figure 9.8.

dragonfly   gravestone   long-legged

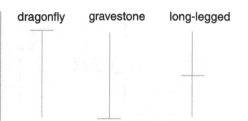

Figure 9.8 Types of Doji Sessions

continuation

an indicator
pointing to
a likely price
movement
in the same
direction as that
of the current
trend, with bull
trend prices
continuing to
move higher, or
bear trend prices
continuing to
move lower.

doji

a candlestick
with a horizontal
line in place
of the more
common
rectangle;
in a doji, the
opening and
closing prices
are identical
or very close
together. In
Japanese, doji
means mistake.

Key Point

A doji pattern is likely to occur often, so its significance should rely not on its frequency but how it works with other sessions before and after.

Because the doji will appear frequently, it should be used in conjunction with other signals as a means for confirmation, but never by itself. Figure 9.9 provides an example of a three-month stock chart in which five doji sessions appear. This does not include the many *near-doji* sessions that are also found on this chart. The near-doji is also called a *narrow-range day* (*NRD*) by swing traders.

Figure 9.9 Doji Sessions on Stock Chart
Source: Chart courtesy of StockCharts.com.

Closely related to the doji is the session with a very small real body. The pure doji has virtually no distance between opening and closing price, but the small real body signal may appear as a square with long upper and lower shadows.

Key Point

a session with a small body is called a near-doji; swing traders also refer to this as a narrow-range day (NRD).

The *spinning top* is an example. The real body may be either white or black, and should appear approximately halfway between the extension of the shadows. Regardless of the color of the real body, the spinning top may be bullish or bearish, depending on where it appears in the current price trend.

The spinning top is illustrated in Figure 9.10.

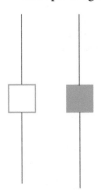

Figure 9.10 Spinning Tops

Another version of the single session with a small real body is an indicator that is called either the *hanging man* or the *hammer* (Figure 9.11). Both of these contain a small real body with a lower shadow that extends longer than the size of the real body. If this appears at the bottom of a downtrend, it is a hammer; when found at the top of an uptrend, it is a hanging man.

This is an unusual pattern in the sense that the color of the real body does not matter. But it appears often enough to be taken as a serious reversal signal, and when confirmed, a strong one as well.

Example

Hanging man or hammer?: You are confused about these two signals because they are identical but they have opposite meaning. It depends on where they appear. It makes sense, though, when you realize that they are reversal signals, bullish for a downtrend (hammer) or bearish for an uptrend (hanging man).

long candlestick

a session with unusually long white or black rectangles, indicating an especially strong price movement upward (white) or downward (black).

dragonfly doji

a single-session candlestick shaped like a capital T, with a horizontal line at the top and a long lower shadow beneath.

shadow

a vertical line appearing above or below the real body of a candlestick, representing the full trading range for the session; the longer the shadow, the more significance it holds, since the trading levels retreated back into the range for a session.

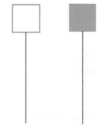

Figure 9.11 Hanging Man and Hammer

Key Point

The hanging man and hammer look the same, but the distinction is based on whether they appear at the bottom of a downtrend or at the top of an uptrend.

The opposite of doji and narrow-range sessions is the long candle. This may be white or black and can work as a reversal pattern. You expect to see a white long session at the bottom of a downtrend to work as an authentic bullish reversal, and to see a black long session at the top of an uptrend to signal a coming bearish reversal.

A long candlestick occurs often, but because scaling of charts depends on the range of prices, what appears long might actually represent a very small price movement; on a different chart, a normal candlestick might actually be long relative to ranges of price on other sessions.

The long candlestick is illustrated in Figure 9.12.

Contrast has to be made between long upper or lower shadows, such as those often found on the doji session, and long real bodies, like those on the long candlesticks.

Key Point

The meaning of size for real bodies versus shadows is completely different. As a general rule, shadows imply weakness in the direction of the shadow, and long real bodies imply strength to the upside (white) or downside (black).

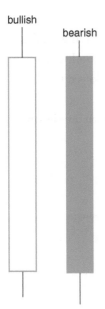

bullish

bearish

Figure 9.12 Long Candlesticks

real body

a candlestick's central white (upward-moving) or black (downward-moving) rectangle, representing a session's movement between open and close; the upper and lower lines of the rectangle represent opening and closing price. In a white candlestick, the opening is at the bottom and the closing at the top; in a black candlestick, the opening is at the top and the closing at the bottom.

A long shadow implies weakness in the direction of the shadow. For example, an exceptionally long upper shadow represents likely loss of momentum among buyers. As price is pushed upward, it ends up retreating as buyers give way to sellers. The same is true for long lower shadows: The price is pushed downward by sellers, but it rebounds as seller momentum weakens and the buyers prevail.

In the case of the long candlestick, the real body is what gets extended. In other words, the distance between open and close is greater than usual, a signal of strength. In a white long candlestick, buyers dominate trading and drive prices higher than on a typical session. In a black long session, sellers are in control and prices are moved downward.

TWO-SESSION INDICATORS

There are dozens of two-session candlestick indicators. Ahead are highlights of some of those that will be found often.

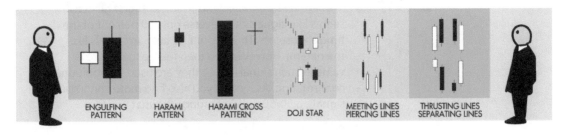

ENGULFING PATTERN   HARAMI PATTERN   HARAMI CROSS PATTERN   DOJI STAR   MEETING LINES PIERCING LINES   THRUSTING LINES SEPARATING LINES

Among reversal candlesticks, one of the more reliable is the *engulfing pattern*. This is a pattern with reverse-colored real bodies, and with the second session longer. It exceeds the open/close range on both sides. The bullish version begins with a black session and is followed by a larger white; the bearish version is the opposite.

The bullish and bearish versions of the engulfing pattern are shown in Figure 9.13.

bullish   bearish

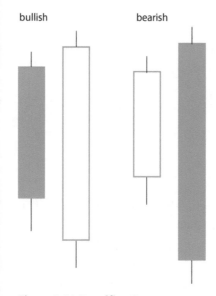

Figure 9.13 Engulfing Pattern

The opposite configuration is known as the *harami pattern*, but it cannot be relied upon because its frequency of reversal is only about 50/50. However, when the harami appears as a confirming indicator, it is more valuable. If it confirms what another indicator reveals, the harami can be applied as an effective indicator.

A variation called the *harami cross pattern* is only slightly more reliable. This is the same as the harami, with the exception that

Example
Is a 50/50 signal worth anything?: At first glance it seems like signals that reverse only 50 percent of the time are useless. That's your first take on signals like the harami. However, you then realize that there is value in such signals when they are used for additional confirmation. As long as you also find more confirmation signals, a 50/50 indicator supports what you find.

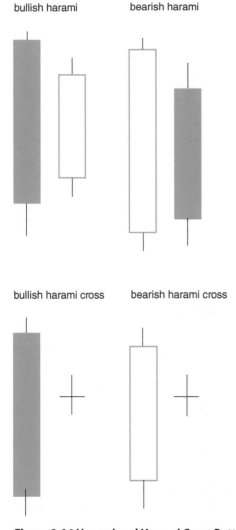

bullish harami   bearish harami

bullish harami cross   bearish harami cross

Figure 9.14 Harami and Harami Cross Patterns

near-doji

single sessions with very narrow trading ranges, close to the doji but with a slight degree of price movement.

narrow-range day (NRD)

a name used by swing traders to describe a near-doji, a session with very little gap between opening and closing price.

spinning top

a single session candlestick with a small real body of either color, and long upper and lower shadows.

the second session forms as a doji. These patterns are shown in Figure 9.14.

Another pattern to look for is the *doji star*. This is a session followed by a gap and then a doji. The gap defines a bullish reversal (when the gap is below) or a bearish reversal (when it is above).

A doji star can also be defined as containing three sessions. This is explained later in the chapter. The two-session patterns are shown in Figure 9.15.

hanging man

a single session candlestick with a small real body of either color and a long lower shadow, working as a bearish reversal and found at the top of an uptrend.

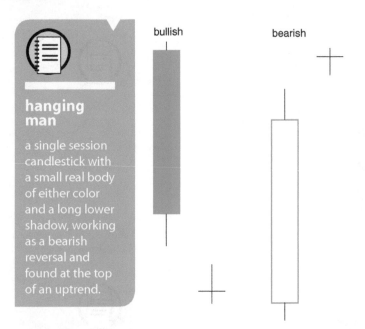

bullish   bearish

Figure 9.15 Doji Star (two-session) Patterns

hammer

a single session candlestick with a small real body of either color and a long lower shadow, working as a bullish reversal and found at the bottom of a downtrend.

The last two bullish reversals (remember, there are many more than those reported here) are the *meeting lines* and *piercing lines*. These involve a relationship between the opening or closing prices on two consecutive days.

In the bullish meeting lines, a black session is followed by a white, with the white opening with a gap below but closing at the same price as the previous day. In the bearish meeting lines, a white session is followed by a black, with the black opening with a gap below but closing at the same price as the previous day.

A bullish piercing line involves a black session, followed by a gap below and a white session that rises to close within the range of the first session. A bearish piercing line is the opposite: a white session followed by an upside gap and a black session that declines to close within the range of the first session.

Key Point

The lines patterns appear often, but their reliability is not particularly strong. So these work best to confirm other signals.

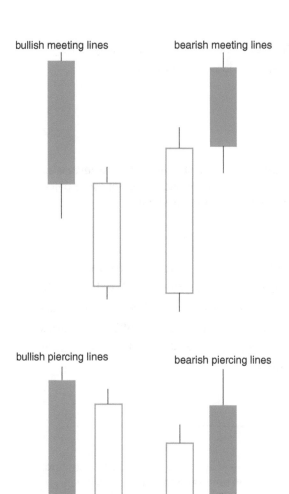

bullish meeting lines   bearish meeting lines

bullish piercing lines   bearish piercing lines

Figure 9.16 Meeting Lines and Piercing Lines

engulfing pattern

a two-session candlestick indicator with opposite-color real bodies; the second session exceeds the real body size of the first on both the top and the bottom.

harami pattern

a two-session candlestick indicator with opposite-color real bodies; the second session is smaller than the real body size of the first on both the top and the bottom.

The meeting lines and piercing lines are summarized in Figure 9.16.

Numerous confirming two-session candlesticks also will be found on stock price charts. When these occur midway in a trend, it forecasts that the trend will continue moving in the same direction.

It is easy to overlook the significance of continuation indicators. With emphasis on reversals as timing mechanisms, continuation is much less inspiring or interesting. However, when you have open trades, you will want to track the price trends carefully, so that you can close the trade when reversals are spotted. Equally worthwhile is locating a continuation

harami cross pattern

a harami, but with a doji in the second session in place of a real body.

doji star (two-session)

a two-session candlestick pattern consisting of a black session, a downside gap, and a doji (bullish), or a white session, an upside gap, and a doji (bearish).

pattern because, if confirmed, it tells you the trend is likely to keep going, and that it is not time to close—not just yet.

Key Point

Continuation indicators are just as important as reversals, but these are overlooked often because emphasis is placed on timing after spotting a reversal signal.

These continuation indicators include many different formations. Among these are *thrusting lines* and *separating lines*. The thrusting lines pattern consists of a white session followed by a higher-opening black session that closes within the first session's range (bullish), or a black session followed by a lower-opening white session that closes within the first session's range (bearish).

Example

Reversal or continuation?: Like many traders, you find yourself focusing on reversal signals but not actively seeking continuation. Reversal is a point where action is taken. But then you realize that continuation is just as strong, even if it only tells you not to close a position just yet. It's another form of information, but trading wisdom comes from an open mind to all of the signals, even those that tell you not to act.

The thrusting lines and separating lines continuation patterns are shown in Figure 9.17.

THREE-SESSION INDICATORS

A three-session indicator is often much stronger than a single-session or two-session one, if only because it takes so much more price pattern movement to create a signal over three consecutive sessions. For this reason, the three-session indicator is found less often; but when it is found, it should not be ignored.

bullish thrusting lines   bearish thrusting lines

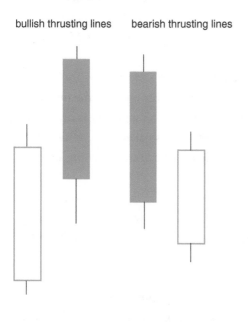

bullish separating lines   bearish separating lines

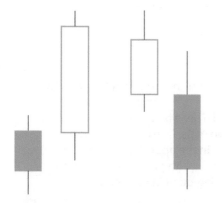

Figure 9.17 Thrusting Lines and Separating Lines

meeting lines

a two-session candlestick pattern consisting of opposite-colored sessions that close at the same price.

piercing lines

a two-session candlestick pattern consisting of opposite-colored sessions, with the second closing within the range of the first.

thrusting lines

a two-session candlestick continuation pattern consisting of opposite-colored sessions with the second gapping to open and closing within the range of the first.

Key Point
Three-session signals may be stronger than others because of what is required to develop a clear signal in three consecutive sessions.

The first of these is the *white soldiers* pattern, also popularly called three white soldiers because it requires at least three sessions. But the signal could take four or more, and the more sessions formed with this pattern, the stronger the likely reversal.

The white soldiers pattern is strongly bullish, especially when it appears after an extended downtrend. It strongly indicates a coming bullish reversal. Nearly as strong is the bearish opposite, the *black crows* pattern. This is strongly bearish.

The white soldiers and black crows are both shown in Figure 9.18.

Another set of three-session reversal indicators includes the bullish *morning star* and bearish *evening star*. The morning star starts out with a black session followed by a downside gap, a smaller white session, and then another white session moving higher. The bearish evening star is the opposite.

Similar to the morning and evening star is the *doji star* (three-session), which looks like the preceding patterns with one exception: The middle session is a doji. It may appear in both bullish and bearish varieties. An earlier version was introduced with only two sessions. Some define the doji star with three.

All three of these indicators are shown in Figure 9.19.

Another strong reversal signal is the imaginatively named *abandoned baby*. This is similar to the doji star with one exception: a gap appears both before and after the middle (abandoned) session.

separating lines

a two-session candlestick continuation pattern consisting of opposite-colored sessions, with the second closing at the same price of the first and following a gap.

Example
Abandoning the baby: You are puzzled at this pattern because it is so oddly named, and you're not sure why it is such a strong signal. Then you recognize the true power of the signal: two gaps. One gap occurs in one direction, and the other in the opposite direction. The baby is that middle session with gaps on either side. It strongly marks the turning point in the trend.

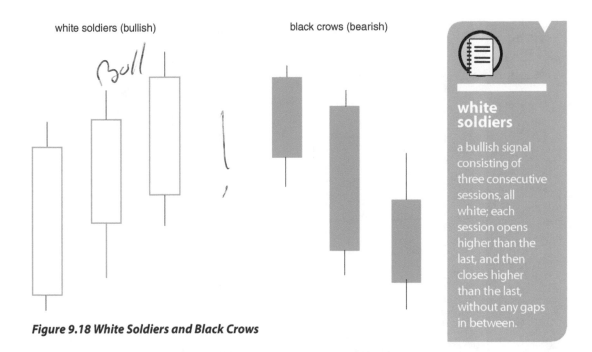

Figure 9.18 White Soldiers and Black Crows

white soldiers (bullish)

black crows (bearish)

white soldiers

a bullish signal consisting of three consecutive sessions, all white; each session opens higher than the last, and then closes higher than the last, without any gaps in between.

This formation is strengthened by the double gap moving in opposite directions. The bullish and bearish versions are shown in Figure 9.20.

The *squeeze alert* is one of the most enigmatic signals, because the color of the sessions is opposite of what you would expect (the first of three is black in the bullish version and white in the bearish).

It consists of three sessions, with each one smaller on top and bottom than the last; thus, each session's range diminishes in both opening and closing. While the color of the first session defines it as bullish or bearish, the color of sessions two and three does not matter.

black crows

a bearish signal consisting of three consecutive sessions, all black; each session opens lower than the last, and then closes lower than the last, without any gaps in between.

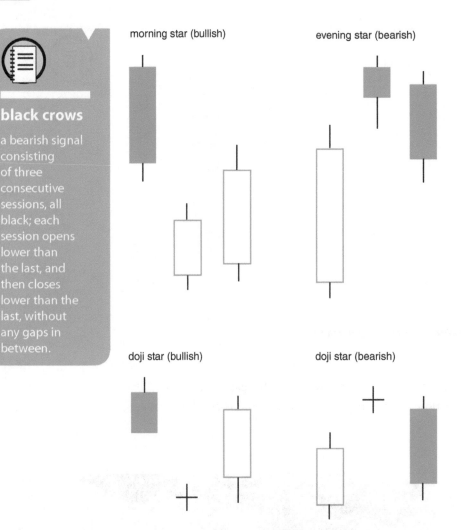

morning star (bullish)

evening star (bearish)

doji star (bullish)

doji star (bearish)

Figure 9.19 Morning and Evening Star and Doji Star

morning star

a bullish three-session signal involving a black session, a downside gap, and then two white sessions moving the price higher.

The appearance of the squeeze alert is shown in Figure 9.21.

In addition to reversal signals, three-session formations can also serve as continuations. One example is the *tasuki gap*.

The word tasuki means a sash used to hold a loose-sleeved shirt in place. It is aptly named if you picture the pattern with this definition in mind. Both bullish and bearish versions of this are shown in Figure 9.22.

A final three-session continuation is the *gap filled* pattern. This is very much like the tasuki gap, with the exception that the range of the third session fills the gap created between sessions one and two.

bullish   bearish

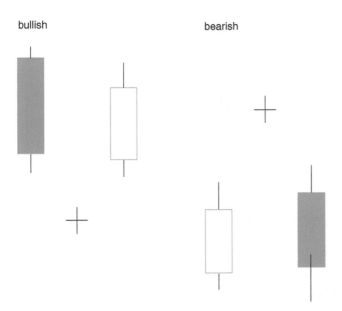

Figure 9.20 Abandoned Baby

bullish   bearish

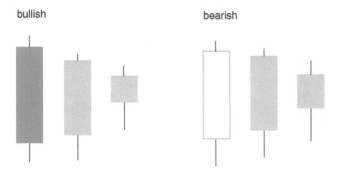

Figure 9.21 Squeeze Alert

evening star

a bearish three-session signal involving a white session, an upside gap, and then two black sessions moving the price lower.

doji star (three-session)

a three-session signal involving a black session, a downside gap, a doji, and a final white session (bullish), or a black session, an upside gap, a doji, and a final black session (bearish)

The gap filled pattern is shown in Figure 9.23.

The reliability of reversal and continuation patterns defines how much you should depend on them for timing of both entry and exit. An in-depth study of how often various patterns are accurate tells the story more completely.[2]

---

[2] Bulkowski, *Encyclopedia*. His study revealed a reliable level of 63 percent (bullish) and 82 percent (bearish) for the engulfing pattern; 82 percent for white soldiers and 79 percent for black crows; and 76 percent for morning star and 70 percent for evening star, doji star, and abandoned baby. Less impressive here are the harami at 50 percent and harami cross at 56 percent; meeting lines, 53 percent; piercing lines, 64 percent; tasuki gap, 55 percent; and gap filled, 60 percent.

abandoned baby

a three-session indicator starting with a black session, a downside gap, a doji, an upside gap, and a final white session (bullish); or a white session, an upside gap, a doji, a downside gap, and a final black session (bearish).

squeeze alert

a three-session indicator with a first session a black day (bullish) or a white day (bearish); the color of sessions two and three does not matter. Session two opens and closes within the range of session one, and session three is smaller than session two.

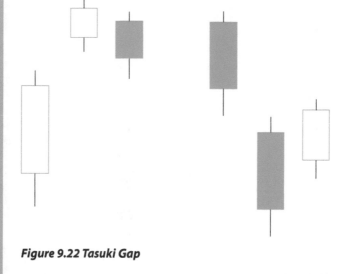

bullish   bearish

Figure 9.22 Tasuki Gap

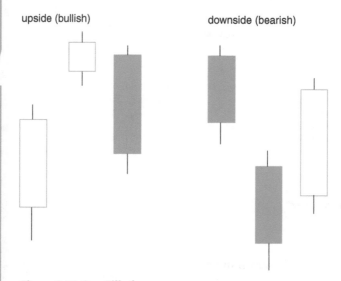

upside (bullish)   downside (bearish)

Figure 9.23 Gap Filled

REVERSAL AND CONTINUATION

Every reversal pattern may serve as continuation, and vice versa. In order to work as a reversal, the pattern has to appear at the expected point in the trend; so a bullish reversal should conclude a downtrend, and a bearish reversal will be found at the top of an uptrend. If these appear elsewhere (bullish signals during an uptrend or bearish during a downtrend) then they are continuation signals.

Example
Which way does it go?: A trader has learned the major reversal signals but is confused. At times, a reversal appears when there is no pattern to reverse. So a bullish signal found during a bullish trend is a contradiction, right? Not really. Any signal may act as either a reversal or confirmation forecast. This complicates matters, but improves your forecasting skills.

Key Point
No signal is *always* a reversal or continuation. Most can serve as either under the right circumstances.

The message here is that no signal is a 100 percent reversal; a signal can work as a continuation as well, so a wise trader will understand that the context for any signal depends on its placement. You can react to a reversal only if there is a trend to reverse.

The same is true for patterns usually identified as a continuation. If the pattern appears during the opposite type of trend, it might provide a reversal indicator. But this can get very confusing, which is why every candlestick indicator needs to be verified through independent confirmation.

This confirmation can be found in several forms:

- Other candlesticks
- Moving average trends and crossovers (Chapter 11)
- Traditional technical signals (e.g., double tops or bottoms, gaps, violations of resistance or support, head and shoulders, triangles, wedges) (Chapter 12)
- Volume spikes or indicators (Chapter 13)
- Momentum moving to overbought or oversold (Chapter 14)

The next chapter examines the nature of trends and how to use them to anticipate price movement, either a reversal or a continuation.

tasuki gap
a three-session continuation signal consisting of a white session, an upside gap, a second white session, and black session moving lower (bullish); or a black session, a downside gap, a second black session, and a final white session moving higher (bearish).

gap filled
a three-session continuation pattern beginning with a white session, an upside gap, a second white session, and a black session that fills the gap created between sessions one and two (upside, or bullish); or a black session, a downside gap, a second black session, and a white session that fills the original gap (downside, or bearish).

CHAPTER 10

TRENDS AND HOW TO STUDY THEM

The trouble with research is that it tells you what people were thinking about yesterday, not tomorrow. It's like driving a car using a rear-view mirror.
—Bernard Loomis, *International Herald Tribune*, October 9, 1985

Technical trends are quite different than fundamental trends. The study of fundamentals involves tracking the dollar values of revenue, costs, and expenses; ratios; and percentages as they change from year to year. Analysts look for leveling off, spikes in the trends, or signs that trends are changing, especially strong and improving trends slowing down or turning negative. Most fundamental trend analysis is based on quarterly or annual comparisons.

Key Point

Technical trends are quite different than fundamental trends. Rather than tracking dollar values, percentages of change, or ratios, technical trends are more about visual information and price trends.

Technical trends are likely to be shorter-term, covering a few days, weeks, or months. Unlike the fundamental trend, in which change is based on ever-moving summaries of revenue, costs, and expenses, ratios, or percentages, the technical side is more likely to be based on patterns of change. These may be bullish, bearish, or inconclusive. The fundamental analyst tends to be numbers-oriented, and the technical analyst or chartist tends to be more visual.

Trends can be defined in terms of shape and movement. This includes trendlines, channel lines, triangles, and wedges. These are the primary tools for technical analysis and for spotting trends. Trendlines and channels define the direction of the trend, enabling you to see when a trend has ended. Triangles and wedges are either bullish or bearish, depending on their shape; so unlike the trendline or channel, triangles and wedges also define trend direction but serve as specific reversal indicators as well.

Example

Shapes and sizes: You have discovered that price movement has not only direction (up, down, or sideways) but also shape. So when you find channel lines, triangles, or wedges, you can observe much more: how quickly they develop, how long they last, how steep they rise or fall. Shapes and speed of change determine the strength of signals well beyond the direction or forecast change in direction.

These trend-specific lines identify changes in many ways—all part of how trends behave. Trends and trendlines are not the same as the lines of resistance and support, which set borders for a current trading range (see Chapter 12). The trading range becomes most interesting to a chartist when the borders are violated, either leading to an immediate reversal or setting up new higher or lower trading ranges. To an extent, these movements of ranges can be anticipated by trends, but the trend itself does not directly influence changes in resistance and support, as it does demonstrate the direction, speed, and angle of a trend.

TRENDS AS INDICATORS OF RISK

In statistics, a few basic observations about trends apply, and these should always be applied to price trends as well—for example:

1. *The spike or exception should be either removed or seen as a key indicator.* In any trend, you may experience a nonrepetitive exception, or a spike. In statistics, the outlying spike should be removed to arrive at a more representative trend or average. This applies to technical analysis as well, but there is an exception. Some spikes, notably in volume, represent key reversal signals; when confirmed, these are among the strongest of reversal indicators. So while adhering to the statistical rule of removing spikes, technical analysis does not always apply the rule in the same way.

2. *No trend continues indefinitely.* A trend is a directional movement that, for the moment, identifies the mood of investors and traders. This may be bullish (moving upward) or bearish (moving downward). But every trend eventually ends, goes flat, or reverses. This is a good general rule for all things, but in the market it provides the reason for continually watching and looking for changes in momentum and the inevitable reversal signal.

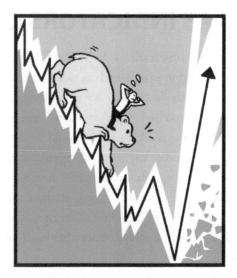

3. *Trends eventually will tend to level out and plateau.* Even when trends move in one direction over a long period of time, the rate of change in that trend cannot sustain the same rate indefinitely. As a result, every trend eventually levels out and reaches a plateau. It's a mistake to assume that a plateau is negative; on the contrary, it is a natural slowing down in the rate of change. But that does not mean the trend is going to reverse—only that it has maximized its rate of change, either upward or downward. A reversal is normally signaled in some manner, based on price, volume, or momentum.

4. *Trends typically go through opposing, short-term retracements.* A retracement is a move opposite the direction of the prevailing trend. This is a normal occurrence. For example, prices moving strongly upward will tend to go through very brief retracements as investors take profits; in the downtrend, retracement occurs when traders think a price represents a buying opportunity. A trend that continues moving in the same direction without any retracements grows dangerously vulnerable to sudden and extreme reversals, so retracements are healthy adjustments in the expansion of even the strongest trends.

Trends are risk-identifying markers. They let you know when current trends are continuing or ending, and by looking back over a chart for several months, you also get a sense of the rhythm. Some trends are very short, and prices tend to rise or fall somewhat predictably as counted by the number of sessions. Other trends are comparatively erratic, forming over the longer term but with a visually clear lack of predictability in the short term.

Key Point

Technical price trends serve as risk markets, showing the duration, slope, and extent of price movement over time.

So as a means for spotting and quantifying risk, a trendline or channel provides guidance by revealing direction, *breadth of trading* (point range from high to low), consistency, and likely points of reversal.

TRENDLINES

In chart analysis, a *trendline* is among the most basic of signals. It consists of a single straight line that continues until price changes interrupt its movement. The trendline may move upward or downward.

Trendlines from the chart of Lockheed Martin (LMT) are shown in Figure 10.1.

breadth of trading

the distance between highest and lowest price points in the current price range, described in the number of points; a relative indicator based on the typical price range (a one-point breadth is substantial for a stock averaging $10 per share, but the same breadth for a stock with price average $80 contains much lower volatility).

Example

Simplicity might work best: A trader had spent a lot of time studying complex signals, looking for the best way to spot a coming reversal. It came down to the simplest of all visual signals, the trendline. The trader realized that as long as a price keeps moving along the trendline, the trend continues—until the price changes and the line runs into the price and then halts.

Figure 10.1 Trendlines
Source: Chart courtesy of StockCharts.com.

trendline
a straight line drawn above a declining trend or below an advancing trend, identifying the direction and continuing until interrupted by changes in price.

The alternating direction of short-term uptrends and downtrends sets up a pattern that could provide a degree of predictability in estimating a likely time for direction changes in the stock chart. For example, LMT's short-term trends have tended to extend between one and three weeks in duration, with two weeks being the most frequent duration. This does not mean there can be any certainty in future trend duration, but this provides some starting points if and when future reversals appear and are confirmed.

Key Point

Trend duration is one visual clue you can use to speculate about the likely timing of future price movements and changes in direction.

The trendline also aids in identifying evolving changes in resistance and support, the borders of the trading range itself. The LMT chart, for example, began with a strong upward movement, but then moved into a pattern of gradually declining trading ranges. From this you might be able to conclude that both resistance and support are evolving in a downward direction.

In evaluating volatility for a particular stock, the slope of the trendline provides further insight into the rapidity of change. LMT, for example, exhibited a tendency for very short-term trendlines, often with steep angles; this slope of change implies that LMT's trading range is typically about 10 points from high to low, but that within that range, price movement often is rapid.

By definition, a trendline must have a specific starting and ending point. The starting point is the end of a previous trendline (bottom of a downtrend at the point prices turn upward, or top of an uptrend when prices turn downward), and the end point occurs when price again changes to intersect with the trendline. It is quite possible, given this observation, to witness consecutive trendlines with a very brief interruption or retracement. For example, in the LMT chart, the first downward trendline consisted of only three sessions, and could be interpreted as a retracement in the existing strong uptrend. That retracement could serve as an early signal that the uptrend was about to top out, as it did before the continuing series of upward and downward trendlines with the price range sliding downward throughout the rest of the period reported. A second consecutive trendline is seen in the last two uptrends, interrupted briefly by two downward-moving sessions.

channel lines

straight lines drawn both above and below the price range when the breadth of trading is the same over time, even while the price range increases or decreases.

CHANNEL LINES

Trendlines can be expanded into *channel lines*, which are marked price movements consisting of lines both above and below the price range. Channel lines are employed when the trading breadth remains consistent even as price levels evolve upward or downward, and also when the resistance and support levels remain level and intact.

An up channel illustration for Caterpillar (CAT) is shown in Figure 10.2. In this case, two distinct channel lines were found, the second one with a greater slope than the first.

Figure 10.2 Up Channel
Source: Chart courtesy of StockCharts.com.

The channel line format, also called the *price channel*, is a type of trend continuation with two important features. First, the breadth of trading remains the same, and second, price levels evolve over time.

Example
A perplexing expansion of the trendline: When you first discovered channel lines, you were not sure how they were different from trendlines. But the pattern is a combination of price direction moving dynamically and a consistent and often limited breadth of trading. That's the big difference.

price channel

alternative name for the channel line.

The two lines are given specific names depending on the direction the channel is moving. In an uptrend, the lower line is called the trendline, and the upper line is the accompanying channel line. In a downtrend, it is the opposite, with the upper line representing the trendline, and the lower called the channel line. However, the key to this indicator is twofold: price is evolving and the breadth remains the same. As long as this continues, the channel lines pattern remains in effect, and any change in the pattern would signal likely changes, at which point you would look for reversal or continuation signals to decide what is likely to happen next.

Key Point
Channel lines move beyond the single trendline to visualize a consistent breadth of trading during a period of dynamic movement in the trading range.

An example of a down channel is found in Figure 10.3. Note the start and finish marks. The down channel began when price topped out, and the channel marked a consistent breadth of 2.5 points throughout the period, even as prices fell nearly 10 points over six weeks. The channel lines ended when the trend turned upward in the third week of April.

Figure 10.3 Down Channel
Source: Chart courtesy of StockCharts.com.

The downside violation of the lower line on March 24 represented a momentary adjustment, a very brief decline. This was identified as momentary because the price range immediately returned to the established range.

A price channel can also be flat, although this is less common. An example of a two-month level channel was seen in the chart of Clorox (CLX), shown in Figure 10.4.

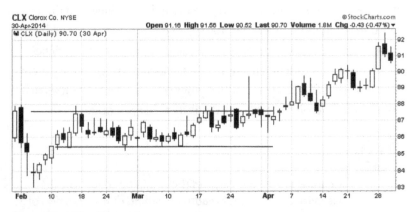

Figure 10.4 Flat Channel
Source: Chart courtesy of StockCharts.com.

The starting point was where price settled down into a very narrow breadth of two points, beginning on about February 10. The unusually large upper shadow near the end of the channel lines period foreshadowed that something was about to change. However, a large shadow like this could indicate weakness among buyers, unable to move price higher; that could mean a new downtrend would begin. It could also forecast an uptrend, which did occur in this case. In situations like this, the shadow is important, but its meaning needs to be confirmed independently. As occurs often, no obvious signals emerged before the uptrend began, so this is an example of confusion on the part of traders, with neither buyers nor sellers able to take control of the trend. Ultimately, the bullish traders won, but the resulting upward movement was not very dramatic.

Key Point

When price patterns are weak or unclear, they often reflect indecision or confusion among buyers and sellers. This is a dangerous period to enter a trade, because the next move cannot be known or even estimated clearly.

Channel lines are subject to interpretation, like all signals. But they provide a view of consistent breadth of trading, which is not always the case with the relatively simple trendline.

Many trend formations do not conform to the channel lines pattern, but involve upper and lower lines reflecting a narrowing breadth of trading. These patterns include triangles and wedges.

TRIANGLES AND WEDGES

Unlike the trendline and channel line patterns, prices do not always move uniformly in one direction or another. A *triangle* formation is either bullish or bearish, and consists of a narrowing price range over time.

There are three types of triangles, each with their own directional indication. An *ascending triangle* is a bullish signal, consisting of a level line of resistance and rising support.

triangle

a trend pattern of narrowing price range, indicating a specifically bullish or bearish signal.

As support closes in on resistance, the expectation is that the top line will give way and a bullish direction will follow. For example, the General Mills (GIS) chart includes an ascending triangle, shown in Figure 10.5.

ascending triangle

a bullish trend pattern combining a level resistance and rising support, forecasting a bullish trend in the near future.

Figure 10.5 Ascending Triangle
Source: Chart courtesy of StockCharts.com.

This formation led to a modest bullish move, but just as important, it broke through the three-week resistance level and allowed prices to rise higher. Triangles such as this occur often but may be difficult to spot unless you are looking for them.

Example
Triangulation of price moves: Why is a triangle such a strong signal? The real reversal or continuation value comes from the narrowing of the breadth of trading, which is expected to lead to the next price move.

Key Point

Triangles occur often but may be difficult to spot. So you need to make an extra effort to identify triangles that can serve as strong indicators for the next price move.

The opposite formation is the *descending triangle*, which is bearish. It consists of a level support and declining resistance, and is likely to allow prices to break below support and to set up a new bearish trend.

An example of the descending triangle is found on the chart of Walt Disney (DIS) (Figure 10.6). The first of two descending triangles is a very short-term example, but the pattern is accurate in anticipating the resulting downward price movement that soon follows. That downtrend is not strong, and as of the period covered, it is not conclusive either. The price range appears to be on the decline, but movement beyond is not certain. More confirming signals should be found before acting on this signal. However, the second descending triangle moving to the end of the charted period is much stronger *and* also serves as a confirming indicator of the first one.

descending triangle

a bearish trend pattern combining a level support and falling resistance, forecasting a bearish trend in the near future.

Figure 10.6 Descending Triangle
Source: Chart courtesy of StockCharts.com.

The third type of triangle is one that can serve as either a bullish or a bearish indicator. The *symmetrical triangle* contains a declining resistance and a rising support level, both narrowing to a decision point. The big question is, what happens next? For this, confirming additional indicators should be located before acting on the signal.

symmetrical triangle

a formation that is either bullish or bearish, depending on confirming indicators that follow; it includes a declining resistance and rising support level. As the breadth of trading narrows, a move in either direction is expected to follow.

An example of a symmetrical triangle is found in the chart of Target (TGT), shown in Figure 10.7.

Figure 10.7 Symmetrical Triangle
Source: Chart courtesy of StockCharts.com.

The February 24 low price point plus the high price point four days later marks the beginning of the triangle. It extends only one month before prices break out and begin a gradual bullish move. The doji session at the narrowing point is a clear indication that a new trend is about to begin. However, the price levels and patterns immediately prior to this end of the triangle are not very clear. This triangle, like many others, requires stronger confirmation before making a new trade.

Key Point

The symmetrical triangle is useful in spotting a coming bullish or bearish trend, but you need specific signals and confirmation, since it can go either way.

Beyond the three types of triangles, additional directional signals are found in the form of the *wedge*. This is a narrowing price trend in which both resistance and support change at different angles, with a new trend expected once the breadth of trading has narrowed.

The ascending and descending triangle are based on resistance or support remaining level while the other side moves closer. The wedge, in comparison, involves narrowing of both resistance and support, but with variation in the angles of each.

A *rising wedge* is a bearish signal, with both resistance and support rising while the breadth of trading narrows.

Example
Wedges versus triangles: You thought at first that a wedge was just another form of triangle. But then you saw that unlike the triangle with a flat side above or below the moving side, a wedge consists of both sides moving at the same time. The breadth of trading narrows until it gives way to the next trend.

wedge
a bullish or bearish signal with both resistance and support narrowing and moving closer together, but at different angles.

An example of the rising wedge is found in the chart for Hewlett-Packard (HPQ), shown in Figure 10.8.

Figure 10.8 Rising Wedge
Source: Chart courtesy of StockCharts.com.

rising wedge
a bearish signal with both resistance and support rising at different angles, with a downward movement predicted once the breadth has narrowed.

The rising wedge lasts over two weeks at a steep slope, beginning with a breadth of three points and ending up with a breadth of only one point. After this narrowing occurred, the expected bearish trend begins.

Key Point

The slope of movement in the wedge should be compared to decide not only the volatility of price but also the likely speed of directional change.

falling wedge

a bullish signal with both resistance and support declining at different angles, with an upward movement predicted once the breadth has narrowed.

A *falling wedge* is the opposite, a bullish signal with both resistance and support falling as the breadth of trading narrows.

An example of the falling wedge can be seen on the chart of McDonald's, shown in Figure 10.9.

Figure 10.9 Falling Wedge
Source: Chart courtesy of StockCharts.com.

This pattern lasts for only two weeks, but it marks the continuation of the gradual uptrend preceding this. As an extended retracement the falling wedge sets up a resumption of the longer-term bullish trend in this stock. Like the rising wedge above, the breadth narrows from three points down to one point before the new uptrend begins.

Key Point

Even short-term wedges can be useful in timing because they appear at a point in the trend where the next step could go in either direction. The wedge might be the determining indicator for either continuation or reversal.

The trendline, channel line, triangle, and wedge are all varieties of visualized trends. However, some short-term trends can be very volatile and difficult to predict. With this in mind, the moving average helps you to smooth out the volatility in a trend and to spot a longer-term trend, either bullish or bearish. By using two moving averages of different duration, you can also identify key points marking likely reversals in the current trend.

The next chapter examines moving averages and how they can be used in chart analysis.

235

236

11 MOVING AVERAGES AND THEIR VALUE

As a rule we disbelieve all facts and theories for which we have no use.
—William James, *The Will to Believe*, 1897

Is the use of averages instructive in charting? Or is it only a means of reassurance that price movement means something?

Averages by themselves are limiting because they include a set of values, but moving average (MA) values are updated with each new entry; chartists have discovered that when two different moving averages are used together, very clear signals can result. This is especially true when moving averages of different duration perform in the same manner or when they cross each other (or move above or below the price range). These changes act as confirmation signals of growing or declining momentum, likely directional change, and subtle but key influences on the current trading range.

SIMPLE AND EXPONENTIAL AVERAGES

average

a value derived by adding together the values in a field, and then dividing the result by the number of values.

In statistics, the *average* (also called the *mean*) is a value derived for a group of values. This allows chartists to even out the otherwise chaotic and seemingly random tendencies of short-term price trends.

The average is easy to compute. The steps are as follows:

1. Add together the values of entries in a field. For example, you are dealing with six values in the field, and these values are 17, 19, 9, 33, 26, and 10. Adding these together results in a total of 114.

2. Divide the total by the number of entries. There are six values, so divide 114 by 6 to arrive at 19, which is the average.

This straightforward calculation is easy because it involves only six values, and a simple two-part mathematical process of addition and division. The process is more complex for variations of the average, and for much larger fields.

mean

alternate term for the average.

🎯 **Key Point**

Calculating the average is a basis for many statistical results. It is easy to calculate for a limited number of entries, but time-consuming for larger fields.

Just adding together a group of values and then dividing by the total number is a *simple average*, so called because of its easy method. None of the values are weighted to give more influence to the outcome. In more advanced methods, some values will be weighted. For example, providing more weight to the most recent entries could make the average more relevant because the newest information has more relevance than older entries.

Averages are useful only for as long as they apply to a current chart. For this reason, a simple average has to be updated regularly. This means the oldest entry is removed and the newest added in. This is called a *simple moving average (SMA)*.

Example

Keeping it simple: You have been studying the different types of averages, and you see that the simple moving average is a starting point for everything else. It consists of adding up a set of values and then dividing the total by the number of values involved.

The SMA is a useful starting point to calculate average over several time periods. A more practical system weights latest information while using a formula to update the average easily. This is called the *exponential moving average* (*EMA*). It is the basis for many stock chart average calculations.

EMA requires three initial steps:

1. Calculate the simple MA. In the previous example, a field of six values had an average of 114.
2. Calculate the weighting multiplier. This is devised by dividing two by the number of periods, and adding one. In the case of six values, the weighting multiplier is: $(2 \div 6) + 1 = 1.333$.
3. Calculate the EMA itself. For this, begin with the new entry in the field, then subtract the previous day's EMA and multiply the result by the multiplier plus the prior EMA. For example, the original simple MA illustration resulted in an average of 19. If a seventh day's value is 26, the formula for EMA is: $(26 - 19) \times 1.333 + 19 = 28.331$.

The outcome of this is to add more weight to the latest values. The simple MA would have produced a result of 20.5 (removal of the oldest value and addition of the newest, then dividing by six). The exponential method gives greater weight to the latest entry, increasing the average by the degree of the exponent.

exponential moving average (EMA)

an averaging method that weights the latest entry in a field more than previous entries.

Key Point

Knowing how to calculate EMA aids in knowing what it provides to you; however, modern online charting sites automatically perform these calculations for you.

For the next entry, only step three is repeated: subtract the latest EMA from the new value, and multiply by the fixed weighting multiplier (for six fields, this is 1.333). Then add the previous EMA.

Fortunately for the modern chartist, MAs are calculated automatically on widely available free charts. By selecting an MA feature, the single or double EMA is entered onto the chart. You do not need to go through the formula for each new session; however, it adds value to your analysis when you understand how the calculation is performed.

One drawback for using longer-term MAs is the so-called lag factor. The longer the period used for an MA, the greater the lag. So a 50-day MA is more responsive to price movement than a 200-day moving average MA because all of those older periods reduce the effect of ever-changing new data.

Even though the long-term MAs are a crucial part of chart analysis, this is why using two different time periods and two MAs makes sense. By observing how the two MAs interact, you can develop useful timing signals and confirmation for likely price trend reversals.

Key Point

Moving averages offer more than just a tracking device for price trends. As the trends change, the MA reflects those changes in how they evolve compared to the price range.

Most chart-based MA calculations are simple. Some chartists may prefer using EMA, but the standard is a simple MA, often based on a comparison between 50-day and 200-day outcomes.

Example

Avoiding the statistician's job: You are concerned about the skill demands and time requirements for computing moving averages, especially those lasting many periods. The good news: You don't have to compute anything. It is instructive to know how moving averages are calculated, but today's online free charts calculate moving averages automatically and instantly.

DURATION OF THE MOVING AVERAGE (MA)

The MA can be created using any number of sessions. A standard offered by most charting services, and serving as the basis for reversal indicators, is the combination of simple 50-day and 200-day MAs.

Key Point

The observed reversal signals based on the MA apply to all versions and durations of averages.

The indications based on the combined use of these two can be applied to any modified MA duration plans. The key to selecting or modifying the duration is that the longer the period, the less responsive the line will be to the latest price changes. For this reason, most of the reversals based on MA change involve the change in the shorter-term MA in relation to the longer-term MA or to price.

These changes are referred to as *crossover* movements, a change in which an MA line crosses above or below the other line, or above or below price.

The selection of a specific time frame depends on your objectives and purpose in the analysis. If you are looking for reversal signals for very short-term price movement (such as swing or day trading strategies), then shorter MA duration makes sense. For example, you might prefer a 5-day and 20-day MA comparison. However, extremely short-term durations such as these might prove less reliable than some longer-term duration choices. It makes sense to try a different duration mix to see what appears to provide the most reliable MA for the purpose.

Many charting services, such as StockCharts.com, allow you to modify MA lines to any periods you want to use. This allows you to experiment and to mix and match a variety of duration selections. The default of 590-day and 200-day MA suits most traders in their quest for reversals and confirmation indicators.

crossover

the change in one moving average (usually of shorter duration) in relation to the other, or the movement of a moving average above or below the price range

DOUBLE CROSSOVER BETWEEN MA LINES

MA crossover signals are excellent confirmation for other reversal signals; however, they might not provide enough of a strong indication on their own to generate trade action. As with most reversal signals, you probably need confirmation before making your move.

MA crossover

a reversal signal based on the shorter MA line moving above the longer MA line (bullish) or moving below the longer MA line (bearish).

Key Point

Before any trade decisions are made based on observations of changes in MA, look for independent confirmation in price indicators, momentum, and volume.

The first two types of crossover reversal signals involve the shorter MA line crossing the longer. A bullish MA crossover occurs when the shorter MA line moves above the longer MA line; a bearish one is the opposite, when the shorter MA line moves below the longer MA line.

An example of the bullish MA crossover is found in the chart of McDonald's (MCD), shown in Figure 11.1.

Figure 11.1 Bullish Moving Average Crossover
Source: Chart courtesy of StockCharts.com.

Notice how both MA lines track along with price throughout most of the period; but as soon as the price begins trending upward, the 50 MA crosses above the 200 MA and begins keeping pace. This is a good example of how more responsive shorter-term MA tends to be to price movement than longer-term MA.

Example

A moving moment: Your chart analysis includes observations about how moving averages behave. You notice that whenever the averages cross above or below price, it is significant. The challenge is in interpreting the meaning of such a move.

An example of the bearish MA is shown in Figure 11.2.

On this chart, the identified crossover point marks the beginning of a downtrend. In this example, the crossover occurs before the downtrend begins. Although MA is invariably a lagging indicator, this

Figure 11.2 Bearish Moving Average Crossover
Source: Chart courtesy of StockCharts.com.

is one case when MA anticipates the bearish move. As long as this could be confirmed, it could provide an initial reversal signal. At the very conclusion of this chart, a crossover is seen in the opposite direction, forecasting a new uptrend.

> **Key Point**
>
> Although MA may anticipate coming reversals, it is a lagging indicator and must be confirmed independently before making trades.

Throughout the downtrend period in this case, the price acted in a very volatile short-term way. This effect, called *whipsaw*, is characterized by sudden movement of the price in one direction and then correcting in the other. While this occurs often during any kind of trend, it typically signals that the trend currently underway could be very short-term.

The double crossover is one form of reversal signal that clearly has to be confirmed by other signals before acting on the information. However, the crossover itself also acts as excellent confirmation of other reversals found in price and momentum signals.

PRICE CROSSOVER SIGNALS

Another reversal signal based on MA changes is the *price crossover*. This occurs under one of two conditions: For a bullish price crossover, price is already higher than the longer-term MA, and then moves above the shorter-term MA. For a bearish price crossover, price is already below the longer-term MA and then moves lower than the shorter-term MA.

An example of a bullish price crossover is found on the chart of ConocoPhillips, shown in Figure 11.3.

whipsaw

a price pattern of sudden and fast movement in one direction, followed by equally sudden and fast movement in the opposite direction, typical of short-term trends likely to reverse quickly.

price crossover

a reversal signal in which the price range is higher than a longer-term moving average, and

(continued)

Figure 11.3 Bullish Price Crossover

Source: Chart courtesy of StockCharts.com.

The price trends above the 200 MA on February 24, and then also moves higher than the 50 MA on March 7, before the price trend begins. Only on March 17 is it apparent that a new uptrend has begun.

A bearish price crossover shows up on the chart of iShares Silver Trust (SLV), shown in Figure 11.4.

Figure 11.4 Bearish Price Crossover
Source: Chart courtesy of StockCharts.com.

Price is lower than the 200 MA and then also trends below the 50 MA, signaling a bearish trend. That trend quickly develops and continues throughout April.

Example

Spotting the change: You have observed that moving averages behave very specifically on the chart. When you see the moving averages confirm one another, it seems to accelerate the price reaction.

then also moves above the shorter-term MA (bullish); or when price range is lower than a longer-term moving average, and then also moves below the shorter-term MA (bearish).

SUPPORT AND RESISTANCE AND MA TRENDS

The shorter-term MA (50 days in these examples) may serve a second purpose beyond crossover signaling reversal. While the role of MA in the trading range is not as reliable as the reversal signals provided, it may be true that the short-term MA is useful for marking or tracking either support or resistance levels.

Key Point

In addition to spotting reversal points, shorter-term MA can also confirm estimated levels of support and resistance, especially as those price borders rise or fall over time.

During an uptrend, the shorter-term MA may mark support. An example of this is shown in Figure 11.5.

Figure 11.5 Moving Average Marking Support in an Uptrend
Source: Chart courtesy of StockCharts.com.

Once the bullish crossover occurs (50 MA trending higher than 200 MA) the shorter-term MA tracks the uptrend through to the end of the period charted. This should be expected since the MA is nothing more than an averaging of price over 50 periods; it is expected to be more responsive than the 200 MA line. Even so, this confirms that the uptrend is holding up and, in the absence of any reversal indicators, it would be expected to continue in the same direction.

During a downtrend, the shorter-term MA may mark resistance. For example, the chart for Cracker Barrel (CBRL) shows this in Figure 11.6.

Figure 11.6 Moving Average Marking Resistance in a Downtrend
Source: Chart courtesy of StockCharts.com.

All the way from two weeks into the year to the end of April, the 50 MA tracks resistance as it declines. Like the support example in an uptrend, this trend is expected based on the nature of MA, a tracking of price trends over 50 periods. But some warning signals can appear. For example, in the middle of March, several sessions move above the MA line, possibly a signal that the downtrend is ending. This turns out to be a false signal, a momentary retracement resulting from the previous month's gradual uptrend within the longer-term downtrend marked by the 50 MA.

Bollinger Bands

an indicator tracking the price average for 20 periods as well as standard deviations both above and below price; the upper and lower bands serve as signal points to make trades in a stock.

BOLLINGER BANDS FOR SHORT-TERM TREND MONITORING

The indicator called *Bollinger Bands* reveals a lot about short-term price trends as well as levels of price volatility. Invented by John Bollinger in the 1980s, the signal consists of a middle line representing the 20-day average of price, and an upper and lower band equal to two standard deviations above and below price.

Example

Banding together: A trader wants to know how to judge when price is trending away from its breadth of trading. Because Bollinger Bands are based on standard deviation, the indicator lets a trader spot these evolving trends quickly and immediately.

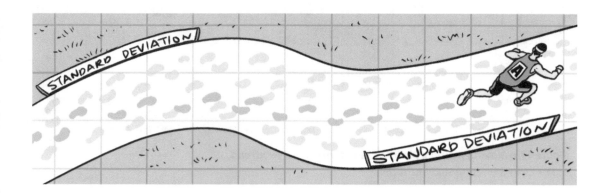

As a statistical analysis of the MA of price, Bollinger Bands are a very effective tool for identifying potential reversal points, and as confirmation of what other price, momentum, and volume signals forecast.

Key Point

Bollinger Bands combine price trends with statistical averaging, making MA more reliable when augmented with standard deviation. This means the upper and lower bands, if touched or exceeded by price, may also mark likely reversals.

An example of a chart with Bollinger Bands is that of General Mills (GIS), shown in Figure 11.7.

The bands typically track price fairly closely, and in this example, the distance between upper and lower bands is only two to four points at most places on the chart. This indicates low volatility on a chart scaled to single-point increments. However, when price moves further than

Figure 11.7 Bollinger Bands as Range Markers

Source: Chart courtesy of StockCharts.com.

usual, as in the beginning of February, the width of the bands follows suit and reflects a broadening volatility level. But like most MA analysis, Bollinger Bands are a lagging indicator.

The best use of this signal is to mark likely turning points. For example, when price touches the upper band, it could serve as a signal to sell, and when it touches the lower band, it could serve as a buy signal.

Perhaps equally effective is a more restrictive use. If the trading signals are recognized only when price moves above the upper band or below the lower band, the indication will be much stronger than merely touching those levels. When price moves beyond the upper or lower bands over a number of periods, it could indicate a likely reversal as well.

For example, in the second half of January, price trends below the lower band several times. This could indicate a turning point to the upside will occur shortly. And in several April sessions, price moves higher than the upper band, possibly signaling a downtrend reversal to follow.

However Bollinger Bands are employed, this tool should be used as much as a confirming signal for other reversals as a signal needing to be independently confirmed.

Key Point

When observing Bollinger Bands, price levels often approach or touch the outer bands. But when they exceed those bands repeatedly, it could signal strongly that a reversal is about to occur.

Moving average is a sound method for better understanding the current price trend, and what it means. In the study of price, there is much more to study. The next chapter explains the many price indicators and how they are used to spot reversals and even to anticipate coming trends.

BUT *WE* WERE HUNGRY TOO. WE'VE BEEN DOUBLE-CROSSED.

INTERESTING USE OF TERMS.

IN TECHNICAL ANALYSIS, A *DOUBLE CROSSOVER* IS AN IMPORTANT REVERSAL SIGNAL...

HEY, YOU KNOW YOUR TECHNICAL STUFF.

THANKS.

I *SUPPORT* BOTH FUNDAMENTAL AND TECHNICAL ANALYSIS, EVEN WHEN I RUN INTO *RESISTANCE*.

AH HAH HA HA HA HA HA

⋛ SNRK ⋚

SUH-SUPPORT *AND* RESISTANCE!

FUH FUH *FUNNY*!

AH HA HAHAHA HAHA!

...

$

12 PRICE INDICATORS

It is always a relief to believe what is pleasant, but it is more important to believe what is true.
—Hilaire Belloc, *The Silence of the Sea*, 1941

Technical analysis is based on observations about price, volume, and momentum. This chapter focuses on price indicators and trends. For many traders, chart analysis and the search for price patterns seems elusive and uncertain, even far from reliable. However, some very specific patterns do emerge on charts, and these can be used to predict future price movements and reversals.

Seeking confirmation for all indicators is essential because there are no 100 percent certainties in price analysis. Short-term price movement is invariably chaotic, random, and inefficient, so a trade should be executed only when two or more confirming signals can be found. It may be a sound policy to also take no action if signals contradict one another, or when no clear directional signals can be found.

SUPPORT AND RESISTANCE

To understand price movement and trends, the first step is to observe the resistance and support trends. Resistance is the top price in the current price range, and support is at the bottom. Movement of these two lines may remain at approximately the same breadth and form a channel; the trend may be rising or falling, and breadth may be widening or narrowing. When this occurs, you are likely to see triangles or wedges (explained in Chapter 10).

Lines of support and resistance take many shapes and sizes. For example, a channel lines formation is a set of movement in a stock that may be rising, falling, or level. The distinguishing characteristic is that the breadth between resistance and support remains the same during the channel period. This is significant because it reveals a tendency toward fixed levels of volatility. If the breadth remains low during a period of rising or falling price ranges, it could mean that volatility levels tend to remain unchanged.

For example, a rising channel is found in the chart of Alcoa, shown in Figure 12.1.

This trend involves two very narrow rising channels with a middle period of less than four weeks in which prices retrace, rally, and retrace once again, before resuming the upward trend. The slope of the second rising channel is slightly reduced from the slope in the first.

A falling channel is found on the chart of AT&T, shown in Figure 12.2.

Figure 12.1 Rising Channels
Source: Chart courtesy of StockCharts.com.

Figure 12.2 Falling Channels
Source: Chart courtesy of StockCharts.com.

In this example, the falling channel also is quite narrow and extends for nearly five months before ending. The stock then moves into a period of rising prices. This is forecast by the double bottom in late January and early February.

A level channel, in the opinion of some, is not a trend at all but a period of uncertainty. However, even volatile stocks go through periods of relative calm (or indecision). For example, Buffalo Wild Wings (BWLD) has a volatile history, but the chart reveals two distinct periods of level channels, the first with a breadth of 8 points, and the second with a breadth of 10 points. This is shown in Figure 12.3.

The period in between is quite volatile, more typical of BWLD's trends and volatility levels.

Managing a volatile stock: You have seen that some very volatile stocks are difficult to manage and time. But you also understand

Figure 12.3 Level Channels
Source: Chart courtesy of StockCharts.com.

that channel lines help manage these stocks, and when a momentary channel appears, you see that it foreshadows the next, more volatile trend. Channels help define reliability on price breadth, identifying trends as moving (up, down, or sideways) without a change in breadth. When you see moving prices with a lot of change in the price breadth, it points to greater volatility and unpredictability. For the purpose of confirming resistance and support levels, channels add a degree of certainty to the price trend.

When the breadth of trading narrows, it has an entirely different significance. It translates to a reduction in breadth, representing lowered volatility. As breadth narrows, you would seek a signal of the next direction in many forms. An example of narrowing breadth is found in the chart of Verizon (VZ), shown in Figure 12.4.

Figure 12.4 Narrowing Breadth
Source: Chart courtesy of StockCharts.com.

This example reveals that as resistance declines, support declines at a reduced rate; as support rises, resistance rises at a reduced rate. These are both wedges.

The first, a falling wedge, is considered bullish, and a bullish move does occur for the weeks starting on February 18. The rising wedge is bearish, and when it narrows by April 7, a price decline does follow as expected.

Key Point

A narrowing of the trading range is a form of declining volatility, and leads to signals for a new price trend to follow.

When breadth widens, it points to increased volatility. Thus, traders should be cautious in interpreting price trends. Higher volatility means greater uncertainty in what will occur next, so the wise interpretation of such a pattern is to require stronger than usual confirmation.

An example of widening breadth is found in the chart of US Steel, shown in Figure 12.5.

At the conclusion of both of the widening periods, the price trend reveals growing volatility. This is anticipated in the widening breadth itself, and this formation is difficult to predict without independent

Figure 12.5 Widening Breadth
Source: Chart courtesy of StockCharts.com.

signals and confirmation. This is a case in which the normal definitions of resistance and support have become chaotic and it is difficult to determine whether either side of the range will hold up in the near future.

 Key Point

A widening trading range represents growing volatility and less predictability about what will follow. This situation requires stronger than normal signals and confirmation.

Yet another phenomenon in the analysis of resistance and support is the *flip*. This is a reversion of resistance to form new support in a rising trading range trend, or of support to become the new level of resistance in a declining trend.

The occurrence of a flip is quite common, and it is worth study because it tends to strengthen the new resistance or support level. This means that a newly established trading range will be more reliable once the flip level is confirmed as a permanent change.

An example of the flip is found in the chart of Boeing (BA), shown in Figure 12.6. This is a good example of support flipping to become a new resistance level during a declining trend.

Figure 12.6 Support to Resistance Flip
Source: Chart courtesy of StockCharts.com.

flip

the reversion of previous resistance into a new level of support during a rising trend, or of previous support to form as new resistance in a falling trend.

The previous support level is quite strong, remaining at slightly above $130 per share for 10 weeks and closing below only once during that time. The large downward gap at the end of January could look like a temporary decline, not only due to the gap but because it moves the price below a strongly established support level. However, within three weeks it becomes clear that the price will remain below that level, meaning support has flipped to become the new resistance price.

Key Point

A flip between resistance and support (or support and resistance) adds strength to the newly established trading range.

The same tendency is likely to be found during a rising trend when a strongly set resistance level is violated and established as a new level of support. The flip is an exceptionally strong signal of its own, tending to set up the new price range more strongly than one without the flip.

double top

a set of two
upper shadow
price spikes
appearing after
an extended
uptrend, and
signaling a likely
reversal and
downtrend to
follow.

DOUBLE TOPS AND BOTTOMS

Price ranges rely on resistance and support, but these also are vulnerable to changes. So traders seek specific technical signals to identify likely reversal points.

A *double top* occurs when price has been rising and then spikes at the top of the trend. This indicates a likely reversal and movement in the opposite direction. In order to qualify as a double top, you need to see at least two price spikes (in candlestick charts, these are found in the form of upper shadows), and it is confirmed if price does retreat after these appear.

Example

Double or nothing: You have found some charts especially difficult to read, and timing trades is challenging because signals are not always clear. One method for overcoming this is to look for those double spikes at the top of an uptrend (or bottom of a downtrend). If you can find confirmation at the same time, you have a good start in knowing when to make your trade.

The double top is found on the chart of BP, shown in Figure 12.7. There are two specific double top formations, both followed by a strong downturn in the price. However, a strong and quick trend often is followed by an equally strong trend in the opposite direction. In both of these cases, the fast downtrend is followed immediately by a new uptrend. These patterns of volatility are difficult to predict, but the

Figure 12.7 Double Top
Source: Chart courtesy of StockCharts.com.

double top indicates loss of momentum among buyers, and often leads to a downtrend. The duration cannot be known, so after acting on the signal, you have to look for the opposite bullish signal to follow.

Key Point

Double tops and bottoms are simple indicators but powerful keys to likely reversal—especially if these occur at or near resistance or support.

double bottom

a set of two lower shadow price spikes appearing after an extended downtrend, and signaling a likely reversal and uptrend to follow.

One of these may be the *double bottom*, the opposite of the double top. This is a pattern of two or more lower shadow spikes at the end of a strong downtrend, which predicts a reversal and a new uptrend to follow.

Figure 12.8 Double Bottom
Source: Chart courtesy of StockCharts.com.

head and shoulders

a technical signal with three upside spikes occurring during an uptrend; the *(continued)*

A double bottom pattern is found in the chart of Cummins (CMI), shown in Figure 12.8.

The overall trend during this period is toward higher prices, but the price decline occurring in the middle of the chart is marked clearly by the double bottom and a resumption of the uptrend that follows. The double bottom is confirmed by the long white candlestick that appears in the next session.

HEAD AND SHOULDERS

The double top and double bottom signals are common, especially in fast-moving, short-term trends. Another reversal signal worth looking for is the *head and shoulders* formation. This is a set of three price spikes at the top of an uptrend. The first and third (shoulders) are lower than the second spike (the head), and this reflects a failure among buyers to move the price higher, resulting in a reversal and a new downtrend.

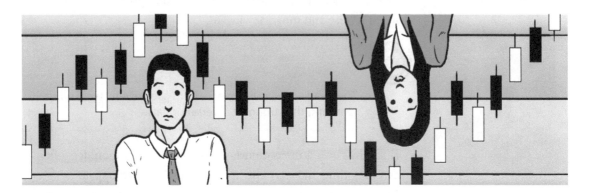

An example of the head and shoulders is found on the chart of US Steel, shown in Figure 12.9.

Figure 12.9 Head and Shoulders
Source: Chart courtesy of StockCharts.com.

first and third
(shoulders)
are offset by a
higher second
spike (head).
After the
formation, a
reversal and new
downtrend are
expected.

This chart was used previously to show a widening breadth formation during an uptrend. However, this reveals even more with the formation of a head and shoulders pattern. It indicates that price movement is about to reverse and move downward.

Key Point

The head and shoulders may form over several weeks, but is among the strongest reversal signals.

This forms over a three-month period. A head and shoulders often takes a long time, but may also appear in a shorter time span.

The reverse indicator, or the *inverse head and shoulders*, appears as a similar formation, but at the bottom of a downtrend, and forecasting a reversal and new uptrend.

For example, the chart of McDonald's (MCD) provides an example of the inverse head and shoulders, shown in Figure 12.10.

Figure 12.10 Inverse Head and Shoulders
Source: Chart courtesy of StockCharts.com.

On this chart, price declines over the first three months and then forms the last shoulder at the end of the fourth month. After this develops, price begins moving upward, extending nearly 10 points from the level where the head appears, to the level at the end of the chart.

Example

Head and shoulders below the rest: You have found a few head and shoulders but find it difficult to spot inverse versions. The problem is not that they fail to appear, but that they are not easy to spot, especially when most traders focus on the more immediate one- and two-session reversals, price gaps, and moves through resistance or support. But they are there.

FLAGS AND PENNANTS

Additional technical signals are found in the forms of flags and pennants.

The flag appears as a short-term retracement formation, moving downward in a period of uptrend, or moving upward during a downtrend. The retracement price trend is common, but when it appears as a flag (meaning the breadth forms as a channel) it confirms that the move is more likely to be a retracement than a reversal.

Key Point

Flags are retracement indicators, and the consistent limited breadth of the flag defines the difference between retracement and reversal.

Figure 12.11 Flags
Source: Chart courtesy of StockCharts.com.

An example is shown in the chart of Macy's (M) in Figure 12.11.

An uptrend was in effect throughout most of the charted period, with two distinct retracement flags during the price movement.

A formation closely related to the flag is the *pennant*, a pattern in which resistance declines and support rises, forming a triangular move and new signals for the next price movement.

The pennant indicates a price breakout, likely to occur once the convergence of resistance and support narrows. For example, the chart of Microsoft (MSFT) (Figure 12.12) includes four pennants, each one predicting a new price move to follow.

The pennants form as expected, and the direction of the subsequent price breakout is determined by other signals. A pennant can lead to either an uptrend or a downtrend, but one of these is more likely than a sideways price pattern. So upon finding that narrowing breadth, the next step is to look for independent reversal signals.

Figure 12.12 Pennants
Source: Chart courtesy of StockCharts.com.

Key Point

The pennant is a signal of a coming trend, but it may lead to either bullish or bearish trends.

So many price-based patterns and signals are useful in chart analysis and for timing of trades. Augmenting the price trend and serving as excellent confirmation is the volume indicator. The next chapter examines several of these and demonstrates how they confirm what you see in price trends.

inverse head and shoulders

A technical signal with three downside spikes occurring during a downtrend; the first and third (shoulders) are offset by a lower second spike (head). After the formation, a reversal and new uptrend are expected.

pennant

a signal shaped like a triangle with declining resistance and rising support on a convergence course.

HE MAKES A GOOD POINT, THOUGH...

...IF YOU APPLY THAT IDEA TO CHART ANALYSIS, YOU GAIN SOME *INSIGHT* AS TO HOW PRICE PATTERNS *EVOLVE*.

YEAH, *SUPPORT* AND *RESISTANCE* ARE THE *WEDGIES* OF THE STOCK CHART, RIGHT?

I GUESS YOU *COULD* SAY THAT. THE THOUGHT PUTS YOU *HEAD AND SHOULDERS* ABOVE MOST ANALYSTS.

THAT REMINDS ME: I NEED TO BUY *SHAMPOO*...

"HEAD AND SHOULDERS"

YOU'RE FULL OF *DOUBLE MEANINGS*, AREN'T YOU?

WHAT DO YOU *MEAN*, MY DEAR?

13

VOLUME INDICATORS

Ideas rose in clouds; I felt them collide until pairs interlocked, so to speak, making a stable combination.
    —Henri Poincaré, *Mathematical Creation*, 1908

Volume—the measurement of shares traded in each market session—is one indicator that may be studied in support of price trends. Some indicators closely track price trends, while others tend to lead, showing up before price actually moves. This provides you with a system for identifying potential reversals before price makes a move.

This chapter explains several *volume* indicators, which are based on how closely volume indicates when price trend momentum is beginning to slow, or as a measurement of the strength of a current trend.

ACCUMULATION/DISTRIBUTION (A/D)

The first indicator measures the level of cumulative dollars moving in and out of a stock. The *accumulation/distribution (A/D)* is a total of each session's volume of how high and low prices relate to the volume of trading.

volume

the number of shares traded for each market session, which may be led by buying or by selling interests, and which can be measured to determine the strength or weakness of current prices.

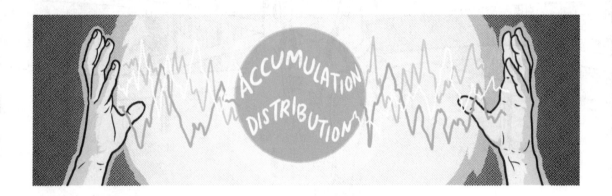

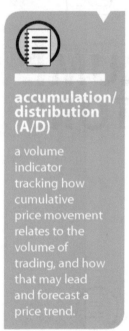

**accumulation/
distribution
(A/D)**

a volume
indicator
tracking how
cumulative
price movement
relates to the
volume of
trading, and how
that may lead
and forecast a
price trend.

Each period's information is added to or subtracted from the previous period's A/D total. To calculate A/D, three steps are involved:

1. Determine the money flow calculator (MFC). This is the net difference between the close minus the low and the high minus the close, with the sum divided by the high minus the low:

$$[(close - low) - (high - close)] \div (high - low) = MFC$$

2. Multiply the money flow calculator by the session's volume to determine the money flow volume (MFV):

$$MFC \times V = MFV$$

3. Calculate the accumulation/distribution (A/D) line by adding the current MFV to the prior A/D:

$$MFV + prior\ A/D = updated\ A/D$$

The continually updated A/D will vary between +1 and −1. The net multiplier calculated in this manner is in the positive column when the stock price closes in the upper half of the range of trading between high and low for the session; it will be negative when the closing price is in the lower half of the high and low range for the session.

Example

A volume of information: A trader has been following a stock's price movement, and a few price-related reversal signals have emerged—nothing compelling,

(continued)

but enough to be interesting. Momentum has also been inching toward the overbought area. The one thing that strongly confirmed all of these signals was a big move in A/D that made the price and momentum indicators appear compelling.

Key Point

A/D is a simple but revealing indicator, based on a multiplier between price range and volume.

Because the indicator measures volume (money flow in and out of the security), a high positive A/D multiplier along with heavier than normal volume indicates buying pressure. By the same argument, a high negative A/D multiplier should reflect selling pressure. The A/D is an effective confirming indicator for price trends, and may also be used to confirm levels of support or resistance.

For example, the chart for Cummins (CMI) reveals examples of A/D leading (or anticipating) price, and also bolsters the support level for the price trading range. This is summarized in Figure 13.1.

The A/D line begins to decline at the start of January. However, price does not start a downward move until two to three weeks later. In this example, A/D is a leading indicator and a trader looking for reversal would next seek confirming bearish signals in the price pattern.

Price bottoms out at the beginning of February, when the A/D line begins rising. Once again, A/D forecasts the reversal and new bullish move. However, price does not make that move until three sessions later. Even though this is a fairly fast response compared to the previous example, it provides traders with a signal that a new bullish trend is about to begin. If confirmed by price signals, it will be possible to enter a trade in advance of the price move.

Finally, the A/D from mid-March through mid-May is level, which serves as confirmation of the strength for the support level then in effect. Without specific and strong changes in one direction or the other, traders in this situation will be able to apply A/D as one form of confirmation for the trading range.

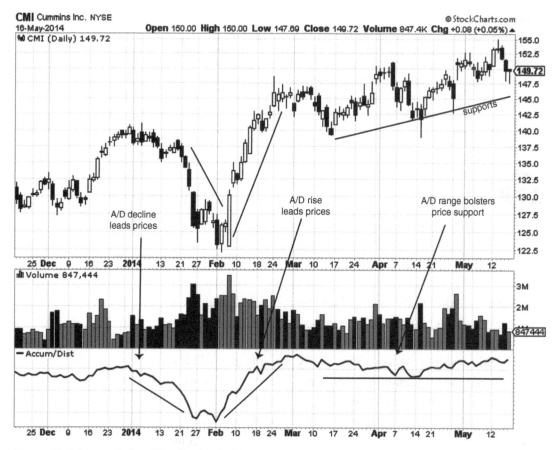

Figure 13.1 Accumulation/Distribution (A/D)
Source: Chart courtesy of StockCharts.com.

Analysis such as this becomes especially effective when treated as one form of confirmation among many others, notably because A/D often anticipates a coming price trend well before it goes into effect.

Key Point

A/D and similar volume-based indicators are wisely used for confirmation, but decisions should not be made based solely on what these signals forecast.

divergence

a situation in which an indicator reveals a specific direction (bullish or bearish) but price moves in the opposite direction.

A/D can also provide clues about price trends in cases of *divergence*, which is the situation in which the indicator (in this case, A/D) indicates movement opposite the price direction. For example, in the last week of December and the first week of January in the CMI chart, the price trend appears bullish even as A/D begins to decline.

The case for CMI is one of *bearish divergence*. The A/D line tells you that a bearish situation is developing, but price holds its level and appears to be moving in a bullish manner. A *bullish divergence* is the opposite; the indicator reveals a likely bullish trend, but price moves downward.

The difficulty with divergence is in how it should be interpreted. Most traders realize that the indicator could be misleading, but so can price. Because of this problem—contradictory indicators—the need for strong and specific confirmation is greater than ever. When A/D supports the price level, it is easily interpreted. When you find divergence, you need more information before acting on what A/D or any other indicator forecasts.

bearish divergence

a situation in which an indicator reveals a likely bearish move but price trends upward.

Example

Diverging points of view: You have been using volume indicators to look for confirmation of both price and volume signals. But the issue gets clouded when you discover bullish divergence along with a set of bearish reversal forecasts in price. Because this is contradictory information, you wisely decide to take a wait-and-see attitude, and to take no immediate action.

bullish divergence

a situation in which an indicator reveals a likely bullish move but price trends downward.

CHAIKIN MONEY FLOW (CMF)

Marc Chaikin developed A/D as well as a related indicator, the *Chaikin Money Flow* (*CMF*). This is also a volume indicator that reveals the positive or negative volume trend over a fixed period of time, normally 20 consecutive sessions.

The CMF indicator is set up with a zero line and CMF fluctuates above or below in a range of +1 at the top to −1 at the bottom. The result provides an idea of buying or selling pressure and which one dominates at any specific moment.

Key Point

CMF labels the current condition as dominated by either buying or selling pressure, based on accumulated volume over 20 sessions.

Chaikin Money Flow (CMF)

a volume indicator consisting of accumulated volume for a period of sessions (normally 20), and indicating whether the trend is positive or negative.

To calculate CMF, three steps are involved.

1. The money flow multiplier (MFM) is derived by comparing the high, low, and close for the session (this is identical to the first step in calculating A/D):

$$[(close - low) - (high - close)] \div (high - low) = MFM$$

2. The MFM is multiplied by the period's volume to arrive at the money flow volume (MFV) (this is also identical to the second step in the calculation of A/D):

$$MFM \times V = MFV$$

3. Finally, the CMF equals the sum of 20 periods of MFV, divided by 20 periods of the sum of volume:

$$20\text{-period MFV} \div 20\text{-period sum of volume} = CMF$$

This is distinguished from A/D since it represents a 20-period average rather than a perpetually adjusted index. The MFM calculated in the first step will be positive when the closing price falls in the upper half of the high-to-low trading range; it will be negative when the closing price falls in the lower half. As a result, CMF is an average that constantly moves between a maximum of +1 and a minimum of −1, compared to the middle zero line.

CMF is unlikely to extend all the way to the extremes in the range between +1 and −1. It tends to fluctuate closer to the middle, indicating the strength of buyers or sellers in relation to one another, with the normal range between +0.5 and −0.5. In order to extend to the extremes, the price would need to experience 20 consecutive sessions closing in either the high or low sector of the daily trading range, and that is rare.

Interpreting CMF is a matter of comparing the index to actual price trends. Buying pressure and selling pressure can be used to confirm what price patterns reveal. Positive CMF indicates bullish tendencies, and negative CMF is likely to point to bearish price trends. However, traders will seek consistency in CMF movement above or below the zero line, and in less certain times the CMF may move back and forth slightly above and below the zero line; when this occurs, CMF is not useful as an indicator. It is only when the CMF trends above or below and remains there for several sessions that it works as a leading or confirming signal of the price trend. CMF at times will contradict the price trend, emphasizing the importance of strong and independent confirmation before acting on what CMF reveals.

For example, the chart of Exxon Mobil (XOM) (Figure 13.2) contains two instances of CMF.

The first highlighted CMF area closely tracks the price trend and works as confirmation that the trend will continue. In fact, price is a leading signal out of the bearish trend, with CMF following soon after.

Figure 13.2 *Chaikin Money Flow (CMF)*

Source: Chart courtesy of StockCharts.com.

Thus, CMF will not always work as a leading indicator or even as one that closely tracks price trends.

The second example diverges from price not just once, but twice. In this case, the divergence presents a serious problem for traders because it demonstrates that using a 20-period average does not ensure that the volume indicator will act reliably. As the price trend turns bullish, CMF signals a bearish change. In a case such as this, when the volume indicator is at a divergence with the price trend, check the technical price signals to determine what action should occur next. In this situation, the February to mid-March resistance level appears to flip over to support as price trends upward. This may be a more reliable indicator and confirmation than the volume indicator.

Example

An uncertain trend: You have discovered strong price reversal signals, and you want to take action. However, CMF has developed into strong divergence with the price trends. Your dilemma: Should you rely more on price or volume trends? You decide to rely on traditional signals, like patterns of resistance and support, and on candlestick signals, as more reliable than volume divergence.

Key Point

Using a 20-session period for volume analysis is reliable as long as volume levels remain consistent; when divergence between price and volume is observed, CMF and similar indicators may be less reliable.

Note also that about half of the sessions during this uptrend closed in the lower half of the trading range, even as the overall price trend continued to rise. This is a flaw in any volume indicator, because the daily high to low affects the calculation even when price gaps in between sessions; but it does not take those gaps into account. This is why the bearish divergence is possible even in a strongly bullish trend.

MONEY FLOW INDEX (MFI)

The *money flow index (MFI)* calculates buying or selling pressure by comparing price and volume over a 14-session period. As an oscillator checking rising prices (buying pressure) versus falling prices (selling pressure), MFI moves in an index range between 0 and 100.

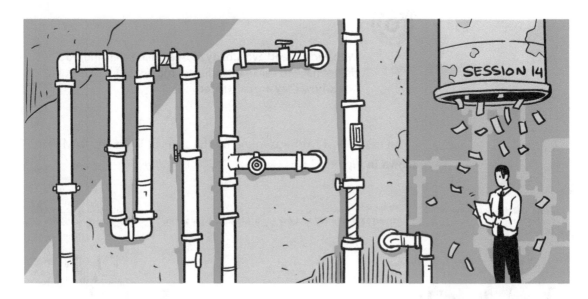

The calculation requires four specific steps:

1. Calculate an average of a session's high, low, and close.

    (high + low + close) ÷ 3 = average price (AP)

2. Figure the raw money flow by multiplying AP by volume.

    AP × volume = raw money flow (RMF)

3. Compute the money flow ratio (MFR) based on 14 periods.

    14-period positive MFR ÷ 14-period negative
    MFR = money flow ratio (MFR)

4. Derive the money flow index (MFI) by reducing the MFR to an index value.

    (100) ÷ (100 ÷ MFR) = MFI

money flow index (MFI)

a volume indicator calculating both price and volume over a 14-session period, used to identify buying and selling pressure.

Fortunately for traders, these calculations are performed automatically when using free online charting services, such as the one used throughout this book, StockCharts.com. Even so, it is useful to understand how an indicator is developed, even though you do not have to perform the steps manually.

Key Point

With widespread availability of free online charting, you do not have to calculate indicator moves, but it is useful to know how they are calculated.

An example of MFI was found on the chart of Walmart (WMT), shown in Figure 13.3.

Figure 13.3 Money Flow Index (MFI)

Source: Chart courtesy of StockCharts.com.

The two instances in which the index moved beyond the middle range are highlighted on this chart. The index value 80 is considered the point at which the stock has been overbought and a reversal is likely; the index value of 20 is considered the point where the stock has been oversold.

Over a six-month period, there was only one instance of overbought and one of oversold. Both remained there (above 80 and below 20) only briefly, and both were followed by a reversal. So the MFI volume indicator is effective at anticipating reversals. When confirmed by other signals showing the same likely outcome, MFI is a useful signal. Making it even more effective for timing of trades, the location of overbought and oversold conditions both preceded the actual price reversal. So MFI, when confirmed, provides a warning signal of reversal likely to occur very quickly.

Example

Volume acting like momentum: You have come to rely on the MFI indicator because, like momentum, it pegs overbought and oversold. However, it comes to this conclusion based on a study of volume rather than price. What does this mean? When both momentum and CFI tell you the same thing, it is strong confirmation.

One market theory states that volume trends precede price. When using MFI, this appears to be true; but no theory can be applied universally and there will be instances in which MFI cannot be used for timing of trades. This is why independent confirmation has to be located before acting on what MFI reveals. The failure swings at times found at either the 80 or 20 index value would typically involve contradictory signals rather than confirming signals. This type of divergence should not be ignored, but recognized as a flaw in MFI and any other oscillator based on volume, price, or both.

ON-BALANCE VOLUME (OBV)

Measuring buying and selling pressure can also be accomplished with a cumulative indicator (versus an averaging one). For example, *on-balance volume (OBV)* moves from one session to another, adding volume on upward-moving days and subtracting volume on downward-moving days.

on-balance volume (OBV)

a volume indicator tracking buying and selling pressure cumulatively, adding volume for upward-moving days and subtracting volume for downward-moving days.

The calculation is based on whether price moves up or down. The formula for upward-moving days (when closing price is higher than the prior closing price) is as follows:

$$\text{Prior OBV} + \text{Current volume}$$

When price moves downward (closing price is lower than the prior closing price), the formula is as follows:

$$\text{Prior OBV} - \text{Current volume}$$

If the price closes at the same level as the prior day, OBV does not change. A flaw in OBV is that it counts a session as an absolute. Thus, a session whose price moves only very slightly is granted the same value as one whose price moves many points. A second flaw occurs when volume is unusually heavy during a particular session even when the price change is only slight, or when volume is light but the price change is substantial. These distortions tend to make OBV misleading in such extreme cases. Given these shortcomings, OBV, like all volume indicators, should be confirmed independently before entering a trade.

Key Point

OBV assigns positive or negative value to a session's volume whether the difference is slight or large. This is one of the flaws in OBV, and should be kept in mind when determining how much importance to assign to what it reveals.

OBV, like many volume-based measurements of buying or selling pressure, assumes that volume trends precede price trends. The indicator is based on volume but is used to predict or anticipate price direction and reversals. However, because OBV changes are based on closing prices, it does not account for the impact on prices of large price gaps, violations of resistance or support, or other significant price indicators that do affect the trend, and may create highly reliable reversal and timing indicators. OBV is not sensitive to these technical price movements, and is focused strictly on volume. Thus, it is a good confirming indicator but it also contains flaws. In addition, a large price spike is an important indicator, often preceding reversals by a single session; but OBV will treat all directional movement in the same manner, so a large volume spike has no meaning within the OBV calculation.

Divergences in OBV should be expected to occur due to the flaws in the calculation itself, notably when volume is heavy, or when price movement does not match the same session's volume levels. The divergence observed between price and OBV may serve as a signal of a reversal to occur soon, with more weight given to the price-based indicator than the volume-based indicator.

An example of OBV is found on the chart of Walt Disney (DIS), shown in Figure 13.4.

The trends on this chart reveal the expected trend in OBV. As the OBV level declines, it closely tracks the downtrend in price. As price

Example

A dubious indicator: You have been interested in using volume indicators to confirm and strengthen what you find in price patterns. However, should you trust OBV? Knowing that it makes no distinction between big and small volume direction, you are uncertain about its value. So you decide to treat OBV as one form of confirmation, knowing you need more.

turns and begins a new uptrend, OBV follows closely as well. In both instances, OBV behaves as expected; it tracks the price trend and confirms the trend.

Another aspect to OBV is seen in the later portion of the chart. The trading range begins trending sideways in a six-point breadth.

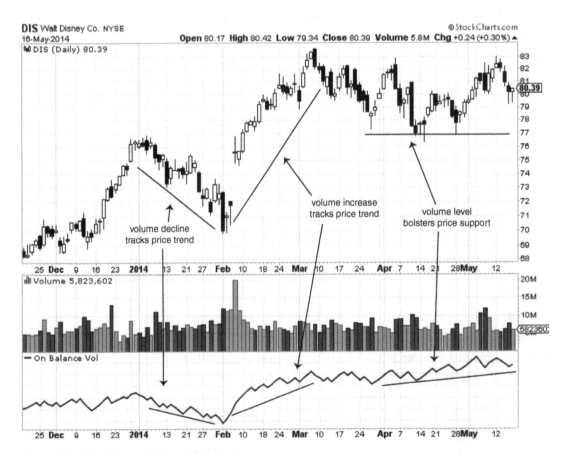

Figure 13.4 On Balance Volume (OBV)
Source: Chart courtesy of StockCharts.com.

At the same time, OBV has very little change, meaning upward and downward days are approximately equal. This volume trend bolsters the price support level, again a confirming signal that volume does precede price. If OBV were to begin trending strongly away from this sideways direction, you would expect price to do the same.

Volume indicators may be based on averaging over a fixed period or on cumulative additions and subtractions. All of these indicators work well as long as volume trends are closely matched to price trends; the divergence or distortion based on changes between volume and price presents more interesting signals, which, when confirmed, may reveal likely reversals.

The next chapter explores a related series of indicators used to measure the strength or weakness of a price trend, in the form of momentum oscillators. These often provide some of the strongest confirming signals of a coming price reversal.

CHAPTER 14

MOMENTUM OSCILLATORS

> *With the only certainty in our daily existence being change,*
> *and a rate of change growing always faster in a kind of*
> *technological leapfrog game, speed helps people think they are*
> *keeping up.*
>
> —Gail Sheehy, *Speed Is of the Essence*, 1971

A *momentum oscillator* measures not the direction of price but the strength and speed of a price trend. This is a key distinction. As a trend evolves, it eventually loses its strength and speed, slows down, and eventually stops; at this point, a reversal signal is likely to be found.

A momentum oscillator may be either a *leading indicator* or a *lagging indicator*, and these distinctions help determine whether the signal should be used as a primary one to be independently confirmed or as a confirming indicator for other signals observed (in the form of price patterns, candlesticks, or volume).

momentum oscillator

an indicator based on analysis of the current price trend that measures the strength and speed of the trend rather than the direction in which it is moving.

leading indicator

a signal that precedes price movement and other reversals, and may be independently confirmed with additional indicators.

Example

A leader or a follower?: A trader has been using momentum indicators, along with price and volume, to find confirmation. Confusion has developed, however, because momentum at times seems to anticipate price, and at other times to follow it. The only solution: Be aware that momentum can lead or lag, and either is useful. But don't rely on momentum to lead a reversal every time.

This chapter examines three key momentum oscillators and displays them on stock charts.

THE NATURE OF MOMENTUM

Momentum oscillators are normally assigned an index value or series of values, based on the outcome of calculations. These are based on price, volume, or both, and in most cases, the reported oscillator index values are the closing prices. However, when you analyze a stock chart during the trading day, the momentum oscillator index values are updated with every change in price or volume.

These calculated indices rely on moving averages, and the selection of a number of periods affects the outcome. Using too short of a period results in an outcome that does not always reflect the true status of momentum; using too long a period levels out the results so that you cannot derive any true value from the analysis.

lagging indicator

a signal that follows price direction, notably reversals, and serves as confirmation for other reversal signals.

Key Point

Momentum is associated not with a trend's direction but with the strength and speed of that trend.

Even though published indicators are based on a set number of periods to calculate the moving average, these can also be adjusted. However, in comparing one stock to another, the same oscillator assumptions should be applied. The current status of an oscillator is most effective when included on a stock chart. It can be listed above or below price, or behind price. The decision is up to each person, and the flexibility of free online charting services enables you to place oscillators where they suit your preferences.

In all instances, you seek some form of movement away from the typical or middle range. Because momentum oscillators measure the strength and speed of a trend, any breakaway move is significant. For example, most oscillators identify a mid-range index value. When the momentum oscillator moves above or below that range, it serves as a potential signal for reversal. This may lead the reversal, subject to independent confirmation; or it may lag behind other signals, and work as one form of confirmation. To many analysts, concurrent indicators (momentum moving beyond the mid-range at the same time as other indicators) may be the strongest reversal flags. This is especially useful when the indicated reversal signal occurs before price itself reverses. This provides you the opportunity to enter a trade in advance of the price change, so you gain full benefit from the reversal.

Key Point

Momentum becomes critical when it moves outside of the typical range based on how the index is calculated; at these moments, reversal is likely due to changes in momentum.

Like all indicators, momentum oscillators are never 100 percent accurate and do fail from time to time. The most reliable system for timing of entry and exit is to seek as many indicators as possible that point to a price movement and confirm the likely change as well. The minimum confirmation you should expect to find is two indicators (initial and confirming). If you can find three or more, that is even better. The more indicators you locate in a short span of time, the stronger the likelihood of an actual reversal.

However, also be aware that if you dedicate too much time to analysis, you are likely to miss the critical timing for the price move itself. There is a balance. You do not want to enter a trade based on too little information; but if you wait for too much proof, you will miss the chance to exploit the reversal. Change is rapid on stock charts, and the stronger the reversal indicator, the faster price will be likely to follow the implied direction.

Example

Excessive information is not a good thing: You have discovered many strong indicators, especially in the realm of momentum. So you decide to review all of them before making trades. Two problems have emerged. First, it takes time to study numerous indicators, and this means you lose the timing to enter the trade itself. Second, you have discovered that the more indicators you review, the higher the chance of contradiction. A better solution: Identify three or four exceptionally strong signals, perhaps one of each type (price, moving averages, volume, and momentum). Focus on these as a first step, and go to more indicators only when you cannot find strong signals in this first step. Also remember, at times no specific signals emerge, and this means you should not take any action.

With these cautionary observations in mind, remember that momentum oscillators do not measure price direction, but the strength (or weakness) and speed of a trend. As these change, reversal becomes increasingly likely. Oscillator levels tend to remain in the mid-range until the momentum level changes.

When the oscillator moves above or below the defined mid-range, it is exceptional and often indicates excessive price movement. A study of stock charts concludes that these extreme movements are not typical and tend to not last long.

The two extremes are termed *overbought* and *oversold*. When a stock is overbought, it means that buying pressure has moved the oscillator above the normal mid-range and that a corrected move will place opposite pressure on price and move it back within range. When a stock is oversold, it means that selling pressure has moved the oscillator below the normal mid-range. A correcting move is likely to return the oscillator to mid-range. Both of these correcting moves are reflected in price reversals, and this is seen consistently on price charts.

overbought

condition when buying pressure has moved a stock price above its mid-range as defined by momentum oscillators, and is likely to lead to a reversal in price and a return of the oscillator below the overbought index value.

Since momentum oscillators measure changes in the strength of a trend and the speed of trend movement, there are two locations where they have the most importance: at or near resistance and at or near support. When oscillators (and other signals) approach these borders of the trading range, reversal signals are at their strongest, and also at their most likely point of success.

Key Point

When momentum oscillators signal reversal at, near, or through resistance or support, the signal is at its strongest; this is the likely location for the reversal to occur.

oversold

condition when selling pressure has moved a stock price below its mid-range as defined by momentum oscillators, and is likely to lead to a reversal in price and a return of the oscillator above the oversold index value.

If the price has made a move above resistance, an overbought oscillator is highly likely to point to a price reversal. And when price violates support and moves lower, an oversold momentum oscillator is also at its strongest.

What does it means when price moves above resistance or below support, but the momentum oscillator remains within its mid-range? Technical analysts recognize that movement through resistance and support is likely to reverse, but the lack of confirmation from momentum oscillators does not always mean that the breakout will succeed and establish a new and permanent trading range. For this conclusion, you need to find strong confirming signals in the form of continuation indicators. Even then, caution is advised because change can develop suddenly. When you see prices developing erratic behavior upon moving through resistance or support (such as price gaps or exceptionally long candlestick shadows), it is a sign of volatility and potential reversal. Momentum oscillators may also move erratically at such moments. A move through resistance or support sets up a most uncertain time on the stock chart; while oscillators are exceptional guidelines for overbought or oversold conditions, confirmation remains a core requirement before entering any trades.

RELATIVE STRENGTH INDEX (RSI)

Relative Strength Index (RSI)

a momentum indicator tracking strength and speed of a current trend based on an index with marked levels when prices become overbought or oversold.

The first of three momentum oscillators examined in this chapter is the *Relative Strength Index (RSI)*. This is a fairly straightforward oscillator and easy to track. It is based on an index value between zero and 100, with a normal mid-range above 30 and below 70. If the oscillator reaches or moves above 70 on the top side, the stock is overbought; if it reaches or moves below 30, the stock is oversold. Neither of these conditions should be expected to last for very long.

Example

Simplicity and strong signals: A trader has been frustrated over the past few months because many signals are complicated and difficult to read. And then he or she discovers RSI. The simplicity of this is appealing. If the index moves above 70, the stock is overbought; if it moves below 30, it is oversold. And these moves are rare, so when they occur, it gives out an exceptionally strong signal, which is also one of the more reliable types of confirmation.

Analysis of momentum may include a study of how the oscillator becomes overbought or oversold. Does the index value gradually approach the 70 or 30 value and then remain at or slightly over the line? Or does the oscillator index jump rapidly and move through 70 or 30 and gain several points of overbought or oversold? The speed of oscillator change and the value above 70 or below 30 indicate the strength of overbought or oversold conditions.

The calculation of RSI spans the most recent 14 sessions. In addition to the straightforward overbought and oversold signals, RSI may also create a divergence signal. This occurs when RSI indicates overbought but the stock price continues to rise, or when RSI indicates oversold but the stock price continues to decline.

Key Point

Just as important as momentum pointing to likely reversal, divergence—when the oscillator contradicts price—is also worthwhile information about what price might do next.

Divergences in RSI are not strong enough to generate a trade. Seek additional confirmation with continuation signals beyond RSI. In addition, be aware that an RSI divergence might represent a delay rather than a contrary signal. It may occur that price reacts more slowly than the momentum of the trend, so in this case you would expect price to eventually correct itself as implied by the RSI signal (overbought leading to a decline or oversold leading to a rise in price).

Many traders recognize that RSI does not frequently move above 70 or below 30, but may approach these index values. As a result, it makes sense to recognize overbought at a level close to 70 (many use the 60 index value) or to recognize oversold close to 30 (40, for example). The observation that the oscillator does not frequently move outside of mid-range makes it sensible to spark an initial reversal indicator at a different index level. However, the speed of movement in the oscillator should also affect how much value is granted to the revised overbought or oversold index value. A rapid move toward those index borders should be granted more importance than a gradual move in the oscillator.

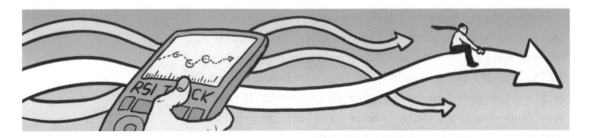

RSI, like all indicators, is calculated automatically on the many free online charts. However, it helps in understanding what RSI reveals if you also know the formula. It involves five steps:

1. Add all upward-moving closing prices in the period.
2. Add all downward-moving closing prices in the period.
3. Calculate the exponential moving average (EMA) for the results of steps 1 and 2.
4. Divide the EMA for upward closing prices, by the EMA for downward closing prices, to arrive at Relative Strength (RS):

$$\text{EMA (upward)} \div \text{EMA (downward)} = RS$$

5. Calculate the index value:

$$100 - [100 \div (1 + RS)] = RSI$$

This produces the index value between 0 and 100. Because the calculated EMA and resulting RSI are based on a comparison between average advancing and declining periods, the outcome is normally going to fall between 70 and 30. In fact, it is rare for RSI to extend beyond these index values, and when they do a fast retreat is the usual outcome. The stabilizing effect of the averaging between advancing and declining sessions is what provides great stability to RSI, so that the extremes (movement above 70 or below 30) are rare but critical as signals for overbought and oversold conditions.

Example

Calculations are easier when you don't have to do them: You have come to understand that it makes sense to know how a calculation is done, if only to further your knowledge of what indicators provide to you. But you find calculations tedious. The good news: These are done automatically for you through free online charts.

Key Point
Due to how it is calculated, RSI is normally found between 70 and 30. When it exceeds these levels, reversal is likely, and the tendency is for RSI to return to the mid-range quickly.

For example, the chart of 3M remained within the 70 to 30 index range for most of a charted six-month period, with exceptions highlighted in Figure 14.1.

The two overbought conditions coincide with the top of uptrends, and also are followed closely by price declines, as expected. In both cases, the index moves above 70 before the price correction occurs. Although acting as soon as RSI goes into overbought will mean missing a few additional points of price increase, this condition—RSI preceding

Figure 14.1 Relative Strength Index (RSI)
Source: Chart courtesy of StockCharts.com.

the price reaction—makes it possible to enter a trade before the price moves. So if you are long in this company's stock, selling as soon as RSI moves above 70 would be good timing.

The oversold condition occurs on a day exhibiting a long black candlestick, which is very bearish. Buying the stock at this point would be well timed. However, if you hesitate, the volume spike occurring in the following session confirms a likely bullish reversal, which does occur right away. The price begins an uptrend that lasts for the remainder of the period shown and moves 17 points higher.

At the end of the chart, two examples are found in which RSI moves close to the 70 overbought level. However, neither of these is the result of a rapid climb in the index, so they do not provide a particularly strong signal for reversal.

MOVING AVERAGE CONVERGENCE DIVERGENCE (MACD)

Another momentum oscillator is considerably more complex than RSI. The *Moving Average Convergence Divergence* (*MACD*) is a useful oscillator that combines three separate moving averages: 12-, 26-, and 9-day varieties.

The signal line appears as a zero line with bars above or below; the 12-day and 26-day moving averages trend above and below the signal line. So there are three separate EMA lines working together, the fast (12-day), slow (26-day), and signal (9-day).

Some generalizations about MACD:

1. When the 26-day and 12-day averages are below the signal line and then cross above, it is a bullish indicator.
2. When the two averages are above the signal line and then cross below, the signal is bearish.
3. Divergences and large swings in either direction indicate stronger than normal indicators, and if confirmed add confidence to the implied direction of momentum. The larger the gap between the 26-day and 12-day averages, the stronger the signal (bullish above signal line and bearish below).
4. The signal line is the average of the other two lines, so the signal line trend is both a summary of the other two and a

Moving Average Convergence Divergence (MACD)

a momentum oscillator based on comparisons and movements of a 12-day and a 26-day exponential moving average, and a signal line, a 9-day exponential moving average.

potential divergence signal. This line is at or close to zero whenever the other two averages narrow or cross one another.

5. The oscillator range is from −1 to +1, with zero representing the signal line.

6. The signal line anticipates the oscillator direction in many instances, diverging from the other averages in advance of price.

Key Point

Although MACD's calculation is more complex than most other oscillators, it reveals and often leads shifts in price due to changed momentum.

Because MACD is actually the signal line's level above or below zero (and the average of the other two), the movement of MACD from the signal line tends to be far less than evolving changes in the 12-day and 26-day averages. Because the trend is based on zero in the center, MACD is referred to as a *centered oscillator*. In comparison, a *banded oscillator* has an upper and lower line, and price resides either within the two or violates the top or bottom band, which generates a trading signal.

centered oscillator

An oscillator that reflects changes either above or below a center line or zero signal point.

Example

A dizzying array of moving averages: A trader has avoided using MACD because it involves too many different averages. But upon realizing that the signal line is the key and the 12- and 26-day averages express moves above or below, MACD falls into places and becomes clear. Although a set of different convergence and divergence signals are possible, the trader concludes that MACD is an excellent momentum test.

banded oscillator

an oscillator consisting of an upper and lower band, with price movement within those bands in a normal range, or trending above or below to generate a potential trading signal.

The value of a centered oscillator like MACD is its visual summary of momentum in terms of both strength and speed of change. It is easily spotted: when the two averages are higher than the center line, the indication favors bullish momentum; when it moves below, the trend is bearish.

An interesting aspect of MACD is its combination of leading and lagging indication. Moving averages are considered lagging because they summarize past direction compared to current price movement. However, by creating MACD as the average of two other moving averages (the signal line), the oscillator also may act as a leading indicator. This average of the averages measures rate of change and may work as a leading indicator, especially when the two averages cross over the signal line.

Key Point

MACD is unique among oscillators because it contains elements of both leading and lagging tendencies.

centerline crossover

the movement of averages from below to above a centerline, or vice versa, considered a bullish signal (crossing from below to above) or a bearish signal (crossing from above to below).

This movement across the middle, or *centerline crossover*, is the strongest element of MACD. The occurrence of the crossover, when both averages move (as they normally do), is seen as a trading signal, depending on the direction. The crossover is a signal that momentum has changed, and when it precedes a change of price direction, centerline crossover can be used as confirmation of other signals, or as a leading signal to be confirmed independently.

The lack of crossover is also worth noting. In a trending situation, as long as the two averages remain far above the centerline (in a bullish trend) or far below (in a bearish trend), the indication is that the trend still has momentum. But once the averages begin moving closer to the centerline, the signal is that momentum is slowing and will end once a subsequent crossover occurs.

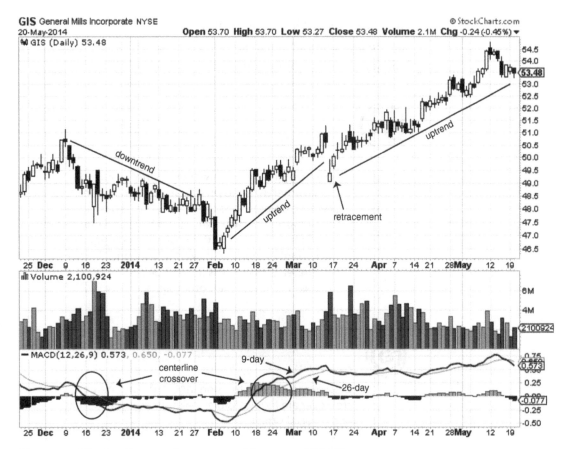

Figure 14.2 Moving Average Convergence Divergence (MACD)
Source: Chart courtesy of StockCharts.com.

An interesting set of MACD signals is found on the chart of General Mills (GIS), shown in Figure 14.2.

This chart contains two crossovers. First is a bearish move from above the signal line to below. Although the crossover occurs after the downtrend has begun, it reveals that the downtrend is likely to continue. The same is true for the second, bullish crossover. The uptrend has begun, but the crossover forecasts that it will continue.

The uptrend lasts for the remainder of time charted. The two averages also remain narrow and stay well above the centerline, revealing that the uptrend will probably not end in the near future. At the very end of the period, the two averages do show a move to the downside, but still remain far above the signal line. In this situation, it would not be necessary to take profits just yet. Once the averages move closer to the centerline, the indication would be reduced momentum among buyers and a likely reversal in the future. Before acting on this, traders would want to find confirmation in price signals and candlesticks, volume indicators, or other momentum indicators, such as RSI.

Example

Keeping it simple: You have been frustrated about how to interpret the movement in MACD. But you have learned to focus on one attribute. When the two averages do not move much but both remain above the signal line, it means the current uptrend is likely to continue; when they both remain below, it signals that the current downtrend is likely to continue. Simple. But remember, these signals need to be confirmed, or to be used as confirmation for other signals.

Key Point

Crossover is the key to using MACD. The moments of crossover are highly visible, making this a key oscillator and reversal signal.

MACD is an exceptionally useful momentum indicator because its crossover signals are so highly visible. It makes the trader's task of timing entry and exit much easier than with many other indicators. Even though it is complex (consisting of two averages plus a third average of the first two), the conclusions you can reach by tracking MACD along with other signals can greatly improve timing of both entry and exit.

Stochastic oscillator

a momentum test consisting of a 14-day average of changes between high and low prices called 3K, and a three-day average of 3K, called 3D.

STOCHASTIC OSCILLATOR

The *Stochastic oscillator* is yet another momentum oscillator, which consists of two calculated moving averages: the first, called %K, is based on comparisons of high and low closing prices over 14 periods, and the second represents a three-session average of 3K and is called %D.

The index developed by the Stochastic oscillator is expressed as an index value between 0 and 100. Like RSI, the Stochastic limits of note are the 80 index line, above which the stock is overbought, and the 20 index line, below which the stock is oversold. The primary distinction between RSI and Stochastic is the combined calculation of high and low prices over the 14 periods, which is expressed as two separate moving averages. In the opinion of many technical analysts, this makes Stochastic more reliable than RSI.

The signal interpretations are useful to anyone tracking momentum. When the oscillator approaches the maximum of 100, it implies a period of accumulation. This may be part of a collective signal for a coming reversal to the bearish side. And when the indicator approaches the low of zero, it reveals a period of distribution. This is seen invariably as a forecast of a bullish reversal.

Key Point

The Stochastic oscillator identifies likely reversal and, when it moves to the extremes, also identifies periods of accumulation and distribution.

The strongest bullish signal is found when the %D line moves below oversold, or an index of 20. If %K moves below oversold and then returns above 20, this is also a bullish signal. Yet another bullish sign occurs when %K crosses higher than %D; but with all of these bullish signals, confirmation is required before entering trades.

The strongest bearish signals are found when %D moves above overbought, or 80. If %K moves above overbought and then returns below 80, this is also bearish. When %K crosses lower than %D, this is also bearish.

Stochastic is calculated in two steps, with the first (%K) based on the 14 most recent periods:

$$100 \left[(cc - lc) \div (hh - ll) \right] = \%K$$

cc = current closing price
lc = lowest close during 14 periods

hh = highest high during 14 periods

ll = lowest low during 14 periods

The value of %D is based on the latest three %K index values:

$$\text{\%K (three periods)} \div 3 = \text{\%D}$$

The outcome helps find reversal points of the chart. For example, the chart of Philip Morris International (PM) is reported with Stochastic in Figure 14.3.

An analysis of price action in conjunction with the changes in Stochastic reveals that in many instances, this is a leading indicator, pointing to reversal before price makes its move. Focusing only on those moments when the oscillator's two moving averages move into

Figure 14.3 Stochastic Oscillator

Source: Chart courtesy of StockCharts.com.

overbought or oversold, there are ample reversal signals, many more than RSI in most cases.

Example

Finding a strong reversal forecast: The mysterious Stochastic oscillator has become easier to understand with your realization that its seemingly complex formula is simply an expression of the trend that often anticipates a coming price reversal. With this in mind, you find yourself relying on this and any other strong momentum signals to confirm what you see taking place in price.

Key Point

The tendency for Stochastic is to identify many more reversal points than RSI, so for anyone interested in high-volume trading, this may be a preferred oscillator.

The first double signal of overbought conditions occurs at the very beginning of the charted period. The first bump above 80 could act as a signal generating a bearish decision (subject to confirmation). The second move confirms the first, but also occurs at the same time that price gaps lower.

The bullish move below 20 acts in the same way, with the first of two moves signaling a coming bullish move (which lasts only 10 sessions). Note how the first of the two moves below the 20 index is broad, and the second is narrow. The broader moves below 20 (or above 80) are stronger indicators than the narrow variety.

Next, in the last week of December, the Stochastic averages move quite strongly all the way from below 20 to above 80 in approximately 10 sessions. This is strongly bearish and anticipates the very strong downtrend that follows three sessions after the first bearish signal.

The Stochastic lines decline rapidly, once again moving into oversold with a two-part move under the 20 index line. These signals are less clear, however, and it is not until the second of the two oscillator declines that prices begin moving upward.

The remainder of the chart includes five specific overbought signals, even as price continues rising. This divergence signal could be interpreted in a number of ways. It could mean the uptrend is losing momentum, notably by the beginning of April, when the move above 80 is broad and lasts longer than the typical move. It could also signal that no decision should be made about entering or exiting trades until momentum changes are confirmed independently.

All momentum oscillators are aspects of changing price trends, and cannot be applied without confirmation, or in a consistent manner. It all depends on the volatility in price, and on what other reversal signals are found (or not found).

In addition to RSI, MACD, and Stochastic oscillators, many additional oscillators may be applied. Confusing to many chartists is the additional fact that many volume and price-specific indicators contain aspects of momentum as well as price reversals. So the distinction between price indicators, volume indicators, and momentum indicators is not always clear. However, the label placed on any of these is not as important as how accurately they predict or anticipate coming reversals, or the simplicity of use for a range of indicators.

In all cases, no single indicator should be trusted by itself to generate a trade. The concept of confirmation—finding two or more indicators forecasting the same price direction—is essential to developing a reliable trading experience. The next chapter examines the elements of confirmation.

THE *TREND* COMES TO AN END AND A *REVERSAL* IS LIKELY.

SO WHAT *EXACTLY* IS AN OSCILLATOR?

IT IS A VISUAL SUMMARY OF MOMENTUM, SUCH AS *MOVING AVERAGE COVERGENCE DIVERGENCE*.

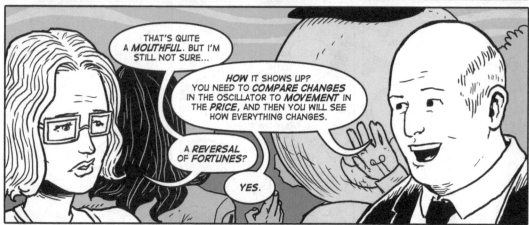

THAT'S QUITE A *MOUTHFUL*. BUT I'M STILL NOT SURE...

HOW IT SHOWS UP? YOU NEED TO *COMPARE CHANGES* IN THE OSCILLATOR TO *MOVEMENT* IN THE *PRICE*, AND THEN YOU WILL SEE HOW EVERYTHING CHANGES.

A *REVERSAL* OF *FORTUNES*?

YES.

DOES THIS MEAN IT'S *MY TURN* TO GIVE THEM A *WEDGIE*?

15

CONFIRMATION, THE KEY TO TIMING

We never stop investigating. We are never satisfied that we know enough to get by. Every question we answer leads to another question. This has become the greatest survival trick of our species.

—Desmond Morris, *The Naked Ape*, 1967

The process of confirmation is the discipline used to improve information, to strengthen the apparent indicator before acting. This is essential as part of the process of analysis, because no indicator will be correct 100 percent of the time.

You will make mistakes. Reliance upon a strong indicator, even with confirmation, will fail at times or offer up a false reversal signal. For this reason, diversifying your risk makes sense. The best way to diversify risk is to limit the dollar amount of each trade, so that on those occasions where you suffer a loss, it will not be catastrophic. This idea—resisting the temptation to be greedy—prevents many losses, and you are better off missing the occasional spectacular gain rather than losing more than you can afford.

Key Point

The most successful traders make mistakes, but learn from them and then move forward to the next opportunity.

So confirmation provides you with a better body of knowledge about the current status of a trend. The stronger the confirming indicator, the more likely the reversal will occur. However, this does not mean you should increase the dollars at risk; it only means you will improve the percentage of well-timed trades by employing confirmation.

Example

Evidence but not proof: A trader had relied on confirmation for timing of trades, but suffered several losses even with strong confirmation. The expensive conclusion: Nothing is a 100 percent guarantee, and even with confirmation, trades do not always come out as you had expected.

WHAT CONFIRMATION IS NOT

Finding confirmation is just a part of the process of timing a trade. A confirming indicator strengthens what the initial indicator reveals or forecasts.

However, confirmation is specific in terms of what it does do. There are several aspects that are not part of confirmation:

    1. *Proof.* A confirming signal is not proof that the forecast change is going to occur. The confirming signal only strengthens

the likelihood of a reversal. Without that strength in the forecast, it does not make sense to take action; but even with confirmation in the form of one or more signals, there is no such thing as proof. Your confidence should be much higher, but this does not justify taking greater risks.

2. *Risk elimination.* Too many traders expect that finding a reversal signal and confirmation does away with risk. Without a doubt, strong confirmation reduces the risk of ill-timed moves, but it cannot remove risk. There are no indicators that will do that for you. Risk is a fact that every trader lives with, the accompaniment to opportunity. Realistically, traders have to accept risk because it cannot be avoided.

3. *Forecast of immediate change.* Another assumption traders make is that the expected reversal will happen immediately. The ideal outcome is for the reversal to hit immediately after the trade has been placed, but individual expectations don't determine when a reversal will occur. A strong move often is followed by an equally strong reversal, but some moves do not reverse until days or even weeks later. A reversal signal and confirmation do not promise immediate results, and the results might not come about when you expect them.

Even with the uncertainties of trading, confirmation contains specific attributes that improve your timing. If you begin with the premise that all trades have a 50/50 chance of being well timed, seeking strong reversal signals and confirmation will only improve these odds. If you can move from a 50/50 outcome to a 60/40 or better, you increase your overall net profits. However, if you accept a slight improvement over the averages, you also need to effectively manage risks. This means keeping your dollar levels consistent for trades. It is not profitable to make a profit on four trades of $400 each and then suffer a complete loss on a $2,000 trade. Risk management requires being aware of trends, recognizing reversal signals, finding strong confirmation, and managing trades to ensure that no single loss will wipe out smaller profits.

PROXIMITY AND STRENGTH OF THE SIGNAL

Not all confirmation is the same. Reversals are especially strong signals when the signal occurs at or near resistance or support; by the same argument, confirmation will also be strongest at these levels.

Key Point

Reversals and confirmation occurring as price approaches or breaks through support or resistance tend to be stronger than elsewhere in the trading range.

For example, a case of multiple confirmation at support and then again at resistance is found in the chart of Kellogg (K), shown in Figure 15.1.

The support test occurs in the first week of February. In the last week of January, price breaks through support for four consecutive sessions. At this point it becomes evident that (1) prices will remain below prior support and set up a new trading range, or (2) reversals will emerge and, if confirmed, lead to a new uptrend.

Figure 15.1 Reversal and Confirmation at Support and Resistance
Source: Chart courtesy of StockCharts.com.

The first reversal signal is the move of RSI into the oversold area below 30. This occurs three sessions before two strong confirming signals appear, a volume spike and a long lower shadow.

This strong three-part reversal with two confirming signals might be enough to generate a trade. However, a subsequent confirming signal is found starting on the next session, which develops into a three white soldiers indicator, a strongly bullish signal. If a trader waits for this additional confirmation, the price will have moved up four points. So as a matter of how much risk to assume in the timing of a trade, the question becomes one of, how much confirmation is enough? For some moderately conservative traders, the momentum signal occurring as a first step, confirmed three sessions later, would be enough. For the more cautious, giving up four points and acting only after recognizing the three-session candlestick confirmation could be the development sparking a trade.

Example

The timing dilemma: A trader has noticed with frustration that by the time signals and confirmation are discovered, the new trend has already taken place. A tough decision: Should you act quickly even without strong confirmation? Or should you be more cautious and stand to miss part of the opportunity? The only consolation is in the realization that this trader is not alone. Every trader faces the same problem.

In either case, note that all of the initial reversal signals occur right after price breaks through below support. This is the area where reversals and confirmation are exceptionally strong, and all of the signals point to a bullish change to follow.

The second occurrence is one of bearish reversals and confirmation, found after an uptrend of nearly two months' duration. The first signal of a bearish change occurs in two parts on the same day: a volume spike and a move in RSI above the overbought level of 70. The volume spike repeats the following day, adding strength to its meaning.

At the same time, a breakout above resistance occurs with very wide breadth and starting out with a long white session. This all appears quite bullish, especially since prices do continue rising another five points. However, the long-term signal is also strongly bearish even though price has not yet reacted.

The rising wedge is a bearish signal that may take time to develop; in this instance, it occurs twice. At the point where initial resistance and support narrow, a change is inevitable. The last five sessions in this initial rising wedge are exceptionally narrow. This is followed only a few sessions later by the start of yet another rising wedge, bearish confirmation. The last six sessions of the chart are once again exceptionally narrow.

Collectively, these bearish signals are very convincing; however, with prices continuing to rise during the last two months, many traders would hesitate at this point, waiting for yet one additional confirming signal. However, if such a signal were to develop, it would make sense at this point to take action and acknowledge the likelihood of a new bear trend.

The fact that both of these reversal signals are confirmed by multiple subsequent indicators *and* both occur with breakouts (first below support and then above resistance) makes these strong signals in terms of proximity to the edges of the trading range. However, in the first case, reversal occurs immediately, and in the second, it is yet to appear.

Key Point

The big question is, How much confirmation is enough? The answer depends on proximity of the signal, your risk profile, and volatility of the price in recent weeks.

This example raises another question: How much confirmation do you need before you act? When reversal and confirmation occur with a breakout below support or above resistance, you probably do not need more than one initial signal and two confirming signals; elsewhere, at mid-range for example, you might require more signals before you act. But this is a question every trader should ask. The answer relies to some extent on how conservative you are, and on how volatile the stock price has been. However, proximity to support and resistance should be the strongest defining factor is knowing when to make a trade. In the case of the Kellogg chart, the level of confirmation is very strong in both the bullish and bearish reversals; both occur with breakouts from the established trading range.

SETTING RULES FOR YOURSELF

Not all reversals are confirmed. You may locate a strong reversal indicator but also be unable to confirm it. In such a case, the best action is to do nothing, at least not until a confirmation signal appears.

In some cases, you will discover a reversal signal, only to find a second signal that contradicts the first. Once again, the confusion between signals should lead to no action. Entering a trade makes sense only when a reversal or continuation signal is accompanied by a confirming signal forecasting the same direction.

Example

A split personality: You have been perplexed at discovering that some signals do not match with confirmation. In fact, you have found many contradictory signals, diverging from the initial reversal. As frustrating as this is, contradiction is just as valuable as confirmation. It warns you to not act.

Key Point

Divergence is just as revealing as confirmation, even though it might be a warning to hold off acting rather than to act immediately.

These cases of divergence can be troubling, because you want to act on the discovered reversal signal. However, all reversals— including candlesticks, volume, momentum, and traditional price patterns—are vulnerable to the false lead. They fail on occasion. The risk of acting with divergence is quite high, because the offsetting and contradictory signals make the trade in either direction a 50/50 one. The chances of bad timing are equal to the chances of good timing.

Taking a cautionary position with divergence is good management. The big threat to this is impatience or overreliance on a signal that has not been confirmed. So your first rule should be:

Enter a trade only when a signal is confirmed.

Another key aspect to confirmation is recognition of where it is within the current trend. A reversal signal at the wrong location may not be a reversal at all, but a continuation signal. But with divergence, placement of the signal itself is a key. The most ideal location is right at resistance in an uptrend, or at support in a downtrend. But knowing where the price is within the current trend itself is a key to effective timing of trades. Another rule:

Acknowledge reversal signals only if and when they appear at a logical point in the current trend.

Another good rule for managing your trades is to understand the breadth of the current trend, and to judge price volatility. A narrow range is low volatility, and a large or erratic range equals higher volatility—and greater risks. Also be aware of how the breadth is emerging. Is it broadening or narrowing? Pay attention to wedges and triangles, especially as they form over several weeks. These can point to likely reversal timing, but they are easily overlooked. When it comes to breadth of the current trading range, remember:

Know the breadth of trading and whether breadth is changing, and be aware of what change means in terms of likely reversal timing.

In articulating the value of reversals and confirmations, employ the tools that clarify what is occurring. These include trendlines, channel lines, and, of course, lines of resistance and support. Attempting to read a chart without these defining tools is very difficult. Drawing lines and defining trading ranges and emerging change all help to clarify the chart and to add some order to what often appears to be random. Another rule:

Use tools to add order to the trend, recognize strength and weakness, and identify how breadth of trading is evolving.

Be certain that you know how to interpret the signals. For example, momentum can be very specific when expressed on an index with overbought and oversold values; however, this is not enough to generate a trade. A starting point is to know what the signals mean, especially for more complex indicators, such as MACD or some candlestick indicators. The next rule:

Know how to read the signals, and apply the interpretation to your timing of trades.

The strength or weakness of any reversal and confirmation depends, invariably, on the circumstances—volatility, proximity to resistance or support, immediate or deferred confirmation, and the significance of divergence when it occurs. Traders may become impatient and forget to apply the commonsense rules to manage their trades; this inevitably results in higher losses in place of higher profits.

Example

Resisting the desire to act: You have gained considerable wisdom with a single realization: Impatience leads to losses, not profits. The desire to make a trade can easily offset the need for confirmation and proper placement of signals. Self-discipline is a worthy trait for traders to develop, and lack of self-discipline is a costly trait.

Key Point

Your greatest flaw may be impatience. Successful traders are those who resist the impulse to make a trade immediately, regardless of whether it is justified by the signals.

Technical analysis is a patient process, occurring quickly and in the short term. However, even fast-moving indicators require patience and caution before acting on what you discover.

Using technical indicators along with well-selected fundamentals helps you to pick strong value investments and then to time trades based on price, volume, and momentum patterns. It is at times more exciting to trade impulsively or on instinct, but in the long run that ends up harming your profits. The slow, consistent building of a working system requires a wide range of knowledge, selection of the right indicators, and the ability to wait out the uncertainties of price patterns.

325

EVEN SO, NOTHING IS *FOOLPROOF.*

THEY COULD *WAKE UP* AT ANY MINUTE AND START THE PARTY ALL OVER AGAIN.

SO *BEFORE ACTING*, YOU NEED CONFIRMATION?

EXACTLY.

CONFIRMATION IS THE *ESSENTIAL* ELEMENT OF *ALL* TECHNICAL ANALYSIS.

SO HOW DO WE *KNOW* THESE TECHNICAL ANALYSTS HAVE *REALLY* GONE TO *SLEEP?*

PLEASE CLEAN UP WHEN YOU LEAVE

YOU COULD *POKE* ONE OF THEM TO SEE IF HE WAKES UP.

NO, THAT'S OKAY. MAYBE *SINDI* CAN DO THAT.

ZZZ

I *WOULD* LIKE TO KNOW IF...

POKE!

THE END!

GLOSSARY

abandoned baby

a three-session indicator starting with a black session, a downside gap, a doji, an upside gap, and a final white session (bullish); or a white session, an upside gap, a doji, a downside gap, and a final black session (bearish).

accelerated depreciation

a method of writing off capital assets based on higher write-off allowed in earlier years, and lower amounts in later years; this is allowed for specific recovery periods as an alternative to straight-line depreciation, or writing off the same amount each year.

accrual

recognition of an expense in the current year when the purchase was made, but when actual payment will not occur until the following period. This places expenses in the applicable year even though actual cash transactions often are not made until later.

accumulated depreciation

the total of each year's depreciation deduction written off as current-year expense each year; the sum of these deductions (accumulated depreciation) is deducted from the basis price of capital assets to arrive at the net asset value.

accumulation/distribution (A/D)

a volume indicator tracking how cumulative price movement relates to the volume of trading, and how that may lead and forecast a price trend.

accumulation phase

the first of three trend phases under the Dow Theory, during which knowledgeable investors begin to buy shares even though the larger market does not recognize the opportunity.

after-tax ROE

return on equity calculated based on net income, after taxes are deducted.

ascending triangle

a bullish trend pattern combining a level resistance and rising support, forecasting a bullish trend in the near future.

auction market
a market such as the exchange market for listed stocks, in which a buyer's bid price is matched to the seller's asked price; execution occurs when these prices agree.

average
a value derived by adding together the values in a field, and then dividing the result by the number of values.

balance sheet
a summary of the company's assets (what it owns), liabilities (money it owes), and shareholders' equity (the net difference between assets and liabilities, or the net worth of the company); the balance sheet is published as of the last date of the quarter or fiscal year.

banded oscillator
an oscillator consisting of an upper and lower band, with price movement within those bands in a normal range, or trending above or below to generate a potential trading signal.

bear trend
a trend characterized by generally falling prices.

bearish divergence
a situation in which an indicator reveals a likely bearish move but price trends upward.

big move phase
the second of three phases under the Dow Theory, in which the majority of traders follow the trend set by a minority, and trade into a stock.

black crows
a bearish signal consisting of three consecutive sessions, all black; each session opens lower than the last, and then closes lower than the last, without any gaps in between.

Bollinger Bands
an indicator tracking the price average for 20 periods as well as standard deviations both above and below price; the upper and lower bands serve as signal points to make trades in a stock.

bond underwriter
an organization that assesses a corporate bond issuer's creditworthiness and helps set the terms of a debt issue, acting as go-between for the issuer and debt investor.

book value
the dollar value of assets as reported on the balance sheet, usually consisting of the original cost of a capital asset, minus accumulated depreciation.

breadth of trading

the distance between highest and lowest price points in the current price range, described in the number of points; a relative indicator based on the typical price range (a one-point breadth is substantial for a stock averaging $10 per share, but the same breadth for a stock with price average $80 contains much lower volatility).

bull trend

a trend characterized by generally rising prices.

bullish divergence

a situation in which an indicator reveals a likely bullish move but price trends downward.

buy and hold

a method for investing, in which high-quality companies are located and shares bought to be held for the long term.

candlestick

a format for reporting stock activity with the same information as an OHLC chart, but visually easier to track.

capitalizing

setting up a transaction as a long-term asset subject to depreciation or amortization over a period of years, rather than being written off in the current year; the tax rules state that capital assets (with a useful life of more than one year) must be capitalized and depreciated, and that current-year expenses are to be written off in the year those expenses are accrued.

cash ratio

a conservative test of working capital.

centered oscillator

an oscillator that reflects changes either above or below a center line or zero signal point.

centerline crossover

the movement of averages from below to above a centerline, or vice versa, considered a bullish signal (crossing from below to above) or a bearish signal (crossing from above to below).

Chaikin Money Flow (CMF)

a volume indicator consisting of accumulated volume for a period of sessions (normally 20), and indicating whether the trend is positive or negative.

channel lines

straight lines drawn both above and below the price range when the breadth of trading is the same over time, even while the price range increases or decreases.

chartist
a technical analyst who relies on price charts to spot signals for price movement, including strength or weakness in a current trend, and signs that a trend is likely to continue or reverse.

comparative statement
an income statement reporting the current quarter and previous quarters in the same fiscal year, or the same fiscal quarter in the previous fiscal year; or reporting the full current fiscal year and the previous full fiscal year.

compound rate of return
a return calculated with partial-year returns rather than the annual stated or nominal yield.

confirmation
The location of a second indicator that provides the same forecast as a first; this may be in the form of a candlestick pattern, price gap, volume spike, momentum oscillator, or other technical signal.

contingent liabilities
estimated dollar values of potential debts—that is, what might become debts in the future; these often include the estimated dollar amount of lawsuits filed against the corporation but not yet settled or determined. They are not yet liabilities but have to be disclosed because their impact on the valuation of the company could be substantial.

continuation
an indicator pointing to a likely price movement in the same direction as that of the current trend, with bull trend prices continuing to move higher, or bear trend prices continuing to move lower.

contrarian
an investor who decides when to buy or sell based on an analytical study of fundamental (and technical) signals, as opposed to following the majority or making decisions emotionally.

cookie jar accounting (*also known as* sugar bowl accounting)
a form of manipulation of financial statements, in which exceptionally favorable profits are put aside in the current year to level out the long-term trend, and to be used in a later year when results are below average

core earnings
the adjusted net earnings of a company after all noncore profit or loss has been removed; developed by S&P, core earnings adjustments remove one-time and nonoperating items from the

income statement. The core earnings number is found on the S&P Stock Reports provided to clients of most online brokerage services.

cost of goods sold

costs directly associated with the generation of revenue, including merchandise purchased, adjustments for changes in inventory levels, direct labor, and other specific costs.

crossover

the change in one moving average (usually of shorter duration) in relation to the other, or the movement of a moving average above or below the price range.

current assets

all assets in the form of cash or convertible to cash within one year (inventories, accounts receivable, and securities owned).

current liabilities

debts payable within 12 months, including all accounts payable, accrued taxes, and 12 months of payments due on long-term debts.

current ratio

a test of working capital, consisting of dividing current assets by current liabilities, and expressing the answer as a single digit without percentage signs.

debt ratio

a test of long-term working capital for a company; the ratio is a comparison between long-term debt and total capitalization (long-term debt plus shareholders' equity).

deferred credits

nonliability credits for revenue received that will not be earned until a future fiscal year; because this income is not properly booked as revenue in the current fiscal year, it is set up under the liability section of the balance sheet and scheduled to be reversed and booked as revenue in the fiscal year in which it will be earned.

deferred or prepaid assets

the value of any cost or expense properly belonging in a future fiscal year; when cash is paid in advance of the proper period for recognizing that transaction, it may be classified as a deferred asset or as a prepaid asset. For example, when a company pays three years of insurance premiums in the current year, two of those years are properly classified as prepaid, and listed as assets to be recognized in the proper later fiscal year.

descending triangle

a bearish trend pattern combining a level support and falling resistance, forecasting a bearish trend in the near future.

direct costs
costs directly related to the generation of revenue, as compared to expenses, which are not directly related; direct costs include merchandise purchase and direct labor.

distribution phase
the conclusion to the excess phase under the Dow Theory, in which a minority of astute investors begin selling shares before the larger market recognizes that the cycle has turned; this is the same as the accumulation phase, but with selling in place of buying.

divergence
a situation in which an indicator reveals a specific direction (bullish or bearish) but price moves in the opposite direction.

dividend achiever
a company whose declared and paid dividends have increased every year for at least the past 10 years, a distinction indicating highest quality among dividend-paying companies.

dividend yield
the percentage of dividend earned, calculated by dividing dividend per share by the original basis in stock.

doji
a candlestick with a horizontal line in place of the more common rectangle; in a doji, the opening and closing prices are identical or very close together. In Japanese, doji means mistake.

doji star (three-session)
a three-session signal involving a black session, a downside gap, a doji, and a final white session (bullish) or a black session, an upside gap, a doji, and a final black session (bearish).

doji star (two-session)
a two-session candlestick pattern consisting of a black session, a downside gap, and a doji (bullish) or a white session, an upside gap, and a doji (bearish).

double bottom
a set of two lower shadow price spikes appearing after an extended downtrend, and signaling a likely reversal and uptrend to follow.

double top
a set of two upper shadow price spikes appearing after an extended uptrend, and signaling a likely reversal and downtrend to follow.

Dow Theory
a set of beliefs about stock price behavior based on the writings of Charles Dow, serving as the foundation for modern technical analysis.

downtrend

a current trend involving a series of progressively lower price levels, also called a bearish price movement or a bear trend.

dragonfly doji

a single-session candlestick shaped like a capital T, with a horizontal line at the top and a long lower shadow beneath.

efficient market hypothesis (EMH)

a market theory stating that the market acts efficiently, and that stock prices reflect all known information at each moment.

elections

decisions made by corporations to treat certain transactions, set up reserves, or determine value, under one of several allowed processes; these elections affect the calculation of net profits as well as capitalization of the company.

engulfing pattern

a two-session candlestick indicator with opposite-color real bodies; the second session exceeds the real body size of the first on both the top and the bottom.

equity markets

the markets for publicly traded stock, or exchanges set up to facilitate trading in equities; an equity holder is part owner of the corporation, compared to the debt markets, in which a bondholder is a lender to the corporation.

evening star

a bearish three-session signal involving a white session, an upside gap, and then two black sessions moving the price lower.

excess phase

the third of three phases under the Dow Theory, in which traders follow the trend and begin to speculate, often at the wrong time in the price cycle; in a bear market, "excess" is replaced with "despair."

ex-dividend date

the date on which dividends are no longer earned; to earn a current dividend, shares must be bought at least one day before ex-dividend date.

exponential moving average (EMA)

an averaging method that weights the latest entry in a field more than previous entries.

falling wedge

a bullish signal with both resistance and support declining at different angles, with an upward movement predicted once the breadth has narrowed.

Fibonacci retracement theory
a belief that a specific sequence of numbers can be used to develop numerals for identifying likely degrees of retracement within a trend.

fifty percent principle
a market theory stating that trends undergo price corrections averaging 50 percent of the gains; for example, a trend that has moved up 20 percent is expected to experience a 10 percent downward retracement, and a trend moving down 30 percent should expect an upward retracement of 15 percent.

fixed or long-term assets
the plant, equipment, real estate, and other capital assets owned by the company, less accumulated depreciation.

flag
a price pattern with a moving rectangular shape like a flag, with a mast on either side, usually representing a short-term minor retracement within the current trend.

flip
the reversion of previous resistance into a new level of support during a rising trend, or of previous support to form as new resistance in a falling trend.

footnotes
a section of the annual report providing explanations of many of the line items of the financial statements, disclosing off-balance sheet items, and showing how estimates were developed.

forward P/E
an estimate of the P/E based not on historical earnings but on estimated future earnings; the calculation involves dividing current price per share by expected earnings per share, usually over the next 12 months.

GAAP
Generally Accepted Accounting Principles, a complex set of policies, standards, and reporting formats used by all publicly listed companies; the system is not centrally located, but is the sum of regulations, published opinions, and policies, as well as long-standing methods for recording and reporting transactions and setting valuation.

gap filled
a three-session continuation pattern beginning with a white session, an upside gap, a second white session, and a black session that fills the gap created between sessions one and two (upside, or bullish); or a black session, a downside gap, a second black session, and a white session that fills the original gap (downside, or bearish).

golden ratio
the strongest ratio in the Fibonacci sequence, also called *Phi*, indicating the most likely point for retracement to occur.

gravestone doji
a single-session candlestick shaped like an inverted capital T, with a horizontal line at the bottom and a long upper shadow above.

gross margin
the percentage that gross costs represent in relation to revenue, calculated by dividing gross costs by revenue; this is a key income statement ratio.

gross profit
the net difference between revenues and the cost of goods sold, representing pre-expense profits.

hammer
a single-session candlestick with a small real body of either color and a long lower shadow, working as a bullish reversal and found at the bottom of a downtrend.

hanging man
a single-session candlestick with a small real body of either color and a long lower shadow, working as a bearish reversal and found at the top of an uptrend.

harami cross pattern
a harami, but with a doji in the second session in place of a real body.

harami pattern
a two-session candlestick indicator with opposite-color real bodies; the second session is smaller than the real body size of the first on both the top and the bottom.

head and shoulders
a technical signal with three upside spikes occurring during an uptrend; the first and third (shoulders) are offset by a higher second spike (head). After the formation, a reversal and new downtrend are expected.

IFRS
International Financial Reporting Standards, a system for the uniform reporting of financial transactions and valuation, which is scheduled to replace the GAAP system in coming years.

income statement
a summary of revenue, costs, expenses, and net profit for a specified period (quarter or fiscal year), covering the period ending on the same date as the published date of the balance sheet.

informationally efficient
descriptive of the efficient market hypothesis (EMH) as an explanation for the short-term price chaos of the market; under this explanation, information is taken into price in an efficient manner even if the price movement or reaction is chaotic.

insider trading
any buy or sell of company stock on the part of key corporate executives, management, or board members.

insiders
individuals who hold or trade shares of stock as primary shareholders or officers of the company.

institutional investors
those investors that are not individuals but larger institutions, such as mutual funds, insurance companies, or pension and profit-sharing organizations.

intangible assets
all assets with value but lacking physical attributes; these include goodwill, brand names, and covenants, none of which have physical value but do have worth. The value of intangible assets may be estimated or assigned at a point of merger or acquisition.

inverse head and shoulders
a technical signal with three downside spikes occurring during a downtrend; the first and third (shoulders) are offset by a lower second spike (head), and after the formation, a reversal and new uptrend are expected.

lagging indicator
a signal that follows price direction, notably reversals, and serves as confirmation for other reversal signals.

large cap
companies with the largest dollar value of market capitalization, which may be either $5 billion or more or $10 billion or more.

leading indicator
a signal that precedes price movement and other reversals, and may be independently confirmed with additional indicators.

long candlestick
a session with unusually long white or black rectangles, indicating an especially strong price movement upward (white) or downward (black).

long-legged doji
a single-session candlestick shaped like a plus sign, with a horizontal line in the middle and exceptionally long upper and lower shadows.

long-term liabilities
all debts due after the next 12 months, including long-term notes and bonds payable.

MA crossover
a reversal signal based on the shorter MA line moving above the longer MA line (bullish) or moving below the longer MA line (bearish).

market capitalization
also abbreviated market cap, the value of a company based on multiplying price per share by the number of shares outstanding.

market order
an order to buy or sell based not on a stated price but on the current available bid price (to buy) or asked price (to sell) for that security.

mean
alternate term for the average.

meeting lines
a two-session candlestick pattern consisting of opposite-colored sessions that close at the same price.

mega cap
a company with more than $200 billion of capitalization.

micro cap
a company with capitalization, defined between $50 million and $250 million.

mid cap
companies with medium dollar levels of capitalization, either between $1 and $5 billion, or between $2 and $10 billion.

minor trend
the changes in price lasting from only a few hours up to a few days, representing the most chaotic and difficult to predict of all market trends.

momentum oscillator
an indicator based on analysis of the current price trend that measures the strength and speed of the trend rather than the direction in which it is moving.

money flow index (MFI)
a volume indicator calculating both price and volume over a 14-session period, used to identify buying and selling pressure.

morning star
a bullish three-session signal involving a black session, a downside gap, and then two white sessions moving the price higher.

Moving Average Convergence Divergence (MACD)
a momentum oscillator based on comparisons and movements of a 12-day and a 26-day exponential moving average, and a signal line, a 9-day exponential moving average.

multiple
the number of years' earnings in the current price per share, based on a calculation of the price/earnings ratio.

nano cap
a company with capitalization below $50 million.

narrow-range day (NRD)
a name used by swing traders to describe a near-doji, a session with very little gap between opening and closing price.

near-doji
single sessions with very narrow trading ranges, close to the doji but with a slight degree of price movement.

net profit
the overall profit from all operating and nonoperating activities and taxes; the bottom line used to calculate net return.

net return
net profit divided by revenue; one of the most widely used income statement ratios, expressed in the form of a percentage.

nonoperating income and expenses
all items outside of operating profit, including currency exchange adjustments, interest income or expenses, nonrecurring and nonoperating items, and other items.

OHLC chart
a stock price chart reporting the open, high, low, and closing price for each session.

on-balance volume (OBV)
a volume indicator tracking buying and selling pressure cumulatively, adding volume for upward-moving days and subtracting volume for downward-moving days.

operating expenses
general and administrative expenses and selling expenses, appearing on the income statement as reductions of gross profit to arrive at the operating profit.

operating margin
the percentage of operating profit compared to revenue, the level of profits from operations and before calculation of nonoperating income or expense or taxes.

operating profit
the remaining profit after operating expenses are deducted from gross profit, representing the profit from operations, but excluding nonoperating adjustments for other income or expenses, and for taxes.

overbought
condition when buying pressure has moved a stock price above its mid-range as defined by momentum oscillators, and is likely to lead to a reversal in price and a return of the oscillator below the overbought index value.

oversold
condition when selling pressure has moved a stock price below its mid-range as defined by momentum oscillators, and is likely to lead to a reversal in price and a return of the oscillator above the oversold index value.

payment date
the date on which dividends are paid to stockholders of record, usually several weeks after the record date.

payout ratio
the percentage of earnings paid in dividends, computed by dividing dividends per share by earnings per share.

pennant
a signal shaped like a triangle with declining resistance and rising support on a convergence course.

piercing lines
a two-session candlestick pattern consisting of opposite-colored sessions, with the second closing within the range of the first.

pretax income

operating profit plus other income or less other expenses, representing the profit from operations before deducting the federal or foreign income tax liability (state and local taxes are deducted as part of operating expenses).

pretax margin

the percentage of profit remaining after adjusting operating margin for other income and expenses.

pretax ROE

return on equity calculated before tax liabilities are deducted.

price channel

alternative name for the channel line.

price crossover

a reversal signal in which the price range is higher than a longer-term moving average, and then also moves above the shorter-term MA (bullish); or when price range is lower than a longer-term moving average, and then also moves below the shorter-term MA (bearish).

primary trend

described by the Dow Theory, the longest-term trend in the market, lasting from under a year to several years in duration.

publicly traded company

a company whose stock is available to the public as investment or for short-term trading, usually through one of the public stock exchanges or electronically.

quick ratio

a test of working capital excluding inventory values; the total of current assets excluding inventory, divided by current liabilities.

random walk hypothesis (RWH)

a theory stating that the market averages cannot be beaten because all movement, up or down, is entirely random and unpredictable.

rational expectation

a belief that, given full information about a stock's price, most people will behave in a rational and predictable manner; this belief is required in order to accept the efficient market hypothesis (EMH).

rational market

a type of market that behaves in a rational and logical manner; for example, efficient market hypothesis assumes the market is rational because it reflects all known information in the current price.

ratios
reduced expressions of financial data, for the purpose of trend analysis and used to clarify the meaning behind dollar values; ratios are expressed as percentages or comparative numerical sets (*a/b*).

real body
a candlestick's central white (upward-moving) or black (downward-moving) rectangle, representing a session's movement between open and close; the upper and lower lines of the rectangle represent opening and closing price. In a white candlestick, the opening is at the bottom and the closing at the top; in a black candlestick, the opening is at the top and the closing at the bottom.

recognition
booking transactions for revenue, costs, and expenses; the year in which these transactions are booked should be the proper accounting period. The process of booking transactions is called recognition because it indicates that all of these are booked into the proper accounting period.

record date
the date on which the stockholder is acknowledged as being eligible for the current dividend; this date occurs two days after ex-dividend date.

recovery period
the number of years provided to write off a capital asset, with the correct period dictated by Internal Revenue Service tables and subject to limited elections.

reinvestment of dividends
a choice made at the time shares are purchased, to use earned dividends to buy additional partial shares of stock, as opposed to receiving a cash payment.

Relative Strength Index (RSI)
a momentum indicator tracking strength and speed of a current trend based on an index with marked levels when prices become overbought or oversold.

reserves
adjustments made to estimate losses or valuation of certain balance sheet accounts, including reserves for bad debts deducted from the balance of accounts receivable; the level of reserve affects the net value of accounts.

resistance
the highest price level in the current trading range, representing the highest price at which traders are willing to buy and sell; price should not easily break through resistance and remain above without reversing.

retail investors
all individuals investing and trading for their own account, excluding institutional investors.

retained earnings
part of total shareholders' equity on the balance sheet, the accumulated balances of all historical profits; each year's profit is added to retained earnings (or losses deducted from it).

retracement
a temporary price movement in the direction opposite the current trend.

revenue
the top line of the income statement, representing earned income of the company, and including cash receipts as well as income earned and not yet received.

reversal
an indicator forecasting a change in the current price trend, to movement in the opposite direction.

rising wedge
a bearish signal with both resistance and support rising at different angles, with a downward movement predicted once the breadth has narrowed.

scaling
the point spread on a stock chart, based on the price range for the selected time period.

secondary trend
a trend, either bullish or bearish, that lasts from a matter of several days up to several months, which tends to contradict movement of the primary trend.

semi-strong form EMH
a variation of the efficient market hypothesis that assumes current stock prices include past publicly known information as well as current information about a company, and that prices change immediately as a result.

separating lines
a two-session candlestick continuation pattern consisting of opposite-colored sessions, with the second closing at the same price of the first and following a gap.

shadow
a vertical line appearing above or below the real body of a candlestick, representing the full trading range for the session; the longer the shadow, the more significance it holds, since the trading levels retreated back into the range for a session.

shareholder services
a department in a company designed to respond to customer questions, and to ensure that financial information is fully disclosed.

simple average
the addition of numerals in a field, then division of the total by the number of numerals, performed without adjustment or weighting.

simple moving average (SMA)
a simple average with updated information, involving removal of oldest values and replacement with the latest values.

small cap
a company with the lowest range of total capitalization, defined as under $1 billion or under $2 billion.

spinning top
a single-session candlestick with a small real body of either color, and long upper and lower shadows.

squeeze alert
a three-session indicator with a first session a black day (bullish) or a white day (bearish); the color of sessions two and three does not matter. Session two opens and closes within the range of session one, and session three is smaller than session two.

Statement of Cash Flows
a financial statement that summarizes all of the company's cash-based transactions for the year, including breakdowns of cash received and cash paid; sources of funds include cash-based income, proceeds from loans or the sale of assets, and nonoperating items, such as currency exchange gains or interest received. Applications of funds include repayments of loans, money spent to buy assets, or any losses.

Stochastic oscillator
a momentum test consisting of a 14-day average of changes between high and low prices called 3K, and a 3-day average of 3K, called 3D.

straight-line depreciation
a method of calculating depreciation in which the same amount is deducted each year; the total basis of capital assets is divided by the number of years in the recovery period to find the annual deduction (with less allowed in the first year based on when the asset was placed in service).

strong form EMH

a version of the efficient market hypothesis (EMF) in which all information, regardless of whether it is known publicly, is immediately reflected in the current price of stock.

support

the lowest price level in the current trading range, representing the lowest price at which traders are willing to buy and sell; price should not easily break through support and remain below without reversing.

symmetrical triangle

a formation that is either bullish or bearish, depending on confirming indicators that follow; it includes a declining resistance and rising support level. As the breadth of trading narrows, a move in either direction is expected to follow.

tasuki gap

a three-session continuation signal consisting of a white session, an upside gap, a second white session, and black session moving lower (bullish); or a black session, a downside gap, a second black session, and a final white session moving higher (bearish).

thrusting lines

a two-session candlestick continuation pattern consisting of opposite-colored sessions with the second gapping to open and closing within the range of the first.

total capitalization

the complete source of capital for an organization, consisting of long-term debt and shareholders' equity.

Treasury stock

the value of stock purchased and retired by the company, and permanently deducted from the shareholders' equity value.

trendline

a straight line drawn above a declining trend or below an advancing trend, identifying the direction and continuing until interrupted by changes in price.

trends

the directional movement of a specific financial statement account balance or ratio that reveals growing or falling strength or profitability.

triangle

a trend pattern of narrowing price range, indicating a specifically bullish or bearish signal.

uptrend

a current trend involving a series of progressively higher price levels, also called a bullish price movement or a bull trend.

value investments

those investments that may be undervalued by the market, but whose fundamental strength is exceptional; the deflated price posture of such companies indicates good timing to purchase shares, and also indicates lower than average risk of loss due to the fundamental strength of the company.

volatility

the degree of movement in price over time, reflecting relative degrees of market risk.

volume

the number of shares traded for each market session, which may be led by buying or by selling interests, and which can be measured to determine the strength or weakness of current prices.

weak form EMH

efficient market hypothesis based on the belief that current prices have taken past information into account, but not necessarily current information.

wedge

a bullish or bearish signal with both resistance and support narrowing and moving closer together, but at different angles.

whipsaw

a price pattern of sudden and fast movement in one direction, followed by equally sudden and fast movement in the opposite direction, typical of short-term trends likely to reverse quickly.

white soldiers

a bullish signal consisting of three consecutive sessions, all white; each session opens higher than the last, and then closes higher than the last, without any gaps in between.

working capital

the amount of funds a company has available to fund ongoing operations, used as a measurement of how effectively it manages its money; the dollar value of working capital is equal to the total of current assets (cash and those assets convertible to cash within 12 months), minus current liabilities (money due and payable within 12 months).

written off

the act of recognizing expenses in the current year, and applying them to reduce net profits; the accumulated annual costs and expenses are deducted from revenue to arrive at operating profit.

ABOUT THE AUTHOR

MICHAEL C. THOMSETT (ThomsettOptions.com) has written more than 80 books on investing, real estate, business, and management. He is the author of several Wiley books, including the nine editions of the bestselling *Getting Started in Options* as well as *Getting Started in Fundamental Analysis*, *Getting Started in Real Estate Investing*, and *Getting Started in Swing Trading*. He also has written numerous other stock investing and trading books, including *Winning with Stocks* (AMACOM Books), *Stock Profits* (FT Press), and *Mastering Fundamental Analysis* and *Mastering Technical Analysis* (Dearborn Press). He contributes regularly to many websites, including Seeking Alpha and the Chicago Board Options Exchange (CBOE), and writes articles for the *AAII Journal* and NAIC's *Better Investing*. He also teaches five classes at the New York Institute of Finance (NYIF). Thomsett has been writing professionally since 1978 and full-time since 1985. He lives near Nashville, Tennessee.

INDEX